MURDEROUS METHODS

MURDEROUS METHODS

USING FORENSIC SCIENCE TO SOLVE LETHAL CRIMES

MARK BENECKE

TRANSLATED BY KARIN HEUSCH

COLUMBIA UNIVERSITY PRESS   NEW YORK

Columbia University Press
Publishers Since 1893
New York   Chichester, West Sussex

© Originally published (in German) Gustav Lubbe Verlag 2002,
English-language edition Columbia University Press 2005
English-language translation copyright © 2005 Columbia University Press
All rights reserved

Library of Congress Cataloging-in-Publication Data
Benecke, Mark.
[Mordmethoden. English]
Murderous methods : Using forensic science to solve lethal crimes / Mark Benecke ;
translated by Karin Heusch.
p.   cm.
Includes bibliographical references and index.
ISBN 0-231-13118-6 (cloth : alk. paper)
1. Murder—Investigation 2. Forensic sciences. I. Title: Murderous methods. II. Title.
HV8079.H6B4613 2005
363.25'9523—dc22
2005041420

∞

Columbia University Press books are printed on permanent and durable acid-free paper.

Printed in the United States of America
Designed by Chang Jae Lee
c 10 9 8 7 6 5 4 3 2 1

In chapter 4 the discussion of decapitation on pages 134–38 was translated from K. Rossa, *Todesstrafen: Ihre Wirklichkeit in drei Jahrtausenden* (Oldenburg: Stalling, 1966), pp. 60–64. In chapter 5 the Denke case presentation on pages 204–216 was translated from F. Pietrusky, "Über kriminelle Leichenzerstückelung: Der Fall Denke," *Deutsche Zeitschrift für die Gesamte Gerichtliche Medizin* 8 (1926): pp. 703–726.

CONTENTS

—"Forensics": from the Latin *in foro*, "in front of the public"

FOREWORD

MICHAEL M. BADEN, M.D.

The forensic sciences have been used to assist investigations into murder and other crimes for the past 150 years. Dr. Mark Benecke puts their uses into a broad perspective. He takes us on a delightful global tour of murders and shows how their investigations have improved during those years as science and police work have come together. He exudes an unabashed enthusiasm for his subject material and has a delightfully inquiring mind for raising and discussing difficult questions such as whether there is some life after decapitation; the pros and cons of capital punishment; how Lenin's body was embalmed; the problems of false accusations; and Hitler's bizarre misuse of genetics.

Dr. Benecke enthusiastically describes his criminalistic studies in violent death, which extend from Europe to the Far East and South America and the United States. He takes us from the heart-removing "Butcher of Cologne" and the sadistic sexual murders of the Düsseldorf vampire to the American cannibal Jeffrey Dahmer and the more recent husband-wife murdering team of Paul Bernardo and Karla Homolka; from the beginning of fingerprinting to Professor William Bass's Tennessee "Body Farm," where studies and the comings and goings of insects are investigated to determine when someone died. Handwriting, facial reconstruction, and the use of DNA in genetic fingerprinting are examined.

Dr. Benecke addresses in some detail the strengths and weaknesses of forensic evidence presented at the landmark trial of Bruno Richard Hauptmann for the murder of the Lindbergh baby. Of particular interest to me was the story of how, in 1865, the father of pathology and the champion of public health for the poor, Dr. Rudolf von Virchow, was almost killed in a duel with the future founder of the German Empire, Otto von Bismarck. The most significant advances in the forensic sciences and the solving of murders are yet to come. Dr. Benecke prepares us for these advances by showing us where we have been and where we are now.   July 2005, New York City

Chief Forensic Pathologist, New York State Police

Former Chief Medical Examiner, New York City

Former Adjunct Professor of Forensic Science, John Jay School of Criminal Justice, New York City

PREFACE AND ACKNOWLEDGMENTS

I would like to show you that sometimes reality is more exciting than a novel. Assume for a few hours or days that you have never heard anything about the sometimes famous and extraordinary cases you will encounter in the following pages. Many of the details are so unbelievable that if they were written in a crime novel, you would consider them unrealistic. Well, sometimes reality is very unreal, too.

If you think you knew all about the O. J. Simpson case, for example, just wait to read some of the more surprising details, and if you think you would have been a good witness or juror in that trial, you may have to think again. Also, the relationship between Johann Sebastian Bach and facial reconstruction might surprise you as much as the bitter fight between the most famous magician, Houdini, and Arthur Conan Doyle over supernatural powers.

Immediately after this book was published in German, numerous fine people contacted me and made interesting and sometimes very moving comments on the cases described in the book. We could not fit many of their contributions into the book without filling another 300 pages, but I would like to thank the contributors for their excellent work, mostly done in their spare time, and mostly without payment.

To mention just two, Armin Rütters went to the former home of cannibal serial killer Karl Denke, discussed this case with me in detail, and allowed me to assemble a case file based on his research. During a visit in 2001, the owner of Denke's house asked him whether he wanted to buy the place, but Rütters resisted the temptation because he felt that the gruesome events that took place there would be too disturbing.

Lydia Schulz managed to track down numerous articles about the Seifert case from Volkhoven that were formerly unknown, and she took hundreds of pictures of the documents. She would make a world-class private eye.

To maintain my personal contact with Luis Alfredo Garavito, who killed more than 300 boys, I completely depend on my friends Claudia Zapata and Miguel Rodriguez y Rowinsky, on Father Didier Amariles Gallego, and, of course, on Luis Alfredo himself. Although much of the Garavito story has not yet been told, the research accumulates while my mind works to organize the chaotic material. I hope to tell this story in my next book.

The folks at Lübbe (my editors in Germany), and Ann Young, copyeditor Carol Anne Peschke, and editor Robin Smith at Columbia University Press played a key role in moving the manuscript from Europe to the United States. (Lübbe feeds me with homemade tiramisu and wine during book fairs, which I greatly appreciate, too.) The only drawback is the long, quiet nights in my research library tracking down the answers to the editor's nerve-wracking yet brilliant questions and comments.

After the German edition appeared, some German TV teams arranged contacts that I could never have made myself, especially Hoggard Films and National Geographic TV. It was great fun to work with you!

If you are a fellow forensic scientist, please note that this is not a scientific textbook but a collection of challenging cases, written for everybody who likes to think beyond the usual suspects and assumptions.

Finally, I send a big thanks to my students all over the world who manage to surprise me every summer with their wild questions, ideas, enthusiasm, and disrespect for bearded men. You are cool.

So thank you all. With friends like you, life is a pleasure, even though mine is immersed in blood, hair, semen, saliva, and insects.

Cologne, Armenia (Colombia), and New York, October 2004
Mark Benecke

MURDEROUS METHODS

CHAPTER 1

ON MY CONSCIENCE

An Atrocity

"He pulled out the heart. The butcher of Cologne-Kalk. Was it a ritual murder? Was he a madman?"

This is what the local Cologne tabloid paper *Express* asked itself and its readers in May 1997 and added, correctly, "Incredibly, the murderer opened the chest and took the heart and other organs out as one might do to an animal. Sixty hours after the gruesome find of the corpse on Kalk-Mülheimer Street, the head and hands were still missing. The upper body, buttocks and thighs are being put together meticulously by the coroner."

The tabloid's sensational account was strikingly close to the truth, but its editors didn't know how close they were; how could they? They followed a completely false trail because they were immersed in a popular culture supposedly familiar with such "satanic" murders.

They immediately called on a criminal psychologist. He suggested that the pulling out of the heart might hint at a ritual murder. Certainly this murderer acted without any feelings, he said. We shall see later whether he was correct.

The residents of the neighborhood of Cologne-Kalk were restless and uneasy; after all, this was obviously the work of a serial killer who was roaming their streets. Renate Kalb, a 33-year-old homemaker, said that she could not sleep through the night and was startled by every noise she heard. Another neighbor, who did not want to divulge his name, said that nobody would be safe anymore.

The excitement began on May 12, 1997. It was an extremely warm and beautiful Monday, and Necmettin Tasci started on his way home by bicycle from his vegetable patch beside the Rhine River.

At the junction of a busy, run-down street he stopped to relieve himself in a nearby thicket. There, he found a blue garbage bag that was larger and sturdier than the usual household garbage bag.

When Tasci kicked the bag, it split open, revealing a human arm without a hand. He quickly cycled to the nearest telephone booth to call 911.

The police assembled the remains on a steel table in the coroner's lab. It turned out to be the upper body and arms of a man without hands, head, and legs. The killer had removed all body parts necessary for a quick identification, including the genitals.

After a tense night, things moved in quick succession for the investigators. On Tuesday afternoon, playing children found another bag, this time in Eytstrasse, in an equally run-down part of Cologne-Kalk. When the children opened the bag, suspecting nothing, they saw a set of human thighs and buttocks.

An hour and a half later, and only 300 yards away, 13-year-old Karl-Heinz Stachowiak found the remaining parts of the legs close to a playground. The bag was lying on the footpath. He called his mother right away. When giving a statement later, the mother said, "It is truly awful when children find things like that near a playground. I get goosebumps thinking the killer is still loose."

Her goosebumps were not without good reason. Ten years earlier, there had been another case similar to this. The press attributed those killings to a butcher, too. The body of Maria Wollenschein had been found, cut into pieces, on the other side of the Rhine, in Ehrenfeld, in a working-class area of this Cologne neighborhood.

That killer had put the body parts in plastic bags and distributed them in that part of town. Because it had never been established who that killer was, the press resuscitated this case and tried to find similarities that connected the two.

The mood was particularly tense because, in addition to *The Silence of the Lambs*, another movie that came out only 2 years earlier was still in the memories of most Germans: *The Dead Maker*. This 90-minute film about serial killer Fritz Haarmann (played by famous German actor Goetz George) was a detailed psychological examination of Haarmann and the original investigation from the 1920s, using the recorded dialogue from the time. This weak and egocentric killer, who was not apprehended for a long time, had frightened the German population ever since. The movie brought the crimes to the surface again; broadcasting the film on all television stations and covering it in the press also made the killer famous. The time was ripe for a Haarmann-like killer.

The Cologne investigators suddenly moved away from the common assumption that the crime was the work of a serial killer. To the utter astonishment of all, a bank statement was found in the cut-up trousers of the victim. This bank statement had a name, Hassan Rhafes, obviously that of the victim.

This was great news for the investigation because in the absence of head or hands it would have been almost impossible to identify the dead person from patterns of bone fractures. One might have to compare the corpse's bones with tens of thousands of X-rays from medical records all over the country to make an identification. Luck was on their side; having a name meant having a firm lead to follow. Other questions were not as easily solved. Foremost was the question of why the organs were removed and why the body was dismembered.

The homicide squad of the Cologne police criminal investigation department proceeded carefully. They announced that they needed to examine names and addresses further before they could make definite statements. The police spokesperson did not mention which people were part of their investigation, but once they knew the identity of the victim, detectives contacted the family.

Some of them lived in an apartment in Cologne-Kalk not 500 yards from where body parts were found. The tenants of the apartment were Mohammed Rhafes, his wife, Aziza, and their 22-year-old daughter, Saliha. Mohammed was the half-brother of 31-year-old Hassan. When interrogated, Mohammed said that it was all incomprehensible to him. At the time of the crime, he was working his night shift with the railroad company in Düsseldorf, a good half hour away.

His daughter knew more. Her uncle Hassan had been in their apartment that day for about an hour and had then left. Saliha's mother, on the other hand, said that her brother-in-law had been at their apartment for only about 5 minutes. This time difference made the investigators suspicious. Before their defense attorneys could tell the family to stop talking to the police, Saliha mentioned that something happened in the apartment.

The phrase "something happened in the apartment" turned out to be an understatement. The police found in the mother's pocket a little bag containing human ashes. In the bathroom they found pieces of the skull and hands of her brother-in-law. When they also found traces of the victim's blood in the otherwise clean apartment, they got an arrest warrant for the two women. Mohammed Rhafes was not taken into custody because police could not prove he was an accessory to the crime. He was free but still a suspect.

Now things began to get complicated. How could two women kill and dismember a strong young man without outside help and without witnesses? How could they bag the body parts and deposit them in Kalkerstrasse and other places? How was it possible that, besides the few small traces found in the apartment, no more blood could be found on the floor or in corners?

The answer was finally discovered in the apartment. Their large freezer was filled with packages of lamb meat. There really was a butcher, not figuratively but literally. Mohammed Rhafes might not have killed Hassan, police thought, but he dismembered the body skillfully. His wife, Aziza, insisted that she alone committed the crime and that her husband had nothing to do with the killing and dismemberment.

In this neighborhood, people often illegally slaughtered animals in their apartments, following an Islamic ritual. Since 2002, this practice has been legal in Germany. Whoever had dismembered the corpse could have done it only by knowing how to slaughter sheep. When a sheep is slaughtered, the organs are always removed, a method the hobby butcher used on Hassan. The expert also knew how to drain the blood with the aid of flat bowls, which were usually used to cook couscous. Finally, he or she ripped the bloody carpet from the floor. This saved the family endless scrubbing and explains how they committed such a crime without leaving large traces of blood.

Who actually killed Hassan Rhafes is not entirely clear, despite the mother's confession. The only thing the 45-year-old woman said in court was that Hassan tried to pull her daughter into the bedroom and rape her. "That's when I saw the knife by the sink." She would say no more. Her defense attorney thought it should be considered a confession.

Aziza described in detail how, in her view, the crime was committed. Her aggressive and drug-addicted brother-in-law Hassan appeared, as he often had done before, at 9 o'clock in the evening and brazenly asked for money and jewelry. When he started to harass Saliha, Aziza grabbed the knife by the sink and stabbed him. While Hassan died, the daughter collapsed. The mother sent her into the living room. She then began to dismember the body.

It took her until 1 o'clock in the morning to put all the body parts in several bags, wiping off all blood traces and keeping the cylindrical stove, which is small but burns hot, in the bathroom going with coal. There she burned the organs, head, and hands, with partial success.

As soon as the neighbors read in the paper about the crime, they suddenly recalled that black smoke came out of the chimney all night and the next morning. This was reminiscent of the Fritz Haarmann story, in which witnesses claimed that oily smoke came from the chimney, although Haarmann never burned his victims. He sold them as meat, and what he could not sell he threw into the toilet of the apartment complex courtyard or into the Leine River.

Dismembering a body is extremely difficult for most people but not for a hobby butcher such as Aziza Rhafes, who took about 2 hours to do the job; in comparison, the inexperienced Haarmann took several days.

Whether parts of the body were transported in a shopping cart through Kalkerstrasse, as Aziza claimed, is anybody's guess. What is certain is that the crime was not the act of a crazy person or of a serial killer without feelings. On the contrary, "He [Hassan] had touched me and my daughter," said the mother to the court psychiatrist; "that caused us great shame." And with this sentence she brought the case to a key cultural point. It is the classic cultural case of an unacceptable disgrace, which was not to be tolerated. There is a real possibility that the mother alone could have committed the crime, without her husband's aid.

The husband also, with a few words, pointed in that direction. As a family member, he declined to give any testimony except "I am sorry I could not protect my wife."

New Technologies and Old Imponderables

About 100 years ago, before the discovery of genetic fingerprinting, a literal print of the fingers was considered a revolutionary advance in forensics, initially not in Germany but by the British government in India and in South American countries such as Argentina. It was used long before in wax seals for documents; documents with "finger seals" date back at least 2,000 years in China. The German police resisted the idea, uncertain whether it would prove helpful. Could one trust the South American investigators who had used this method with great enthusiasm since 1891? How could one possibly use all that information from the lines in the fingers in a uniform way, to make a useful comparison?

The officials in charge were so doubtful that Paul Koettig, police chief of Dresden and a certified criminologist, had to act decisively. He did not want the police to ignore this new and excellent investigative tool. On March 30, 1903, he ordered his people to begin using the new fingerprinting method the next day.

In the United States, it was a long time before fingerprints were used regularly. The first case was the one of a thief who was caught in a New York City hotel in 1903. Because his identity could not be determined, his fingerprints were sent to London, where they were found to be those of a known professional thief who had recently stolen a large sum of money from the wife of a well-known writer in England.

However, it was another 7 years before fingerprints were used as a tool for forensic identification inside the United States and used in a court of law. The two trials of the *People vs. Jennings* (in Chicago, for homicide) and the *People vs. Crispi* (in New York City, for burglary) were well covered and brought the technique to the forefront of criminal trials and investigations.

Fingerprints were used for civilian or military purposes before this, however. For example, the U.S. Army and the Navy started to fingerprint recruits in 1906 to detect deserters or men dishonorably discharged who tried to reenlist. They were also used to identify dead soldiers. In 1910, the Inferior Criminal Courts Act mandated the fingerprinting of prostitutes in New York City's magistrate courts. Between 1910 and 1913, the magistrate court recorded fingerprints of more than 12,000 women arrested for prostitution. The magistrates found that "approximately 629 women are constantly walking our streets for victims and these repeat offenders constitute a large proportion of the business in the Woman's Night Court."

In 1913, the New York City magistrate court also started to fingerprint men arrested for intoxication and vagrancy and soon also men arrested for disorderly conduct, pickpockets, mashers or "persistent insulters of women in New York City," and "degenerates." The central office for fingerprint records at that time was at 300 Mulberry Street. "By this means," the magistrate said, "it will no longer be possible for a defendant to plead sympathy on the ground that he is a first offender when as a matter of fact he has been convicted previously."

By 1915, the magistrate's court files held around 80,000 sets of fingerprints. In 1919, the New York City Health Commissioner asked for fingerprinting of drug addicts. "The primary object was, and is, to . . . crush out the 'regulars' or 'repeaters' or 'professionals' by successively lengthened sentences, thereby serving as a deterrent for others to drift into that class," according to City Magistrate Joseph Deuel.

After World War II the United States promoted the idea of internationalizing identification for criminal cases. Long before, the U.S. National Bureau of Criminal Identification had already been set up in Washington, D.C., but it received photographs and fingerprints from only about 150 U.S. police departments on a regular basis. Until 1922, large parts of the United States still did not use or deliver fingerprint records to the bureau; for example, Cincinnati and Cleveland sent only mug shots to the office. From the summer of 1919 until the summer of 1920, only 15,000 fingerprint sheets had been sent to the bureau from the whole country.

In September 1922, the police conference in New York tried to remedy this problem, inviting colleagues from England, Belgium, Argentina, and Canada, where fingerprints were already used on a large scale and collected nationwide. Congress finally mandated the exchange of fingerprints. In 1924, the Federal Bureau of Investigation (FBI) established the Identification Unit, and by 1946 it had processed 100 million fingerprint cards in manually maintained files.

Wherever method was used, its success was quickly apparent. To this day, fingerprinting is still the most commonly used method in crime scene investigation, and it accounts for about three-fourths of all trace evidence. In 2001 Simon Cole, a theoretician from the humanities—with the help of a large press following—tried to attack these methods in the United States from a theoretical standpoint, challenging the basic concept of a "match," but there was no way back. The fingerprint is here to stay, and it continues to provide excellent evidence.

New forensic methods are easily embraced today but are often called into question as soon as they are introduced. Especially in the United States, new methods have been adopted quickly, although a longer trial period might be prudent for some methods, which take years to develop for reliable courtroom use. There have been problems with facial reconstruction and genetic finger-printing, for which scientists have misjudged the limitations of their methods. Much of Europe was spared from using new technologies too early only because its bureaucracies prevented quick implementation of new methods.

Despite these new techniques, investigators often seem to be banging their heads against a brick wall. Witnesses' testimonies show so many memory gaps, misjudgments, and prejudice that they are often useless. On the other hand, sometimes the testimony of mentally ill people is disregarded even when it happens to be the only promising lead. This book not only shows the process of forensic science but also shows how, whenever humans are involved, events may go in unpredictable and strange directions.

Ways of Thinking

Attitudes and habits often made it difficult for forensic scientists of the past to recognize new methods as useful. Social constraints also limit their ability to clear up homicides. The reason is simply this: Many offenses that today are considered criminal were at one time considered normal, socially accepted ways of dealing with people. It took decades, sometimes even centuries, for society to recognize that certain habits are wrong or cruel. A look into the past should make this clear.

Dueling came to an end only in the nineteenth century. By the end of that century duels were forbidden and were even punishable by imprisonment, but bans did little to prevent most duels.

It was not just military officers and students but also politicians, poets, artists, and representatives of all professional groups who took to the sword or pistol when something was perceived as a question of honor. Often, a misunderstood remark, an ironic smile, a disdainful look, or a simple disagreement could lead people to risk losing their own life or taking that of a fellow citizen simply to obtain satisfaction.

The tradition of fighting duels was so ingrained that even opponents of duels forgot their teaching and writing against dueling and immediately resorted to weapons to defend their own honor. Men and sometimes women saw lost honor as stolen property, much as today losing family heirlooms would hit us hard. Challenging someone to a duel was felt to be the only way to restore lost honor. An example of this is the duel of two famous men of times past. It had an absurd beginning and came to an unexpected end.

Rudolf von Virchow Versus Otto von Bismarck

Otto von Bismarck, who in 1871 became the first chancellor of the German Reich after unifying the German states, was vain and stubborn. Even before he began his law studies in Göttingen, he was involved in minor squabbles in Berlin. When a fraternity brother laughed about his foppish attire, he responded by calling the fraternity brother "stupid boy," which is harmless enough. But four fraternity brothers challenged him to a duel, and Bismarck accepted. The "stupid boy" withdrew, which turned out to be the smart thing to do because Bismarck was not only a good dresser but also an expert fencer.

Otto von Bismarck was a descendant of an old noble family, so it was expected that at the beginning of his student years he would join a fraternity. Fraternities still exist in universities throughout Germany but are quite out of fashion. They are generally conservative and emphasize "Life with Tradition." Following the fraternal ideals, there is no commitment to any political party or group. Every member is free to decide in accordance with the principles laid out in the motto "Ehre, Freiheit, Vaterland" ("Honor, Freedom, Fatherland").

For example, the large Deutsche Burschenschaft began nearly two centuries ago, in 1815, in the university town of Jena as a "revolutionary movement for freedom and unity of the German nation. Against small state feudalism, for freedom of speech and citizens' participation in political life." In 1815, Burschenschaften had only about 200 members. Today the Deutsche Burschenschaft alone is a federation of about 15,000 young and old members in more than 120 fraternities in Germany, Austria, and Chile. They describe themselves as a community that lasts for a lifetime. They are characterized by the unity of young students and the "old boys," or alumni.

Becoming a fraternity member is more than just joining a club. The situation is similar to that found in many U.S. universities today. Above all, it means the voluntary duty to support the nonmaterial aims laid out in the slogan "Honor, Freedom, Fatherland." Furthermore, today students are encouraged to examine nonmaterial moral concepts and achieve an interdisciplinary general education.

Fraternity brothers, both young and old members, the actives and the old boys, keep in touch after having finished their studies. This guarantees a continuous interchange of thoughts and experiences between generations and professions. Thus Burschenschaften are also a system of establishing long-lasting contacts that may become useful, especially in political and official careers and businesses.

In former times, it was also quite common for members to fight one another. In Bismarck's case, he socialized with the Hannover Corps, where his challengers were members, and the Braunschweig Corps. During his 3 years as a student at the university, he was involved in at least two dozen duels. As a grown man he was proud of his dueling scar, which was an important badge of honor among fraternity students of the time.

Despite the high status of dueling scars, the university condemned the fencing that produced them, and he was subsequently punished. He and other dueling students accepted these punishments with pride, and Bismarck found that he did not have to stop dueling.

The life of Rudolf von Virchow began differently. As the son of a bourgeois family in Pomerania (one of the states in Germany at the time), in 1840 he studied medicine at the hospital of the Berlin Military Academy. This saved his parents a lot of money: At that time, German universities charged tuition, but the military academies were free.

Later he worked as a pathologist and anatomist. He was a great champion of the public health system, in which he engaged with great enthusiasm, particularly for the plight of city employees who had to work under disastrous conditions. When he pointed out a little too vehemently that epidemics could be prevented only through better living conditions for the poor, he lost his teaching post at the University of Berlin. He then taught at the University of Würzburg for 7 years before he was called back to Berlin. Many of his students became professors, a clear indication of his excellence in teaching.

Rudolf von Virchow became famous not only as a physician but also as a politician. In 1861 he was a cofounder of the Liberal Progressive Party, of which he remained a member for more than 40 years. He also had a seat in the Prussian State Parliament for 51 years and in the German Reichstag for 13 years. It was after a debate on naval forces in the Prussian Parliament on June 2, 1865, that our tale in crime begins.

Rudolf von Virchow, considered a liberal, had for years put the proud Prime Minister Bismarck in a difficult position by contradicting him during parliamentary debates on naval matters. Ever since the Treaty of Vienna had been signed between Germany and Denmark, the subject had been a heated one. A councillor of the state of Oldenburg, Hannibal Fischer, was asked in 1852 to auction off old naval vessels that it was thought had no use in peace-time. This upset many Germans, not only those in the military but also many taxpayers, who, after all, had paid for the fleet in the first place. Fischer was later called a ship salesman. This was considered a slight against his honor be-cause selling was not an appropriate occupation for a gentleman. He was also called a "rogue" and an "adventurer" who had dirtied his hands by working on such a project. In reality, Fischer only did what he was told to do by his govern-ment. But among friends of the navy, his name had a negative connotation.

The naval debates were always heated in Parliament. Today, we can only imagine how aggressive Virchow's verbal attacks on Bismarck must have seemed. From a modern perspective his words seem mild or at least only slightly cutting. But the code of honor was different in those days, and the years of quarrels between these two opposing characters had embittered them both. According to the stenographer's notes, Virchow said the following: "I can only assume that the Prime Minister [Bismarck] did not bother to thor-oughly read the report. I furthermore assume that it was enough for him to review only the end of the report as far as these delicate questions are con-cerned. But if he did indeed read the entire report and asserted that there are no sympathetic statements in the report, then I truly do not know what to make of his [Bismarck's] truthfulness."

This was too much. Virchow not only stated that Bismarck had not read an important file but, worse, accused him of lying about it. A few days later, Bismarck requested his second, Herr von Keudell, to call on Virchow and of-fer a challenge. There was no getting around it with honor, so Virchow had to find a second also, and he asked a Herr von Hennig. The situation had become dangerous because both men were prominent politicians, and nobody wanted to see either killed. On the other hand, because the two men had such different philosophies of life, many people were secretly looking forward to a duel.

But on June 8, Herr von Forckenbeck, the mayor of Berlin, tried to reduce the tension by addressing Parliament and stating that a parliamentary issue must not be fought over outside Parliament. Forckenbeck also pointed out that it was impossible to hold a duel inside Parliament because the law and social mores forbade it.

The president of Parliament, Herr Grabow, agreed and said dryly that the delegates had to abide by the laws of the House. "The decision is made and an-nounced, and the issue is herewith taken care of," said Grabow.

Minister of Defense Herr von Roon, the politician most injured by the sale of the naval vessels, took Bismarck's side. Although he was not a supporter of duels, he still thought that every person had the natural right to defend his or her personal honor, despite the law. No power on Earth, certainly not the rules of Parliament, could weaken one's code of honor. If Virchow did not apologize, it would be Bismarck's prerogative to choose the means of regaining his honor. According to von Roon, Parliament could not forbid anything once a quest for satisfaction was formulated. The only thing left for Virchow to do was to choose the weapon. This was an extraordinary viewpoint: The minister of defense put personal honor not only above the law but also above the legislative assembly.

The conservative party was delighted. They let it be known through their speaker that essentially any dispute in Parliament could be finished outside the House by any means suitable, even an illegal duel. The newspapers had a field day with the controversy.

Because there was no agreement by the members of Parliament and because they essentially disregarded the speech by its president, there was no decision for or against the duel. The next day the minister of defense sent a note to Virchow and asked what he intended to do.

In the official institutional history of the University Clinic of Berlin (Charité), where Virchow worked, it simply states that he was challenged to a duel and declined to accept because of his belief that weapons are not a solution to political questions. But of course this was too simple.

In reality, Virchow finished the argument with a strategic master stroke on June 17, two weeks after the verbal attack on Bismarck, by saying that his speech at the time had included an apology. He still believed that Bismarck had not read the report. If that were the case, then the chancellor could not have found anything positive in the (unread) report and therefore could not have lied about the content of the report. No one can knowingly lie about something unknown.

Finally Bismarck gave up grudgingly and accepted the half-hearted apology. The minister of defense let Virchow know that Bismarck no longer demanded satisfaction. The duel of the two stubborn opponents wound up as nothing but a battle of words.

A Question of Honor

Haluk Kaya, the Frankfurt police's expert on foreign nationals, collects startling newspaper headlines from around the world. Here are some samples: "Because he was called a homosexual, a man took revenge by killing him with 17 deadly knife wounds without showing any remorse"; "A 55-year-old man

Honor and Redbeard

At the beginning of the twentieth century, lawyers realized that there is no such thing as objectively defined honor. The concept depends on the individual case. Not even listing all the merits of a person yields a definition. What makes a person honorable, or what honors or offends someone, depends on his or her environment. The different hierarchies of the famous Cologne Carnival in Germany illustrate this: The position of the "carnival prince," the head of the festival committee, and the choice of the "triumvirate," who are chosen to serve on the festival committee, are extremely important honors and are taken seriously. However, such an honor in Cologne is of little interest to people in other parts of Germany and might even evoke a patronizing smile or total ignorance. But who insults whom in this context?

The penal code distinguishes between insults aimed at honorary titles, club member presidents, or decorations, and derogatory remarks about another person that attack his or her reputation or self-esteem. Therefore one can only offend people, but not businesses, institutions, or administrations. There is no such thing as an insult to a telephone company, the municipal streetcar system, or a treasury; only their workers can be personally insulted. Cologne's "carnival prince" can hardly be insulted by a grumpy coastal resident in Friesland. He has no following there that might honor or dishonor him.

Insult against a single person can result in jail time for up to 2 years; libel in Germany can be punished by up to 5 years. In 1983, there were about 8,000 convictions for personal insult, 200 for malicious gossip, and 98 for libel. The code of honor today is not quite as important as it was a hundred years ago.

Germans pay dearly if they make offensive hand or finger signs in traffic, which are deemed particularly obnoxious. A man in Bavaria had to pay 600 Euros because he "gave the finger" to a surveillance video camera set up by the police. Such a sign shows vulgar disdain for the people who have to inspect the pictures taken by the camera, according to a judge of the Munich Regional Court.

Even more bizarre, one can be prosecuted for an insult that is not perceived at all by normal people. In 1961, a Stuttgart Superior Court ruled the following to be an offense: A man nicknamed Redbeard told a woman that he could get well again only if she performed fellatio on him. This cunning man did indeed have an illness, an infection of the eye, dating from World War II. He maintained that only the desired acts would keep him from turning completely blind. Furthermore, he said that this affliction could also lead to dementia unless he received the "cure," via oral contact.

When the woman realized 7 months later that he had deceived her, she went to court to bring charges against him. The district court sentenced him to prison for continued insults against the woman, citing paragraph 185 of the German penal code. The appeals court upheld the conviction. Today it may seem unbelievable that a person who committed what seems to us as a bizarre joke would have to go to jail.

The case went to the next level of appeals court, where it was demonstrated how vital it is to interpret the law competently. Laws usually are written in a general way because the details of every case cannot be foreseen. Obscene actions are considered offenses under paragraph 185 of the German penal code, but they lose their illegality—and therewith the character of an insult—when the offended person is a willing participant. Nobody disputed that the woman had been prepared to do what was necessary to get Redbeard well again. Therefore, his prank could not be seen as an insult.

The court came to a wise conclusion; otherwise, adultery would be an offense according to paragraph 185, an insult to both the spouse and the person with whom the adultery was committed. When two adults are willing partners in an illicit affair, according to the law, the act is consensual. Socially it is still an unacceptable offense by which they forgo the protection of the honor of marriage. This is not to say that we can renounce higher levels of honor, such as that of human dignity and the right to life.

In the Redbeard case the courts went a step further. The woman who performed the "therapy" did so only because she believed the lie she was told; therefore, her consent was legally not binding, and Redbeard's sexual act became punishable. This decision was well meant but still amounted to nonsense because the woman was of clear mind and was able to reject the bizarre wish of her partner. Common sense cannot be prescribed by law.

Within limits, each person has different ideas about what is normal and what is disreputable. In Redbeard's case, this fellatio therapy was given by several women when he invited them for a joint session. According to the woman's own statement, she was glad that she no longer had to shoulder the entire responsibility of maintaining his health.

kissed the murder weapon with which he had killed his neighbor after finding him in bed with his wife"; "Angry father killed a 16-year-old boy and his 49-year-old father because the 16-year-old tried to rape his daughter."

Such cases appall most of us; we are often quick to say that they reflect foreign cultures and habits. Indeed, these crimes were all committed by members of the Turkish community in Germany. They had killed and showed no remorse. In their minds it was always a matter of honor. Much as it was 100 years ago, they did not feel bound by laws. They were convinced that they had done the right thing for their and their family's honor.

To understand the psyche of murderers and their crimes, it is advisable to look at the emotional driving force of the criminal. In these examples, the driving force is the code of honor. The traditional Turkish family differentiates between three forms of honor. One form of honor can be injured without touching the other forms.

The Turkish form of honor a person assumes in social and sexual contexts is known as *namus*. Society determines where a given person is on the social ladder and how that person is to behave sexually. Women must remain celibate before marriage and show decorum when meeting men. This more active role of honor in Turkish culture is called *irz*. Men do not have to abide by these rules. *Namus* is also the recognition of a person's social standing and how to preserve it. *Irz,* on the other hand, demands demure chastity and virtuous restraint in particular.

A third form of honor is *şeref*, which comes closest to the Western sense of personal honor. It relates to a person's value as recognized by others, or one's good reputation, which comes from honesty and good deeds. *Şeref* plays a secondary role in the criminal cases in this book.

Sexual advances toward women and deliberate adultery on their part diminish their *namus* and *irz* and the honor of their family. In this case, the male family members, especially the brothers, are required by tradition to protect the family against any loss of honor. In the past, such loss of honor led to social and economic disadvantage. Therefore it is understandable that the protection often is carried to extremes. After all, we are talking about the survival of a family.

There is a warning system that is supposed to prevent these attacks. Through their traditional family structure, Turkish men show that they will not condone violations of *irz* and *namus*. In their original cultural circle, potential troublemakers are thus scared off. At the same time, the precautionary behavior of these proud men is designed to prevent possible rumors that they give in too easily or that they are weak and unmanly or, even worse, *namussuz,* which means without *namus.*

To the Western mind, this behavior seems harsh, patronizing, or even brutally macho. This behavior is no longer valid in today's cultural context. Although different ways of life and habits are adopted quickly these days, forensic scientists and criminologists are still confronted with crimes that older ideas of conscience dictated for the protection of traditional honor systems as outmoded as dueling seems to us today.

CHAPTER 2

TRACES

Bones in the Forest

In the Rhafes case, the body parts were easily reassembled. But it is not always so easy to find a connection between the crime and the bodily remains. A typical example is when bones are found in a forest.

Every year, many bones are found, but unlike in the movies, sometimes it is not immediately apparent whether they belonged to a human being or an animal. Sometimes it is also impossible to determine how long a bone has been there—a month, a year, or a century. Were the bones dug up by animals and carried away? Would it be worthwhile to conduct a search with dogs or search poles? Search poles are used to search an area inch by inch.

The results of such a search determine whether any bones found are connected to a missing person report or a murder case. If there is no match with the register of missing persons of someone of that stature and there are no traces of stab wounds or other evidence of homicide, then further investigations may be fruitless.

Until a few years ago, bones such as these would be brought to a storage place in the basement of an institute for legal medicine. In the United States, such bones usually would have a piece of paper attached to them with the words *forensic anthropologist* written on it. This means that a forensic bone specialist should investigate the skeleton to try to determine the approximate time of death, the way the person died, or how the corpse was stored before it decayed. Unfortunately, there are very few forensic skeleton experts in the world. There is little overlap between archeology and forensic medicine, and there are only a handful of independent bone experts.

One of the few training places in forensic anthropology is the Body Farm. Its actual name is the Forensic Anthropological Research Facility (ARF). Its laboratories are hidden under a football stadium at the University of Tennessee. It therefore has an unusual address: 250 South Stadium Hall, University of Tennessee, Knoxville. Formally, the Body Farm is a subdivision of the anthropology and forensic archeology departments of the university.

Like most research institutes that deal with corpses, the Body Farm is squeezed into an academic backwater. This in itself is not a bad thing because at the interface between the different disciplines, interesting things are being investigated. The place is famous now; even the dry German weekly *Die Zeit* gave the Body Farm the poetic name "The Forest of Corpses." Once in a while, the effects of insects on corpses are studied here, too, so I have had the opportunity to work there.

The history of the Body Farm has become a modern tale for researchers and crime novelists. It began in 1971 when William Bass was assigned to start bone research at the university. He remained head of the anthropology department in Knoxville until 1995. In the beginning, Bass needed space and materials for his anthropological forensics group. The research was aimed at improving the rapid identification of corpses, even those in states of advanced decay. All forensic researchers depend on exact data to infer age, ethnicity, and time of death. The more exact this information is, the more efficient and accurate the subsequent investigations will be.

Forensic anthropologists do not always answer difficult questions, such as the time of death. One of Bass's first cases occurred when he was still a student. He had to identify the corpses of two truck drivers whose trucks had collided in Kentucky. To everybody's astonishment, the investigation showed that the parts of the two corpses were actually the parts of three bodies. The third person was a female, who probably was dead before the collision and was being transported by one of the trucks.

Even before Bass arrived on the scene, the art of skeletal examination rested on a solid foundation of knowledge. This is because an enormous number of skulls from all over the world have been measured for many decades in science museums and anatomical institutes. The examination of these skulls has produced many useful charts of characteristics and variations of human growth, and important conclusions have been drawn about the living body.

Many anthropologists in Europe were enthusiastic about racial anthropology before World War II. If not, they were compelled to become enthusiastic by the Nazis. After the war, few researchers wanted to go into this field. Physical anthropology had acquired a bad name, not so much because of bad data collection but because of its appalling connotations of genocide and racial purity. In German-speaking institutes of forensic medicine, there are still too few qualified bone specialists. The position of forensic scientist, as portrayed in U.S. books and films, is very unusual in Germany.

To interest and teach students, Bass started his own bone collection from scratch in 1971. For his data files, the skeletons were exactly measured and the data systematically recorded in tables according to sex, age, geographic background, illness, and all other pertinent information. When an unknown skeleton is found, the characteristic features of the person in life can then be inferred because these exact charts help to determine what body features were once associated with this skeleton.

Bass wanted more. His institute also researched the processes of decay. For that purpose, Bass and his students had to drive to a farm, where they kept the decaying material, and this was complicated and took hours of driving. The students had to examine their experiments several times a day. The police also were supposed to be able to attend the classes on bone identification, but given the location of the farm, all of this was unrealistic.

Bass told the dean of his school that he needed a permanent space at the university where he could store and research corpses. It would be so much easier to research the natural decay process over time if Bass could continuously observe it. This work could help determine the "age," or postmortem interval, of any given corpse.

In the spring of 1981, Bass was given an area on campus where the university's garbage used to be kept before incineration. Because open air garbage incineration was no longer allowed in the United States, the university had no use for that area. That was the day the Body Farm at the University of Tennessee was established.

"Such an outdoor area was necessary; it was a question of knowledge or ignorance," Bass explained many years later. The first question the police always ask is, "How long has the body been lying there?" Only then do they ask, "Who is this person?" Only by looking at the body's state of decay can one determine how long it has been there. Looking only at the bare skeleton does not help.

Because Tennessee was more densely populated than Kansas, where Bass had worked before, he had no problem getting corpses for his daily research, before they became skeletons. That was another good reason for having the Body Farm there. Whoever dies in Tennessee usually was discovered earlier because of the odor, while still in a state of active decomposition aided by insects. In the less populated state of Kansas, corpses lying in remote areas usually were found much later. Those bodies often were already completely decayed, and a tissue investigation was no longer an option.

Bass concentrated more and more on the forensics of decaying tissue. He also had several research projects in other areas of anthropology, but the Body Farm was a unique research center known internationally, and it became his pet project. Even after his retirement, he remained the head of this open air subdepartment. In 1995 he handed the farm over to his successor, Murray Marks, who is in charge to this day.

The Body Farm was not without its troubles in its early years. In the first year of the lab's existence, FBI special agent William Rodriguez began to research insects on decaying bodies. When the parking lot of the university clinic was extended in the direction of the Body Farm, the press got involved. One of the construction workers told the local television newscaster, "I am being harassed by a swarm of flies that came directly from one of the dead bodies."

Rodriguez and Bass were concerned about overnight trespassers into the research facility, so in 1986 Rodriguez moved into a tent on the Body Farm. The dean was kind enough to authorize the building of a barbed wire fence around the Body Farm.

As part of his insect research, Rodriguez put corpses into wire cages mounted on posts a few centimeters above the ground. The wire kept foxes and other vertebrates away from the bodies. It also allowed him to collect the insects that were underneath the bodies. Today, decomposing corpses are no longer elevated because maggots cannot climb; they simply fall off the corpses. It is more realistic to keep the corpses in contact with the ground, as occurs in real life.

Interestingly, Rodriguez realized that his corpses were infested by the same insects that had been reported decades earlier to be present on animal cadavers. There were minute differences in the species and the time they spent on the corpses, but that could be attributed to the different environments. His work and that of others led to the recognition of forensic entomology as a form of scientific and criminalistic research in the United States and Canada. Since then, insect specialists at a dozen North American universities have taken up the study of forensic entomology.

Local excitement over the presence of the Body Farm died down after a year of Rodriguez's research. Although there may be thirty to forty corpses on the farm, which at times give off an odor of decay, everybody soon realized that it had become a useful and peaceful research facility.

(Since this book was first published, I have become a member of the extended ARF family. In the summer of 2003, I was an FBI instructor in forensic entomology. This was an extremely happy time for me, and I enjoyed my interactions with the special agents. I also learned so much from colleagues Murray Marks and Richard Jantz that I collected enough material for the many additional courses I teach in Germany.)

News from the Body Farm

The details of many decay processes are well understood. Body Farm researchers are still investigating new environments in which to observe decay, particularly those that might be found in real cases. For example, corpses may be left in a shaded area, under water, or under a layer of concrete. It is astonishing to see how even the tiniest change in the surroundings can change the decay. I worked on such an experiment during a rainy summer in Canada and observed that a pig corpse left near a walkway had been skeletonized after only 2 weeks, whereas a similar pig placed only a few feet away, hidden under a bush, was comparatively well preserved after the same time period.

The Body Farm researchers are constantly experimenting with more sophisticated measuring equipment see whether they can accurately determine how long a corpse has been there. Entomological methods have already been mentioned; more recently, "artificial noses" that detect gases and measurement of the chemical composition of the corpse are being used to pinpoint a corpse's age.

These forensic anthropological experiments, performed under realistic circumstances, are not only scientifically appealing. They also teach us to avoid extrapolating from our previous work to new situations when the surroundings are different. Most importantly, the Body Farm, together with police procedures, can test the implications of the scientific experiments. Real cases can be different from controlled experiments, however, even if the temperature and ground condition are known exactly. This is often how misunderstandings happen during investigations. In an experiment, we only try to understand exactly when a bacon beetle or a gold fly, for example, appears on a corpse. But in a real case sometimes the question for the scientist is reversed: The decomposition stage of the body is known, but it is unclear why a certain insect approached the corpse.

Every year, the FBI sends a squad of special agents to the Body Farm, where they take an introductory course in forensic anthropology. There they learn not only how long it takes for a corpse to decay but also how to correctly and efficiently excavate a burial site. During an ongoing investigation there is no time for a detailed archeological reconstruction, but one should not be hasty and use an excavator, either.

When students come to the scene of a possible burial site, the first thing they are taught to do is to probe the ground carefully with sticks. Later the corners representing the area that has been probed are marked. The soil is then taken out with plastic shovels, bit by bit, and run through sieves. One must never stab directly into the ground; always remove the soil using movements horizontal to the ground. The soil is examined for evidence, either from the victim or from the killer.

You can tell the people who are taking this class for the first time by their despairing looks and soft curses. Why? The rule is that if a trainee misses even a minute piece of evidence buried in the earth, the entire area is filled in, and they have to start all over again.

Because the class is such a success, in some years it is exported to the FBI Academy at Quantico, Virginia. All FBI agents, regardless of their duties, can get involved if they wish. Next to the careful searches by hand and by sieve and other tools, they must learn how to find bones that lie below the fall foliage in the forest surrounding the academy, which stretches as far as the eye can see. At Quantico, the participants are told the same rule: You have to start all over again if a single bone is missed. These new gravediggers are rewarded with a small plaque with a joke written on it, attached to the buried skeleton.

The importance of the combination of science and criminal investigative practice is demonstrated by the fact that William Rodriguez, the former Body Farm scientist, now heads excavations for the United States on international missions such as those in the former Yugoslavia and in other war crime scenes.

Murray Marks's team at the Body Farm is, first and foremost, trying to study the stages of decay. Students periodically take tissue samples as the bodies decay. (Incidentally, most of these students are women; male students are rare both on the Body Farm and in my lab. Could it be that women have stronger stomachs?) These tissue samples are examined later in the lab. Maybe one day there will be a machine to do this work. Such a machine could be extremely helpful, not only to find buried corpses but also to determine burial time more precisely. This is important because, as we have seen, the decay process depends on many outside influences.

Let me add a word about the former head of the Body Farm, William Bass. He is by no means an odd or strange man. At 75, he remains full of energy and humor. Some of his visitors find his sober dealings with corpses during investigations rather strange. "A criminal case has nothing to do with grief. As an investigator, grief doesn't come into it," says Bass. "When I do experiments, I want to test myself and find out if I have enough knowledge to be able to identify the person and that person's fate."

A look behind appearances of this scientist makes his ways understandable: "I have lost two wives, both to cancer," Bass says. "Therefore I can't stand

Corpse-Tracking Dogs

The Body Farm does not deal only with dead bodies. In connection with the 1995 bomb attack in Oklahoma City, in which 168 people died in a federal office building, tracker dogs were being tested on the Body Farm in Tennessee to see whether they could work in such surroundings. Contrary to what we see in crime thrillers, four-legged helpers are quite difficult to handle.

Dogs are trained to look for bodies or body parts through a search and reward game. Tracker dogs must be very playful and enjoy the game; otherwise, they would not do this dull work. However, being so playful means that they quickly lose interest in the search. You cannot force them to do it; you have to understand them. In order to understand dogs and to get them to do their job, you have to find out what their stress level is in an environment of corpses.

Dogs live in a world defined by smell, and they are trained using the odor of corpses. That is why a collapsed office building full of dead bodies often is too much for them. There still is no satisfactory solution to this problem. Therefore, the dogs should be used only for a short while at a time. Each dog needs its own trainer, so this becomes an expensive proposition. Maybe studying the psyche of dogs can help us to find ways to use them for longer periods of time.

mourning. I don't like death, and I loathe funerals." On the other hand, Bass often holds small memorial services for the corpses at the institute. His colleagues find this slightly odd; usually, there is a service once a year for corpses at most institutes and departments of anatomy in Europe.

THE CRIMINALIST'S TOOLBOX

As with most scientific results, we can infer only a certain amount from the victim's bones about what happened to him or her. If there are no scrapes or fractures, that might mean that no strong force was applied to the body. But it could also mean that the person had been suffocated or stabbed in the abdomen. This lack of knowledge is annoying in that it runs counter to the criminalist's rule formulated by Sir Arthur Conan Doyle's character, Sherlock Holmes: "When all other contingencies fail, whatever remains, however improbable, must be the truth."

Investigators try to use as many techniques as possible from their criminal bag of tricks. These techniques can either confirm or refute the sequence of the crime. Not all methods are used every time, but it is helpful to be able to use the right method at the right time. Special techniques are taught to the FBI special agents who choose to stay current through rigorous training courses. Criminology is a social science. A criminalist will never be a forensic medical doctor or a forensic biologist, and vice versa. Their jobs are different, and so are their ways of thinking when working on a case. This is the way it should be. A scientific experiment cannot unmask a pickpocket, and a house search cannot determine how long a corpse has been lying in a certain location. Therefore, close cooperation is needed between the different investigators, whether they wear a uniform, a suit, a leather jacket, or a lab coat.

FACE AND IDENTITY

As we have seen, two questions are vital at the beginning of an investigation: What is the age of the corpse, and who was she or he?

The identification of the corpse by itself does not tell us what happened, and how long the person has been dead is of the greatest importance in questioning suspects effectively. The more exactly the time of death can be established, the more useful the witnesses' testimony will be. This is especially true in establishing people's alibis. On the other hand, it can be just as useless to know the postmortem interval of the corpse if it cannot be identified.

Forensic scientists take great pains to search for distinctive marks on the body. The face, above all, is crucial, because this is the thing witnesses remember best: A written description of the person often produces no response from the public, but as soon as a face is publicized on posters, the public responds. This is not astonishing; after all, a face gives much more information than any description possibly can.

There are three ways to reconstruct a face: It is possible to do facial cosmetics if the corpse still has some tissue, police artists can use witnesses' descriptions to create an accurate sketch, or the face can be reconstructed directly from the skull.

The art of cosmetically treating a corpse is an ancient one, almost forgotten in Europe because today dead bodies are rarely displayed in mortuaries or funeral parlors there. In the United States the dead are more commonly displayed at a viewing or a wake. Undertakers are able to make a face look peaceful and to keep a corpse from decaying too quickly. One simple way is to close the mouth, which often is wide open in a dead person. An open mouth does not look peaceful or dignified at funeral services. Worse, it makes the features unrecognizable and therefore more difficult to identify. The undertaker therefore either puts a book under the chin or sews the mouth shut before rigor mortis sets in. Today, undertakers, or embalmers, know many such cosmetic techniques, an art that remains mysterious to most of us.

Facial features change immediately at the time of death because all muscles relax, regardless of what the person last saw or what happened to him or her just before death. The facial muscles are controlled by the brain and therefore slacken with death. When dentures are taken out, the face also changes. Relatives and friends often are astonished at how little the dead person, whom they may never have never seen in deep sleep, resembles their relative or friend when alive. At the scene of an accident or crime this often leads to a problem: Spouses sometimes cannot immediately identify their partners, and investigations can then go in the wrong direction.

With the 1981 publication of the novel *Gorky Park,* one method of corpse identification became well known to the public: the reproduction of a face directly from the skull. After death a face not only slackens but also, because of the ongoing decay, can change in color to green, red, or black. The face may sink in at the same time, but it may also puff up as gases build up in the tissue. It takes a lot of patience and technical know-how to keep a face from decaying. The best example of face preservation is Lenin's corpse.

Of all Soviet politicians who were embalmed, only Lenin's face has been so well preserved. Joseph Stalin was also embalmed, but after de-Stalinization,

LENIN'S CORPSE

"Comrades, workers, and farmers, I come to you with a request. Don't let your grief change into a superficial devotion to the personality of Vladimir Ilyich. Don't build palaces or monuments in his name; he never felt such matters were important during his life. He even found them embarrassing. You know how much misery and chaos we have in this country. If you want to honor his memory, build kindergartens, houses, schools, and hospitals. Even better, live in accord with his teachings." These are the words of Lenin's widow, Nadezda Krupskaya, written on January 29, 1924, to *Pravda,* the only major Soviet newspaper at the time.

Lenin had died 8 days before this appeal, after a long struggle with arteriosclerosis, cerebral hemorrhage, and maybe also syphilis. Krupskaya suspected that her request would not be heeded. It was not the will of the Soviet government. Also, no nation would let a great leader rest in peace. Even the films of Charlie Chaplin and Albert Einstein's documents were preserved after their death, not destroyed as they had explicitly asked.

There was to be no quiet resting place for Lenin: His successor, Stalin, wanted to pave his way to autocracy with the full power of a state parade. The pleading of Lenin's widow was as ineffective as the wish of the deceased, who also did not request an elaborate funeral or memorial to him.

Three months before Lenin's death, the Politburo had discussed in a secret meeting how to keep Lenin's body preserved. It didn't matter that Stalin had gone a long way toward neutralizing Lenin's residual hold on power; in that crucial meeting, he presented himself in an amiable way and said ingratiatingly, "Some are of the opinion that modern science is able to preserve his body permanently, or at least long enough so that the people get used to the idea that he is no longer among us."

Two members of the Politburo, Trotsky and Bukharin, begged to differ. "Trotsky is right," noted Bukharin; "if we preserve his remains as a relic, we offend his memory! Really, we cannot take this possibility seriously." A few days later, Trotsky was charged with activities undermining the unity of the party. His voice had lost its weight. Nobody dared to contradict Stalin.

On January 23, 2 days after Lenin's death, the chief of police gave the official view of the Politburo to the newspaper *Pravda:* "Kings are being embalmed because they are kings. As far as I'm concerned, the main question is not whether we should conserve the body of Vladimir Ilyich, but rather, how it will happen."

Four days later, Lenin's corpse was brought to a provisional mausoleum. Workers had dug into the frozen ground a 10-foot shaft into which
they lowered the body. This was lucky, because in this way the body was
frozen. In summer, the body would have begun to decay right away. There
was no refrigeration available to keep corpses; the Soviets had to order re-
frigerators from abroad. In the freezing temperature, Lenin's body dried
up, which meant that bacteria could not grow. At low temperatures bacteria
develop only very slowly, if at all. The result is that the corpse undergoes a
kind of freeze drying that naturally preserves the tissues.

To further preserve the corpse, anatomist Abrikossov put 6 liters (21
pints) of a mixture of alcohol, zinc chloride, and glycerin into Lenin's veins.
This mixture acted as an antifreeze. As a result his blood vessels, which at
higher temperatures would have been a very effective conduit for the spread
of bacteria and other germs, were blocked off.

Nevertheless, the spot where Lenin's skull had been sawed open in order
to take out his brain turned brown. The rest of the skin turned more and
more black. In the meantime, a political committee, with no expert knowledge, argued about the correct way to preserve the tissue.

After days of argument, the committee finally commissioned Vladimir
Vorobjov, a professor of anatomy, to put together a dissecting team and get
started. Vorobjov was afraid for his life, and rightly so. If he made a mistake and could not successfully preserve Lenin's body, it would be close to
treason. On the other hand, if he refused to do the work, it would certainly
cost him his head.

Vorobjov was lucky that he had already tried a conserving method de-
vised in 1895 by pathologist Melnikov-Rasvedenkov. It used the following
ingredients:

240 liters (63.5 gallons) glycerin (to keep the tissue flexible and to prevent freezing)

110 kilograms (242.5 lb) potassium acetate (to bind the water in the tissue)

150 liters (39.6 gallons) water

1 or 2 percent chlorine and quinine (as a disinfectant)

For this work, the mausoleum was closed for 4 months, and Vorobjov's assistant, biochemist Boris Ilyich Zbarski, was hired. Ten years later,
Zbarski's son Ilya joined the team. He swears that to this day, it is Lenin's
real body that is still on display, not a wax replica.

But what did the first team do in only 2 months in order to restore
the corpse, which was already beginning to discolor, to an apparently good

state? Even today, their work seems like a miracle of preservation, even if it is a chemically produced miracle.

Because everyone on the conservation team knew that a single mistake might cost them their heads, Vorobjov removed all organs from the chest and stomach cavity because they are most prone to decay. He then rinsed the open body parts first with water, then with formalin, and finally with vinegar.

Freed of all material susceptible to rapid decay, the cleansed corpse was put in a formalin bath and thawed for the first time. A radiator kept the temperature at 16°C. It was unfortunate that the otherwise agreeable temperature caused the sharp odor of formalin to leak out.

Worse, the formalin did not penetrate all the way through Lenin's body. At first, Vorobjov was afraid to make further cuts into the corpse so that the formalin could seep deeper into the body. He told his colleague Rosanov, whose formal consent he needed to make these cuts, "I am afraid not for the dead but for the living." Needless further cuts into Lenin's body might also result in a death sentence. The problem was that Vorobjov needed to cut not only Lenin's shoulders and back but also his hands and fingertips. Vorobjov's colleagues refused their consent.

Luckily, Vorobjov had the courage to make the cuts anyway. He also raised the alcohol level of the bath, which made the body more porous and gave it more color. When they put Lenin's body into the final bath mixture of glycerin, water, and calcium acetate, everything went well. The body became flexible again (as it remains today) and looked realistic. Slight discolorations on the skin were bleached with peroxide, and mildew was removed by phenol.

The rest was routine. The lips were sewn shut, the eyes were replaced by glass eyes, and the eyelids were drawn. When Lenin's brother Dimitri Ulyanov looked at the corpse in the glass coffin, he said, to everybody's relief, "It takes my breath away. He looks the same as when I saw him a couple of hours right after he had died, maybe even better." The preservationists had saved their own lives.

Ever since, Lenin's corpse has needed constant attention. The tip of the nose, the ears, and the fingers dry out quickly and discolor to a dark, mummy-like hue. For this reason, the corpse wears a tailor-made, fine-quality rubber corset under which preservation fluids are injected regularly.

In May 1997, President Boris Yeltsin announced that times had changed, and Lenin would soon be removed from the mausoleum and transferred to his mother's tomb in St. Petersburg. The protests came immediately. The Communist hardliners met and came to the conclusion that because Red

Square, where Lenin's mausoleum is, was about to be named a World Cultural Heritage Site by the United Nations, the corpse could not be moved. They used a new law that forbids any change to the buildings of Red Square. But even Ilya Zbarski, who was able to preserve the corpse for decades, now feels that although the durability of Lenin's corpse is an unequaled scientific achievement, any further conservation would be barbaric, out of keeping with modern culture. The only people who are being permanently preserved today are anonymous corpses, used for anatomical instruction, and dangerous Russian felons, whose Mafia associates consider this a stylish practice.

started by Khrushchev in 1956, his body was removed from public display next to Lenin in 1961 and buried in a grave 300 feet from the mausoleum.

The facial tissue of corpses normally decays quickly, especially in summer and when outside, where animals have access to them. Bluebottle flies and other blowflies lay their eggs on a corpse hours or sometimes minutes after death, so that the tiny maggots can easily scrape off the tissue at moist places and wherever there is thin skin. Certain body parts are slow to dry out, such as the eyes, inner ears, nose, and mouth. This means that the parts most important for identification of a corpse are the first to be destroyed.

When maggots have begun to eat away at a face, it no longer makes sense for the investigators to preserve the tissue. The holes and the loss of tissue do not allow effective restoration. Rather, the investigators need to start anew from the underlying bones to calculate what the face must have looked like. But how is this done when no soft tissue is left?

The scientific–medical charts are the key to the face. Travelers have realized for centuries that faces differ in different parts of the world. For example, Africans tend to have flatter noses and thicker lips than Europeans. These characteristic features have been measured and documented for a long time. The obvious and the sometimes subtle differences in physique add to the fact that we are able to derive the geographic origin of a person, often from scant remains. It is not only the bones that have been measured in modern times but also the soft tissues such as skin, fat, connective tissue, and muscles.

Such measurements are made using measuring needles stuck into the dead body or X-rays and ultrasound images of living people. The thicknesses of the tissues of different origin may be very similar, but often there is a slight difference that is significant. The average differences are important in trying to reconstruct the face on a skull.

Figure 4 shows twelve important measuring points that were used in an investigation in 2001. The facial surface is measured perpendicular to the bone or the teeth, and the same is done diagonally. The area where the tissue thickness is known to be most telling for the reconstruction of an artificial face is of course most important.

For all these body features there are always variations. A favorite statistical tool of the scientist is helpful: the median value, in this case the average thickness of soft tissue above the bone. The average thickness of this tissue at several places on the cranium gives the first clue for facial reconstruction.

Skin thickness changes with age, particularly in children and adolescents. But it also varies with the geographic and genetic origin of the person. Fortunately, the bone structure of a skeleton gives additional evidence about the geographic origin. Furthermore, the skeleton can tell us a lot about the person's age and sex. Today, we can pretty well establish the age of a person with an X-ray of a hand bone. Perhaps surprisingly, the skeleton does not tell us whether the person was slim or heavy-set.

In criminal cases it is rare that there is only a skeleton. With a burnt corpse the face usually is badly distorted, but the rest of the body often is not so badly affected. During burning, the high temperature on the surface of the body decreases rapidly the deeper you go inside the body. The heat is blocked by the fat and the high water content of the body. Even medical students are astonished when they see the well-preserved heart and other inner organs of a corpse that is badly burnt on the outside. Even if the skin is completely charred and the face is destroyed, measuring the thickness of the thighs can tell us how much fat the body had. In other words, the soft tissue tells us about the body weight of the dead person. This and the median tissue thickness are the basis of any subsequent reconstruction.

It is much more difficult to reconstruct the lips and nose. There is no reliable mathematical method to determine how thick or curved these facial parts once were from the underlying bone, but this shortcoming is being addressed. It is hoped that additional measuring points and faster computers will help us develop better data for lips and noses.

INVESTIGATION AND GUESSWORK

Noses and lips are not the only imponderables in facial reconstruction. Hair color, eyebrow shape, and hairstyle all are important in identifying a person. That is why it is often enough to wear a hat in order to get lost in a crowd or to avoid being recognized. A reconstructed face almost always wears a relaxed and serious expression, which a casual acquaintance may never have seen.

In a sense, it is impossible to reconstruct fully a person about whose life we know nothing. Perhaps a certain facial expression unique to that person would be enough to enable others to recognize him or her. Like every other criminological method, facial reconstruction has its limits.

In the last 100 years the uncertainties of soft tissue reconstruction have resulted in lively discussions about the usefulness of the technology. In 1999, two Australian anatomists, Carl Stephan and Maciej Henneberg, researched whether facial reconstructions can truly be successful. The two authors wrote, "This study aims to determine if any of 16 facial approximations, built using standard techniques, are sufficiently accurate to produce correct identifications of the target individuals above chance." The result was shocking.

The Australians used plaster casts of four human skulls, which they christened Sam, Fred, Kate, and Jane. They constructed faces for each skull using different but uniform methods. The first method was by a simple drawing, something like a police artist's sketch. Besides the skull, the sketch artist used no other clue to identify the person. There were no descriptions from witnesses. The artist had nothing to work from but the average thickness of the soft tissue. From this he had to deduce the form and size of the nose, lips, forehead, and chin. The artist made a drawing, not a model, but his basic calculations were the same.

In another experiment, pictures of the skulls were digitally constructed on a computer. There, the calculated images were superimposed on the skull so that they corresponded exactly to the calculated thickness of soft tissue. The reconstructed images then fit perfectly onto the underlying skull.

In the third method, thirty-four holes were drilled at designated spots and wooden pegs were put into a plaster cast of the skull. These wooden pegs were cut to correspond to the median thickness of soft tissue, which forensic medical expert Richard Helmer had measured by ultrasound in the 1980s. The outer ends of the pegs were either tied together with the help of computer software or simply embedded in plastic. The figures received artificial eyes. Men received eyes with a diameter of 26 millimeters, and women's were 25 millimeters wide. The width of the nose was a rough estimate based on measurements performed on living people: The nose typically is two-thirds as wide as the skull's nasal cavity opening. The eyelids were also based on an estimated value. The size of the outer ear was extrapolated from the length of the nose. Some of the results are shown in figure 6.

Because the wooden peg method seemed too simple, the Australian researchers also used another classic modeling technique: The skull is first given facial muscles in the reconstruction. Because these are positioned on the skull in living people, some of them leave visible traces behind. These traces can indicate the thickness of the muscles or, better still, their distinctive features. Unfortunately, this is not the case with all facial muscles. The exact position of the cheek muscles and the muscles used to open and close the lips cannot be derived from any markings.

It took weeks to develop faces for the four skulls using the various methods. Two of these faces were drawn, the other two modeled. None of them had hair. Then the experiment got exciting. The anatomists showed sixteen pictures of the reconstructed faces to thirty-seven volunteers, all medical professionals. They were supposed to compare these pictures with ten photos of real faces, some of which were of the people whose faces had been reconstructed.

The results were disappointing. In almost 500 attempts, the skulls were identified correctly only thirty-eight times. This would not necessarily have been a bad result because even an imperfect identification could give helpful clues. It would mean that a modeled face would not be recognized by all witnesses but maybe by one out of ten. Even that would be a step in the right direction.

Much more serious was the fact that "witnesses" in this experiment made wrong attributions in more than 300 cases. In more than two-thirds of these cases the facial reconstructions were assigned to photos that were of random people who were not actually reconstructed. In a real case, such mistakes would send the investigation in the wrong direction.

The high number of errors in these lab trials probably occurred because we are used to connecting cause with effect, even when such a connection is obviously absurd. We start from the assumption that in an experiment or a criminal case, the person we are looking for is one of the people in the pictures presented to us. Otherwise, why would we be shown the pictures? But unfortunately this is not always the case. The selection of the images depends on the status of the investigation and whether the person we are looking for is among the suspects. Also, it depends on the availability of photos: Could there be a more recent or a better photograph of that person?

Another reason why the Australian investigation had such poor results was that the "witnesses" could not connect the reconstructions with the real people without characteristic facial features, particularly if they were shown without hair. The result was that in many cases they simply guessed instead.

The Australian anatomists wrote that only one in sixteen facial recognitions was better than a random guess. This implies that facial reconstruction is an inexact and unreliable method of identification, which contradicts the rare isolated cases in which facial reconstruction is helpful in investigations. This result cannot be reconciled with the high success rate often claimed by facial reconstruction experts; their results seem better than they actually are because solved cases attract much more attention and publications than the many failures, which of course are not even published.

Furthermore, facial reconstructions are unscientific because they leave so much room for artistic license. After all, several different guidelines and methods are used in facial reconstruction. It is up to the artist to decide which method or combination of methods to use. This is an additional source of errors. Also, hairstyles clearly cannot be derived from looking at the skull.

Given all this, one has to wonder why facial reconstruction is still being used. What follows is a case that should help to illustrate why the Australian experiment produced such disappointing results. The problem lies largely with life's complexities and realities.

MURDER IN MANNHEIM

Friday, August 20, 1993, was a beautiful summer day in Mannheim, a city in southwestern Germany on the Rhine. A few curious people were waiting to see an old U-boat that was being transported up the river to a museum in Speyer. The local paper, the *Mannheimer Morgen,* noted that horror spread among the crowd when in the cornfields some 50 meters south of the Theodor Heuss Bridge at the north end of the city, the burnt body of a man was found. The startled onlookers called the police. When the body burned, the tendons of the dead man shortened, bending his arms and legs into an unusual contortion. The cornfield directly around the corpse was scorched, and there was a bloody trail leading to the body. Obviously, a crime had been committed.

Police helicopters circled above the gruesome scene, and forensic scientists were summoned from nearby Heidelberg University. They discovered that the dead man's skull was damaged before he was burned.

As early as the next day an analysis of the textile and hair remains suggested what the man would have looked like when alive. He had brown, wavy hair. He was wearing white socks and brown wingtip shoes, black jeans, and a turquoise-colored shirt. This clothing would have been more fitting for the 1980s than for the 1990s. Beyond this, the corpse was not further identifiable because of the severe scorching.

Because the corpse was lying next to a paved path, it is very unlikely that it was put there in the middle of the day. It was probably left there the night before.

An autopsy was performed. The dead man must have been between 25 and 35 years old and weighed about 130 pounds. His teeth were in very bad condition. On his upper left arm he sported an odd, unprofessional tattoo that depicted a dog, or possibly a dove, or even a halberd (a pike-like weapon from the late Middle Ages). He also had a mustache. All these clues pointed to a person who might have had connections to blue collar and criminal circles. The next day, Monday, the police set up a hotline where anyone could give anonymous hints regarding the corpse and the crime. A reward of about 2,500 marks ($1,600) was offered, a standard reward that has not been increased by the police since the end of World War II.

As was expected, no clues came from the criminal underground. The police got a lead when 2 weeks later they investigated the murder of an elderly couple in the city of Solingen, more than 130 miles away. These two art collectors were ambushed and shot dead. The criminals robbed them of watches, coins, and jewelry valued at more than 200,000 marks (about $100,000). Just before the crime, two people who appeared to be Eastern European had been asking questions about this couple.

The crime resembled another crime that had been committed in July, only a month earlier. Some Eastern European men had ambushed a coin collector in the town of Hanau, close to Frankfurt. The two men had demanded, at gunpoint, that the coin collector let them into his apartment. The collector was then tied up, and the criminals got away with a number of valuables, driving off in his car. They did not kill their victim, so the investigation moved quickly.

The duo drove to a rest stop near Viernheim, parked the car, and disappeared. Mannheim police put two and two together: The rest stop was close to the cornfield where the burned victim had been found. The man had features that are common in Eastern Europeans, so he could well have been from Eastern Europe. Maybe the dead person belonged to a criminal gang and then became a victim? The fact that he had been shot in the head and his body had subsequently been burned made this plausible. But that brought the investigators to a dead end. The criminals probably had returned to Eastern Europe a long time ago. For about 6 months, there was no further news about the murder in the Mannheim cornfield.

Working from tips phoned in by viewers of a television program about the case, the police began to focus on two Polish citizens who were registered in Mannheim. They also concluded that they were looking for members of a gang or possibly contract killers. As it happened, the Polish police also were looking for these two, in connection with a murder in Lublin.

Recent and older photos of these men were published in the press. A few superficial changes in their appearance made them look very different at different ages. In one photo, the younger of the two looks like a street thug; in another, he more resembles a hard-nosed businessperson. The other man had grown a mustache, making it difficult to track them by photographs alone. The chances of catching these two were slim because they also had fake ID cards. However, the police discovered that one of the two wanted men, whose actual name was Robert Kwiek, had several aliases: Darius Sosnowski, Waldemar Peasecki, and Marius Czerwinski.

Successful Facial Reconstruction

As important as the search was for the killers was, the problem of identifying the victim was just as important. Luckily, forensic specialist Richard Helmer managed to complete a facial reconstruction (see figure 6).

Helmer is a pioneer in forensic facial reconstruction. One of his scientific predecessors was Russian anatomist Mikhail M. Gerassimov (figure 5). Gerassimov had dreamed of reconstructing ancient faces, especially those of primitive or prehistoric humans, and he wanted to reconstruct them from skeletons. He wrote a book on this subject that was translated first into German and later into English. Gerassimov died in July 1970, at age 62, shortly after publishing his book.

In contrast to Helmer, Gerassimov was interested in famous people from the past, such as Tsar Ivan IV "the Terrible," Friedrich Schiller, and the so-called Heidelberg Man (*Homo erectus heidelbergensis*), an early ancestor of modern humans. At the time, anatomy specialists such as Professor von Eggeling from Germany and Professor Sur from Czechoslovakia believed that because of the many unknowns about these skulls, it would be impossible to reconstruct their faces even approximately. It was only when Gerassimov began to work successfully on murder cases that it became apparent, after years of experiments, that he could reconstruct faces from skulls. At the end of his life, he wrote, "In these last years, many portraits that were derived from my work on human skulls became famous. They are displayed in scientific collections and in various museums. They are considered plausible; the truth of the reconstructions is proven by the photos of the living people themselves. The agreement between the facial reconstruction from the skull and portraits or photos of certain people often has been explained as being due to my personal ability, and my 'phenomenally developed' instinct. It is very flattering to have such exclusiveness credited to you, but this does not fit the facts. The success of my students, who use my recommended methods, proves that this method is correct in its main elements. They not only produce portraits of people from the Stone Age and Bronze Age but also systematically solve problems of identifying unknown people from the recent past."

The "instinct" Gerassimov mentions is nothing but a nicely phrased reproach that every facial reconstruction specialist is subjected to: that he has additional but uncredited information that helps him get the anticipated result. The fact that this is a routine forensic procedure seems not to occur to many lab scientists.

BACH, RAPHAEL, AND THE SCATTERED SKELETON OF A BOY

Since 1867, several anatomists have tried to restore faces to skulls. These are not crime victims but the faces of famous people or those found in archeological discoveries. Friedrich Gottlieb Welcker (1784–1868) worked on the reconstruction of the skull of German poet Friedrich Schiller. He also worked on the skulls of Dante and Raphael. He always compared his reproductions with drawings of these people or with other clues to their appearance, such as Raphael's own work.

The first anatomist to use a method close to modern forensic practice was Wilhelm His, working in 1895. There was a question as to whether a skull ascribed to Johann Sebastian Bach was truly his. His's facial reconstruction was a close match to a portrait of the composer.

The forensic application of these methods was suggested in 1899 by Hans Gross in the journal *Archive for Criminal Anthropology* (*Archiv für Kriminalanthropologie*). But still missing were sufficient soft tissue data for the different facial areas. Then there was the persistent question as to whether a facial reconstruction could point to just one person. Today, scientists can guarantee at least a reasonable resemblance to the face of a given deceased person.

Gerassimov's first case occurred in 1939 in Leningrad (now St. Petersburg). The bones of a person were found in a field, scattered over an area of some 12 by 15 meters. However, animals also scatter bones like this. And sure enough, the corpse showed traces of possible wolf bites. The skull and lower jaw were found 65 feet away. Only traces of cuts were found on them, and they could not be from animal bites. Thirty years later, Gerassimov remembered,

"When I entered the room, the investigative magistrate was just about ready to discontinue the procedure. He looked at me in an unfriendly way and asked: 'What do you want?'

"I answered: 'Lieutenant Gudov from Department I of the Militia Administration just told me that you have a skull of an unknown person.'

"'Yes, and?' the investigator replied.

"'I have been working for more than 15 years on problems of facial reconstruction, and I believe I could help you with the identification.'

"The judge growled: 'Nonsense. Nobody can help. But since you're here, you can pack up these bones. We have nothing to lose. Anyway, I have 12 hours until I have to turn in a draft of the order to dismiss the process, and it doesn't matter whether the bones go to the crematorium or to you.'

"Thirty minutes later I was seated at my desk. I took a large piece of paper and carefully placed the bones on top. The skeleton, including the long bones, was not complete. There were only a few ribs and vertebrae bones. The skull was in good condition, but earth and grass were sticking to it. There was also earth inside the skull. When I began to clean the skull carefully with a brush, I saw there were many small hairs on the underlying paper. They were reddish blond and short.

"When the skull was cleaned, it revealed on the left side of the frontal bone the trace of a blow with a blunt weapon. On the right side of the back of the head, slightly above the mastoid process of the temporal bone, I saw traces of cuts indicating numerous blows that must have been inflicted with a tool that had a very thin and sharp blade.

"There was no doubt, this was murder. The crime had obviously been committed with a small, light hunting axe. The blow to the forehead could have been applied by the back of an axe. It was my job now to determine the age and the sex of the victim as exactly as possible and then to mold the face onto the skull.

"The incomplete bone formation of the skull, the entirely loose joints between the bones of the cranium, the low degree of wear and tear of the teeth, and the absence of the back molars all led to the assumption that this must have been a youth no more than 12 or 13 years old.

"It was much more difficult to determine the sex, since it was a young person who did not yet display the sexual characteristics on the skull very well. But certain things like the stronger streamline of the relief of the bone structure above the eyes and the back of the head at the mastoid process of the right temporal bone, the relatively strong lower jaw bone, as well as the strong micro-relief of the entire face skeleton led me to believe that this was a boy's skull rather than a girl's. This assumption was emphasized by the relatively massive structure of the ends of arm and leg bones.

"Two hours later, I already had some indication of the appearance of the dead person, and I conveyed it immediately to the investigative judge by telephone. I asked him, 'Among the missing people, are you looking for a boy of 12 or 13 years, of small but sturdy build, stocky with an oblong face, and a long back to the head, with reddish blond hair cropped short, it must have been cut about a week prior to his death?'

"The astonished judge asked: 'Why a boy, why reddish blond?'

"I answered: 'I vouch for everything I just said. I'll explain the reasons later.'

"I did not want to tell him on the phone that, with a little care on his part, he could have found the hair himself and that the dead person indeed had short reddish blond hair.

"The reconstruction of the boy's skull needed specific preparatory work. Luckily I already had some material. Among the collected X-ray photographs, there were about a dozen pictures of boys aged 9 to 13. So I was able to form a pattern of the soft tissue parts after the profile.

"Only then could I actually begin the work of reconstruction. It was tedious and it took all my attention plus a lot of agility; first, the bite and the lower jaw needed to be put together correctly. This was not so easy in this case, because after his death so many teeth were lost. After that the most important chewing muscles were reconstructed out of wax, since they determine the facial form. Glass eyes were put in the wax face.

"The profile was developed on the median line [an imaginary line drawn down the middle of the face], and I paid attention to the existing data on the soft tissue thickness of children of that age, in addition to the specific features of the skull relief, the nasal bone, the jaw (bite), and the chin: They all had to be taken into consideration. Slowly, the head of the boy was formed. He was snub-nosed and chubby-cheeked; he had a steep forehead, thick upper lips, and protruding ears.

"The next day, at 11 o'clock in the morning, I appeared in front of the investigating judge. Together with him I drove to Lieutenant Gudov of the Militia Administration Department. It was there that it would be decided in which way the investigation should continue. Expert opinion of my kind had never been given before. One thing was certain: It was impossible to just show the reconstructed skull to members of the family. The reconstruction in wax could not simply be shown to either the father or the mother (assuming they did not know their son was dead). They would be very upset, and an objective identification would no longer be possible. On Gudov's advice, we planned to show photos of different children. They would not show the actual reconstruction to the parents but rather photos of it among many others. In order to make them look as much as possible like the photographs of living persons, we photographed them from many different angles, wearing a coat and a cap, as well as photographs without a cap. Seven photos were finally made of the reconstructed head of the dead boy. It was apparent only by very close inspection that the seven photos did not show a living face.

"Five days later, the unknown person was identified in my presence. The investigating judge meanwhile established that 6 months earlier, in the village of K. not far from the place where the bones had been discovered, a boy was missing. He had run away from home several times, so the parents were not alarmed. Eventually, they thought, he would reappear. After all, where could he go? The relatives believed that, as adventurous as the boy was, he probably was still roaming about. The child's father was summoned to an investigating court in Leningrad. At that meeting, he said that his son was 12 years old, had red hair like his mother, was very bright and a good student, that he liked to read, and he did not like farming. He also said that the boy constantly threatened to run away to the city. The father was convinced that his son was still alive.

"After the questioning, as agreed upon, about thirty photos of boys aged between 12 and 13 were shown to him, including the seven of the reconstructed head of the dead boy. Without hesitation he pointed to all seven photos of the reconstructed face. It never occurred to him that these photos did not depict the real face of his son. Looking at one photo he said, 'Oh, what a nice coat he has; the cap seems to be new. He must be doing all right.' That is the way the murdered boy was objectively identified. It was the first experiment in which a facial reconstruction was used in a criminal case, and with splendid success. The remaining work of the investigating judge was done without me. I merely recall that the case was closed in 1941."

Another team in Auckland, New Zealand, also uses facial reconstruction in criminal cases. In 1999, for example, they succeeded in identifying a decayed corpse that was found without any markings in Manukau Harbor (in the north of New Zealand, close to the capital, Auckland). Because they believed it to be the body of a sailor from the Polynesian island Kiribati, different objects from his home were requested for comparison. The genetic fingerprint taken from hair from his home could not be compared successfully with the DNA from the corpse because the corpse's DNA was too degraded. So a facial reconstruction was made using the skull. It was digitally scanned and overlaid on photos of the missing man on the computer. The agreement was sufficient for the identification. Finally, the sailor could be declared dead.

Gerassimov's claim that he solved practically every case he worked on was met with disdain by his colleagues. They forgot that Gerassimov had at his disposal a totally different forensic research system in the Soviet Union. Their police force was not bound by the same rules of law as the police in the West are. For example, the police could spy and tap phones routinely despite a lack of hard evidence. Living in a "police state" naturally gives the police tremendous power. This gave Gerassimov substantially more information about cases than what scientists received in the West, which helped him solve them more easily. More importantly, crimes committed in Iron Curtain countries (if they were officially acknowledged to happen at all) would be declared solved on orders of the government, whether they were or not.

Richard Helmer also has performed many experiments on facial reconstructions for criminal investigations in the 1980s and 1990s. He has also investigated how photos of dead people could be assigned to a given skull. Helmer has shown that both reconstruction and superimposition are good investigative tools when other methods reach their limits.

In the Mannheim cornfield case, facial reconstruction was helpful because there were few clues as to who could have known the victim. A photo therefore would help the investigators in their search because, with this in hand, they could ask many people with some likelihood of getting some useful replies. They were successful. Witnesses reported that a man named Krzystof had been staying in Mannheim the previous August. Mannheim was a way station on his journey from Lublin, Poland, to Italy. The Polish police then searched among the people in the circle of suspect Robert Kwiek and his partner, Paul Bielawski, for somebody called Krzystof; they found out that there had been a Krzystof Rejak, residing in Lublin, and he knew both of them. After that, the still partially recognizable corpse in the cornfield was immediately fingerprinted and compared with the Polish records. The identification was successful: Krzystof was the corpse in the cornfield.

The comparison of the facial reconstruction with a photograph of the real Rejak was interesting. Because Richard Helmer knew the hairstyle and hair color of the corpse, he was able to come up with a description of the missing person that was very close to reality (figure 6). If you compare the work of a makeup artist with that of pure facial restoration without hair, you will realize quickly why the Australian anatomists felt that facial reconstructions were of little use: Without hair, even Helmer's excellent reconstructions probably would have been unrecognizable or of little use. Fortunately, a lot of corpses keep their hair for a long time: Hair does not decay.

Richard Helmer said, "A well-reconstructed face, photographed as if for a portrait, can look almost lifelike. An observer who does not know that it is a reconstruction may not be able to detect that he is looking at a reconstruction." It was clear to him that such a photo is an aid to the investigation and nothing more, but also nothing less. "A plastic facial reconstruction should and will give only clues. Proof of identity must be established by other methods."

This is true for all forensic methods. Not even an absolutely certain genetic fingerprint can be the only piece of evidence used to convict a suspect. There must be other facts leading to the conclusion that the suspect indeed committed the crime. Every piece of evidence must be put into a reasonable context by the criminalist's conclusions; otherwise, even if the conclusions are correct, they may not stand up in court.

The End of the Story

Fugitive Paul Bielawski was apprehended on May 12, 1994, 9 months after the murder in the cornfield. He had absconded to Antwerp, where jewelry and gems are traded on a grand scale. The international search had been hot on his heels after the police has received several clues that Bielawski was staying somewhere in the Benelux countries, and Antwerp was the obvious choice for a criminal of his prominence. Whereas his smarter colleague, Kwiek, had gone back to his home area, Bielawski was caught with a stolen and altered ID card. It bore an alias that he had used before in other crimes. Therefore it made no difference whether he used his real documents or a fake one: He was on the search list with either name.

After the Belgian police's great success in capturing one of the two criminals, their Ukrainian colleagues began to get busy, and Kwiek also was trapped by documentation requirements. A year after the burnt corpse of Krzystof Rejak was found, Kwiek wanted to marry his girlfriend. To accomplish this he posted, very law-abidingly, his intention to marry at the city hall of Dnjepropetrowski, a Ukrainian city of more than 1 million inhabitants. After a quick look into his records, this almost-groom was arrested on his way to the wedding.

East Meets West

The economic plight and open borders of Eastern European countries after the collapse of the Communist bloc in the 1990s drove professional criminals such as Kwiek and Bielawski to the West, if only for a short time.

The eagerness of these criminals to resort to violence was something unknown in Germany. The criminals often were caught, albeit after extensive investigations, if they moved around. They were easily spotted because even in the underworld, the rules and social requirements varied from town to town. Kwiek and Bielawski felt a little too secure. The idyllic small-town atmosphere in Germany fooled them into thinking that they had settled comfortably into their new environment without attracting attention. But this was certainly not the case.

It was different for contract killers: They came, did their job, then left the area quickly. Such criminals were hard to catch; they left few or no traces behind. One such case, investigated by police in Hannover, in northwestern Germany, may illustrate the problems investigators have in tracking contract killers.

An Almost Perfect Crime:
The Case of the Wholesale Market

Thirty-three-year-old kindergarten teacher Suzanne K. and her parents lived in a fairytale world where everyone is good. In 1985, she met Hans-Jürgen, and they got married 3 years later. They moved into a duplex apartment, for which they took out a big mortgage. Their new home was in plain view of her parents' house.

On Wednesday, February 18, 1998, Suzanne drove her husband to his job at the wholesale produce market at 3 A.M. because Hans-Jürgen's car had been in the repair shop since Monday. After she dropped him off, she drove home and went back to bed.

At 8 A.M., Suzanne's mother found the motionless body of her daughter on the downstairs floor of her house. The worried mother had opened the door with a spare key. She had seen Suzanne's car standing in front of the house, although her daughter should have been at work at the kindergarten.

A pool of blood had formed around the head of her prostrate body. The mother immediately called the emergency medical service. Shortly after 8 A.M., she called the wholesale market where Hans-Jürgen worked and told him in a 13-second phone call, "Hans-Jürgen, come home quickly! She is lying in her blood."

The husband came home right away. But before he left, he told two of his co-workers that his wife had been attacked. When he arrived at his home, he was so distraught at what the emergency medical service told him that he had to be admitted to the hospital; there, he was placed in the psychiatric ward for fear that he might kill himself.

The next day he appeared to have recovered somewhat. He told the authorities that burglars must have been looking for the 27,000 marks (around $15,000) he had borrowed from a colleague to buy shares in the wholesale market, mostly in 1,000-mark bills. His colleague confirmed his testimony. The investigators were astonished that the dresser in which the money was supposed to be appeared untouched, but the money was gone, together with two expensive Rolex watches. The burglars clearly were extremely careful when looking through the dresser, taking the underwear out carefully and putting it on top of the bed, stacking it very neatly. The safe in the basement had been left untouched even though the key was in a hiding place on top of the heating pipe near the safe. The door to the house showed no sign of forcible entry. Was this the work of an amateur or a very shrewd professional?

A Happy Marriage, a Parked Car, and a Brothel

Suzanne's husband, Hans-Jürgen, and Suzanne's parents described the 10-year marriage as perfect when talking to the police. Never once did they stray to other partners. They did not take out any large life insurance policies. Neither would profit from the death of the other.

Hans-Jürgen seemed like a poster boy for marriage. Even in a sudden outburst of rage, he could not possibly have committed such a crime. The drive to and from the wholesale market took almost an hour, and his disappearance from work at peak business hours in the early morning certainly would have been noticed. On top of this, his car was being repaired.

Still, whoever committed the crime must have had a connection with Suzanne or Hans-Jürgen. Who else would kill a kindergarten teacher in the early morning in a peaceful residential neighborhood? Or was the intended victim the husband? Did the criminals make a mistake in figuring out his daily routine? The next day, Thursday, homicide detectives were stunned to learn that the day before the crime, Hans-Jürgen had called a certain brothel seventeen times, and other brothels, too. All these brothels had the same owner, who was known to the police for his close connection to the Eastern European underworld. The police discovered this after routinely investigating the telephone calls to and from the house. But things were to get even stranger. The head mechanic at the garage where Hans-Jürgen's car was being serviced told investigators that tests showed that nothing was wrong with the car and that it was in perfect condition. But instead of picking up the car, the owner had asked only for the keys and the papers and then walked away.

The investigators also found that in 1995 Hans-Jürgen went on a vacation to the Caribbean with an unknown woman. He had introduced this woman as his wife. But according to Suzanne's parents, that could not have happened because as far as they knew, their son-in-law went by himself on a business trip, not for a vacation.

Further investigations the next weekend came up with new and unexpected information that got Hans-Jürgen into deeper trouble. In the brothel to which Hans-Jürgen had made all those telephone calls, the police showed Beata, one of the prostitutes, a photo of Hans-Jürgen and asked whether she knew him. She said she did not. This contradicted the testimony of one of Beata's colleagues from a neighboring house, who said that Hans-Jürgen was Beata's regular client. After that the police brought in Hans-Jürgen for another interrogation. This time he appeared insecure and got tangled up in a web of contradictions, which later in the interview he could not clarify. He was arrested, even though the police thought he could not possibly have killed his wife.

The following weeks brought further interesting clues. A salesperson in the nearby town of Hamelin remembered that Hans-Jürgen had bought two Rolex watches. Hans-Jürgen had already submitted the authenticity and warranty certificates to the police, for insurance purposes. But the salesperson knew even more. She told the investigators that a man from a "Mediterranean country" had originally wanted to pay for the watches, but he had wanted to pay by check, and she could not accept checks.

The police soon found out that the "Mediterranean" man was Greek. He was one of Hans-Jürgen's clients at the wholesale market, and he apparently was the real owner of the two Rolex watches. Hans-Jürgen advanced him the money to buy the watches, but he paid him back almost immediately. The Greek man had not heard from the nice man from the wholesale market for quite a while. Hans-Jürgen was to send the certificates and guarantee of the watches to him, but so far he had not done so.

Things were getting dangerous for Hans-Jürgen. He always bragged about the value of his watch collection, mentioning that it was worth some 100,000 marks ($60,000). But after the robbery, when his wife was killed, he could produce the certificates for only two Rolex watches, both of which were really owned by the Greek man. What about the receipts for the other watches in his collection? The answer was surprising: Hans-Jürgen's watches were all fakes. In reality, he spent his money not on watches but on women. Since 1992, he had had relationships with almost twenty women, including several prostitutes. They all said that he was a show-off who squandered his money on them.

At this point, all of Hans-Jürgen's testimony was reexamined. When the police asked people at the wholesale market about the 27,000 marks that Hans-Jürgen had said he always kept in his dresser drawer, supposedly to buy shares in the wholesale business, they were met by silence. It turned out that there were no shares of that size. Two days before the crime, Hans-Jürgen had bought just one share worth only 2,000 marks.

The Phantom Male Prostitute, "Frank"

Although all these revelations proved that his life was a sham, the investigation was about a murder, not financial irregularities. However, Hans-Jürgen had another problem: Why did he make a hotel reservation in Hannover only 2 days before the crime?

On that day, at 3:30 P.M., he reserved by telephone a double room with breakfast. Forty minutes later he showed up at the hotel, signed the registration form, and left. But somebody in his room watched a pay-per-view movie at 6:15 P.M. At 11:15 the next morning, one day before the murder, someone returned the room key. For whom was the reservation made? Hans-Jürgen's explanation was odd, to say the least.

Early that afternoon, he said, he was wandering about the train station and was approached by a male prostitute called Frank. Because a threesome at his favorite brothel was too expensive for him, Hans-Jürgen took Frank to the hotel room, where Frank stayed overnight. A police artist's sketch of Frank was shown around the prostitution scene in Hannover and in other cities, but no one had ever seen him. This story was indeed strange because Hans-Jürgen had been leading a strictly heterosexual life until then. The male prostitution story therefore sounded unbelievable. It was exposed as a lie when it turned out that at 4:45 P.M., the hour of the supposed tryst, Hans-Jürgen withdrew money from an automated teller machine near the wholesale market. The plot thickened further when the police followed the lead of a Latvian telephone number that Hans-Jürgen had called several times the evening before the crime. The owner of that telephone number was a prostitute called Solvita. She once worked near Hannover for a while but was later deported. This was an important clue that might help explain why Hans-Jürgen had contacts with so many prostitutes all over Eastern Europe.

All this came to nothing in July 1998 when the Superior Court in the town of Celle had to release Hans-Jürgen because of insufficient evidence. The police were frustrated, but even they had to admit that Hans-Jürgen could not have shot his wife when he was at the wholesale market, no matter how many lies he had told them.

Beata Is Annoyed

Hans-Jürgen settled comfortably back at home, continued to enjoy relationships with several women, and went back to work. Then the police got a lucky
break. Investigators in another case were once more led to talk to the prostitute
Beata. She mentioned in passing that Hans-Jürgen still owed her money. She
had to hire an attorney in the case against him, when she was held in custody
for questioning. Hans-Jürgen had agreed that he would pay the attorney's fee,
but he had reneged. Now all he said to her was that he did it "for both of us."

A few days later, he told Beata that he had planned the murder much earlier. This failed to impress her. She wanted to see money. Beata then told the
whole story to the police on the case, so the "perfect murderer" was found
simply because he was too cheap to pay her attorney's fee.

The police and prosecutor had already wondered how Hans-Jürgen could
have known immediately that his wife had been attacked when his mother-in-
law had spoken only of blood. Hans-Jürgen was arrested again.

Nothing he said convinced the court. It was obvious to everyone that he
was the one who pulled the strings in the background. He must have used his
Eastern European connections to arrange a murder for hire. Police commissioner Werner Eckermann recalls that at the time there was still no clear motive for the crime, although "there were a number of small motives. Suzanne's
death brought him some financial advantages, such as the full ownership of the
apartment and a small life insurance payment."

More importantly, further investigation revealed that in December 1997
she had collapsed in her chiropractor's office, telling him that her husband
had had an affair. Apparently she had written her husband a note, saying she
would not try to keep him if he wanted to get out of their marriage. "But Hans-
Jürgen could never have continued his excessive lifestyle after a divorce," says
Eckermann. "He would have to pay alimony and would have lost the financial
support of his parents-in-law, who up to that time gave them 100,000 DM."

On top of that, his ego was hurt. The idea that his wife could so easily let
him go was a hard thing for this conceited man to swallow. His numerous
girlfriends agreed with a psychologist who said that he was abnormally jealous.
Although he had had numerous affairs, the idea that Suzanne might leave and
go to another man was an unbearable slight to him.

"Whatever actually happened remains unsolved," continues Eckermann.
"It is likely that Hans-Jürgen reserved the hotel room for two criminals and
that the crime was to have been committed the night before, Monday night.
Since this did not happen, for whatever reason, Hans-Jürgen had to keep his

car in the shop for another night. This also meant that Suzanne had to drive him to the wholesale market on that night, providing him with an alibi in the process."

Solvita, the Latvian woman, was interrogated in July 1998 in Riga at the German Embassy. She admitted her contacts with Hans-Jürgen. She also told them that she had last seen him when she worked in a bar near Hannover. The telephone calls turned out to be unimportant and did not bear on the case. Her participation in the crime could not be proven. The search for the killers has been unsuccessful to this day.

Unsuccessful maybe, but not unpunished. The Hannover Superior Court, using only circumstantial evidence and witness testimony, sentenced Hans-Jürgen to life imprisonment in June 1999 for incitement to commit murder. The Federal Appeals Court rejected his appeal, and the ruling remains final.

An almost perfect crime was not so perfect after all. The testimony given purely by chance by a prostitute who did not want to pay an attorney, the excessive number of phone calls on a cell phone, the use of credit cards, and the collection of fake Rolex watches all brought Hans-Jürgen down.

Say It with Pollen

Cases involving contract killers often are hard to solve. Even when witnesses recognize the criminal, it rarely helps because the perpetrators are long gone.

But not all cases that seem hopeless really are. It is important to consult forensic and criminal experts early. The killer cannot prevent insects, fungi, or pollen from leaving their telltale traces. Many of these tiny organisms cannot be seen by the naked eye, and even many biologists know little about them.

A good example of the value of forensic science occurred when a construction crew in Magdeburg, Germany, happened to uncover a mass grave in February 1994. The skeletons appeared to have belonged to young men. The skulls showed that many of their front teeth had been forcibly knocked out. These skeletal remains appeared to be those of soldiers who had first been tortured and then shot, the most likely explanation for a mass grave with such young male victims. But why was it found in the middle of the city?

There were two possible explanations. The area was first used by the Nazi Gestapo and then by the Soviet Secret Police (GPU). The Gestapo performed many executions shortly before the end of the war in April 1945. Whatever had been done in concentration camps earlier had to be done in the backyard of the Gestapo building because the concentration camps had already been abandoned. It was also known that in the German Democratic Republic (DDR), the GPU killed the people they held responsible for the summer uprising in 1953. The question was, Who was responsible for these skeletons: the Gestapo or the GPU?

The gruesome history of the site offered an investigative advantage for forensic scientists. There were only two possible dates: April 1945 if it was the Gestapo and June or July 1953 if it was the GPU. Was it possible to differentiate these two dates by biological methods?

Pollen was taken from the nasal cavities of the skeletons. The reason for this was obvious: Different trees and grasses bloom in April and May than in midsummer. Spring pollen would not have been inhaled in the summer. At the time when the Gestapo crimes were perpetrated there would have been mostly oak and linden pollen on the skeletons. If the crimes were committed in June, however, birch pollen or pollen from the summer plantain grasses (*Plantago* species) would be found. This would prove that the dead were victims of the GPU.

Forensic specialists Reinhard Szibor and Christoph Schubert scheduled a plan of action at the Institute for Forensic Medicine at the University of Magdeburg. First, they had to find out whether any pollen was left in the nasal cavities of the corpses. It could also be that year-round pollen would be found. This was conceivable, because pollen has a very hard shell that does not decay easily. On the other hand, the hard shell is irrelevant if the body expels it through normal mucus flow.

The Magdeburg scientists were able to show in a series of experiments that most year-round pollen must have been expelled. To arrive at this result, over a time period of a week, Schubert blew his nose into a handkerchief four times. Then he washed the pollen out of the handkerchief, washed it with boiling sulfuric acid, and arranged it according to shape and plant type, using a powerful microscope.

It was evident that the body very quickly ejects the pollen it has inhaled. The frequency distribution of the different types of pollen in the air does indeed match that found in the noses of corpses, thereby indicating the season.

Pollen grains can play an important role in forensic science: Long after the death of a person, during the decay of body tissues, pollen grains remain in the bone cavities. If a corpse is in a grave in the ground and therefore protected from water currents, the pollen grains can be retrieved from the nose cavity decades or sometimes centuries later. Therefore this becomes a very good means of determining the season or even the month of death.

The forensic scientists followed these lines in their investigation. Together with colleagues from the Magdeburg Institute of Material Science, they established the relative amounts of the different types of pollen from the skeletons in the mass grave. In four skulls they found between 74 and 464 pollen grains from plantain. They also found some linden pollen and a few grains of birch pollen. The pollen was all from the summer, not the spring. To be absolutely certain that the pollen was not part of the surrounding soil where the corpses were found, the scientists compared the results from the nose cavities with spot checks from bones in the pelvic area, where no pollen was found.

If the assumption that the mass grave is either the Gestapo's or the GPU's is correct, then it must have been the GPU's because of the summer pollen. The dead bodies in the center of Magdeburg therefore were those of victims of the DDR uprising.

There are other cases in which fungal spores can indicate where a person took his or her last breath. The Magdeburg group used mushroom spores from the nasal cavities of a corpse to make such a determination. There were mushrooms growing close to the place where the corpse was found. It was assumed that the person must have killed himself or herself in this area of the forest, or at least the corpse was not transported there, because the person could not have inhaled the mushroom spores after death.

CHAPTER 3

WITNESSES, COINCIDENCES, AND MEASUREMENTS

The previous chapters showed that investigators and technology may err, but in the end, investigations do tend to lead to a useful solution. There are many reasons for this. One reason is the forensic scientist's instinct; another is a collaborator I'll simply call the detective's instinct.

Scientists mistrust investigative aids that are not used in a controlled or predictable environment. But some particularly clever or particularly stupid criminals often can't be caught with other methods.

Cases of blackmail and kidnapping with ransom demands often prove this point. Both of these acts force the criminal to disclose parts of his or her character: The criminal has to formulate demands and plan the handing over of the money. In the case of abductions the investigators have to not only determine who is responsible but also find the victim quickly. The pressure on them is enormous.

In a perfect Hollywood scenario, both things happen simultaneously: The perpetrators and the victim are found together. The cases in this chapter prove that, at times, state-of-the-art criminal technology gets investigators nowhere, but coincidence and intuition often are all they need.

THE MARRIED DECORATOR

"When we asked him in for questioning," remembers detective Anton Kimmel from Karlsruhe, a city in southwestern Germany, "he was just decorating the window of a department store. He wiped the sweat from his forehead, permitted himself to be driven to the police station, and only then turned white when he learned that the criminal investigation department suspected him of attempted blackmail. But when he recovered from the shock, he reacted exactly as an innocent citizen would do: He said he knew absolutely nothing."

But the decorator could not be as innocent as he made himself out to be. The police had watched him for some time and had found out several astonishing things.

At the end of July 1961, a year and a half before his questioning, a rich widow found an unpleasant letter in her mailbox. She was to place 10,000 marks (about $6,000) in a plastic bag next to a certain corner pillar of her fence between August 8 and August 9. The letter threatened, "If the money is not placed there on time, the recipient of this letter might next be found mutilated." The dropoff place was true to the style of the note: It was close to a cemetery.

On August 8, around noon, the woman placed the money at the corner pillar of her fence. Eleven hours later, a young man sneaked toward where he assumed the money would be. He felt the grass around it but left without taking the money. The widow inadvertently had put the money in the wrong place. The police, who observed all this, were astonished at how quickly the man came and left. He disappeared into a nearby apartment complex.

The police were now on the lookout. At a quarter to nine the next morning, the man came out of the building and drove into town. At noon he returned and left his car on a side road. He looked very suspiciously at the conspicuously parked police car. The man then drove back to the apartment complex, honked his horn twice, and left again for the city.

The next day, the 22-year-old suspect was taken into custody and ordered to give a handwriting sample. This proved to be pretty close to that of the blackmail note. When the police confronted the man with his bank debt of 10,000 marks, the decorator told them a wild story. He said that he was not looking for something at the fence; rather, he was placing something on the grass: a used condom. He had no knowledge of money or blackmail.

The police didn't believe a word he said. But when they searched the area, they did find the condom. Embarrassed but with the courage of desperation, the suspect now stated that on the evening of August 8, he had had sex with a waitress at his parents' restaurant. Afterwards he put the used condom in his pocket in order to throw it away on his way home. At home he realized that he still had the used condom in his pocket. To get rid of it, he went to the corner pillar of the garden fence and put the object in an open drain covered by grass.

Although the waitress admitted, without batting an eye, that she had had sex with the married son of the restaurant owners, and although a condom in the less permissive 1960s was embarrassing, the story was still pretty far-fetched. There was a lantern at the corner of the fence, and the corner could be seen from his master bedroom across the street, so his wife easily could have seen him placing the condom there. Still, the judge had to lift the arrest warrant because there was no other evidence. The decorator was free.

Two days later, the widow, and this time her sister too, received another blackmail note. The writer of this note threatened not mutilation but rather a hydrochloric acid bath.

The blackmail money was not paid, whereupon five other wealthy people in town received similar letters. Two letters included a death announcement. A certain portion of the text, where relatives mourned the sudden death of a family member, was underlined in red.

The police arranged for several money transfers, but not one was collected. The suspect—the decorator—kept quiet. Not the slightest useful hint could be found about whether he was involved with the threatening letters. Besides committing adultery with one of his parents' employees, could he be innocent?

The case ended quickly and unexpectedly. On the third Sunday in February 1963, a retired woman in the same town opened her door. She found an unstamped letter demanding 10,000 marks; otherwise, she would be killed.

Stinginess or a shortage of money brought about the criminal's downfall. Apparently, he delivered the letter himself, because several neighbors described a man who sneaked up to the door at the time in question. The description was familiar to the woman: It was her son's chess friend.

Police inspector Kimmel summarized, "The evidence that we found in the 18-year-old chess friend's apartment was enough to arrest him for nine attempted blackmail cases, for a series of burglaries, and for acts of indecency with children." The series of blackmails was brought to a halt, and the other crimes were now cleared up.

The chess player remained taciturn during the interrogation. He did say, "I just needed the money for my new car." But every time he wanted to pick up the money for his dream car, he lost his nerve. He then wrote another blackmail note. The police also found a bottle of hydrochloric acid in his room. He did not divulge the reason for having it.

The decorator had nothing to do with these crimes. But his affair with the waitress and the forgotten condom brought him 4 weeks of detention and some awkward questioning by his wife. After that, all was quiet, and the case seemed to be solved.

After a year and a half, the chess player was prematurely released from juvenile detention. A few days later, on April 8, 1965, the postmaster received a letter telling him to deposit 10,000 marks in a specified place. If he did not comply, his 5-year-old daughter would be raped. The return address showed a company logo of an engineering plant in town. The letter was handwritten.

The police, expert in matters of money transfers and surveillance, once more began their investigation. But, once again, the ransom was not collected. The police had a sense of déjà vu.

Suspicion naturally fell on the chess player. He was immediately interrogated and asked for a handwriting sample. While he did that, a detective remembered during an earlier search having seen a stamp in the man's room with the machinery plant logo on it. The chess player had once worked there as an apprentice.

Further investigation brought three results. First, the stamp on the blackmail letter was not identical to the stamp found in his room. Second, the writing sample definitely matched that of the handwritten letter. And third, the chess player immediately admitted the crime to his probation officer. The probation officer hoped that because his ward admitted his guilt right away, the judge would be lenient when sentencing.

Strangely, the number of blackmail letters then increased explosively. Twenty-five clients of the machinery plant received insulting and sexually threatening letters, many of which ended in blackmail attempts, all under the real letterhead of the company. In additional letters, the writer wrote that the clients were bad and insolvent. Curiously, all these letters began with the words "You pigs." The writer seemed to be losing control.

The chess-playing electrician also seemed to lose control. He was identified as a fake a few days after his interrogation. Everything seemed to come together, except the fact that the stamp in his apartment was not the stamp on the letters. It was also hard to believe that, as an apprentice, the suspect could have stolen dozens of letterhead sheets, produced dozens of insulting letters in advance, hidden them, and then sent them off intermittently.

This mystery ultimately led to the machinery plant. The stamp in question had recently been stolen from there. Nobody realized the significance of the theft at the time. The lost stamp was used only in the incoming mail room, and not for any other use, and therefore was a useless thing to steal. With all these inconsistent leads, the police did not want to go in the wrong direction again, so they interviewed every worker in the plant. In the process, they came across a 17-year-old apprentice who knew neither the chess-playing electrician nor the married decorator. The apprentice admitted that he alone was the letter writer. He felt sexually stimulated by writing these insulting letters and sending them off, which explained their increasing number.

Now the electrician revoked his confession. He said that when new blackmail letters appeared shortly after his release, his probation officer advised him to admit everything in order to avoid trouble. In this case even the probation officer had been fooled by the logical train of coincidences, which seemed so compelling. The parole officer also believed that a person who had committed blackmail once would do so a second time.

In February 1966, the 17-year-old apprentice was sentenced to 6 months' probation by the Karlsruhe district juvenile court. Only then did the blackmail stop.

From then on, the Karlsruhe police proceeded in cases like this with much more care, especially when there were handwriting samples. In both blackmail cases, the experts had apparently conclusive handwriting tests, and in both cases they were wrong. It was prudent that the police and the judiciary did not trust the "irrefutable" evidence of experts but rather acted according to their own premonitions, following Sherlock Holmes's rule: "When all other contingencies fail, whatever remains, however improbable, must be the truth." Only when all the results of the investigation make sense together can we be sure that we have the perpetrator. The results often resemble a puzzle that, in its finely woven elegance, is like those found in an Agatha Christie or Georges Simenon thriller.

CONCRETE FOR THE BEER BREWER: THE HEINEKEN CASE

Police intuition is in high demand; it is needed to keep investigations on track and going in a sensible direction.

When beer brewer Alfred Heineken and his driver, Ab Doderer, were kidnapped in 1983, the case was not only about the enormous ransom of 35 million Dutch guilders (about $18 million) but also about saving their lives.

Within a few days the police collected about 700 clues. One pointed to a Chinese restaurant where, day after day, someone picked up two take-out meals. This person was "suspiciously careful"—admittedly a feeble lead. But when the Amsterdam police followed him, they got a surprise. The man brought the meals to a corrugated iron shed in a former industrial park at the Amsterdam West Harbor. The shed was behind a wall, and according to the sign, it belonged to a furniture company. Two rice dishes for one man seemed odd. Day after day, eating in an old corrugated iron shed? Was this a strange quirk, or could it be the key to solving the case?

After the man left the hut, a police squad of ten examined the shed more closely. It looked pretty innocuous and almost unused. The front was covered with a board, presumably to keep burglars out. The officers knocked on the walls and called out but heard no sound coming from the inside. Feeling that their suspicions were not sufficient to warrant breaking into the shed and possibly inviting a claim for damages, they called off the search. The team, in contact by radio, told the station that the search was unsuccessful and that they would therefore return to base.

However, police inspector Geert van Beek still thought there was something fishy going on. Before he gave up, he knocked once again on the side of the shack and was startled when the knocking indicated a hollow space. The hardboard on the side of the shed was not nailed flat against a door but was covering a small anteroom. Why, he asked himself, would someone want to cover the entrance in such an obvious way?

There were two concrete cells inside the shed, and Heineken and his driver were sitting in the cells. The two could not speak to or hear each other because the cells were soundproof. This was why the police did not hear any sound coming from within, and the locked-up men could not hear the police.

Because it was winter, the kidnapped men had only two wishes: to be freed from the chains that tied them to the concrete walls and to get warm. The kidnappers were caught shortly thereafter. But they refused to say where the already-collected ransom money had been hidden.

After Heineken was freed, people strolling near the town of Zeist, some 30 miles from Amsterdam, found dozens of hundred-dollar bills. Instead of keeping the money, these honest Dutch people went to the police. When the site where the money was found was dug up, they found about 17.5 million guilders. More than half of the ransom money could be returned. Thanks to intuition and luck, the case had a happy ending.

As a postscript to this case, three of the offenders, Cor van Hout, Willem Holleeder, and Jan Boelaard, served their prison term in the Netherlands, but the fourth kidnapper, Frans Meijer, escaped and lived in Paraguay for years until he was discovered and imprisoned. In 2003 Frans Meijer stopped resisting his extradition and was transferred to a Dutch prison to serve the rest of his term.

Boelaard is in prison again for killing a customs official.

Holleeder was released in the early 1990s. He was arrested again in 2003 for possession of an illegal weapon but has since been released.

Van Hout returned to prison on a drug-related charge and was murdered there in 2003. His elaborate funeral procession through the streets of Amsterdam, complete with a horse-drawn hearse and many fancy limousines, drew the scorn of many who thought the funeral more appropriate for royalty than for a criminal.

Blind Luck Versus Five Dozen Eyewitnesses: The Case of Manuela Schneider

It is not always just the details that blackmailers overlook. Kidnappers are neither especially intelligent nor particularly unintelligent. Greed and hunger for power are found equally among clever and not-so-clever people.

A criminal who is smart and releases the hostages can even win public sympathy. The more tricks criminals use, the more they divulge their character. This may help investigators devise an effective strategy for negotiation and thereby bring the case to a speedy conclusion. There is no truly perfect blackmail scheme. The cleverer the criminals, the more they may want to play with their opponents, which may give them away.

But plenty of criminals are just plain stupid. They do everything wrong, but still, they may leave no useful clues.

It can be impossible to understand the mind of a confused criminal and foresee his or her next step. Put another way, the connection between all the known facts and clues seems to make no sense, often because it really is not logical. The following kidnapping and ransom case illustrates exactly this point. It was handled by detectives Helmut Wälter and Norbert Westphal in the city of Essen, in the Ruhr Valley of western Germany.

For 12-year-old Manuela Schneider, the trouble began on the way to school. Usually, at around 7 A.M. she walked with her older sister to the bus stop. But on Thursday, May 5, 1994, her sister had just started an internship, so Manuela did the 10-minute walk alone. The bus stop was on a busy road, just outside of town. Usually the bus drove her near the school, where she got off and met a girlfriend in a flower shop before school started. However, today Manuela neither entered the shop nor attended classes.

Manuela's mother was the first to notice the disappearance when she waited to meet her immediately after school. When Manuela didn't show up, her mother called Manuela's father, who in turn called her teacher. Nobody had seen her. The child could not be found.

Only when Manuela's older sister received a telephone call in the late afternoon from a man who said he was holding her sister and told her not to contact the police was the alarm raised. Manuela's father immediately called the police. When all attempts to find the girl had been exhausted, a special police task force was formed that night.

The kidnapper had demanded that there would be no police, so the task force went undercover. It appeared to the public and to the kidnappers as if the police were not involved. That night, everybody who knew the child was questioned. The parents' telephone was tapped, and the press was asked not to report it. Until the second evening, there were no further clues and no further telephone calls. Meanwhile, the police obtained more information about the missing girl. She was shy and introverted. She grew up in a small rural town with her parents and sister, and until the age of 10 all seemed well. Then her father was hired as a caretaker for the estate of a wealthy family in Essen, and she and her parents moved into a house on the estate. In her exclusive new surroundings, Manuela found no new friends. At school, the newcomer was teased, ignored, and excluded by her classmates.

Manuela had told her only friend of some ruins near her house. Police thought she might be there, but all they found were the expected spiders and dust.

It turned out that at school Manuela once wrote an essay about a boy's fictitious kidnapping. Manuela's essay mentioned a girl hiding in a haystack. She had also written letters to relatives in Iserlohn, a rural town 30 miles from Essen where she had lived before, in which she claimed to want to return there, saying that Essen seemed strange to her. Could it be that Manuela took the train to see her relatives? Maybe she was walking along the country roads? Was she really kidnapped? If the child just ran away, why would a strange man call and frighten the family? Yet if it was truly a kidnapping, why was there no ransom demand? The case became even more mysterious when the bus driver told the police that the bus did not stop at Manuela's stop that Thursday. He said that when he saw nobody was waiting and no one on the bus wanted to get off, he preferred to save time and just continue to the next stop. He clearly recognized Manuela from the photo the police showed him as the girl who, together with her sister, usually got on the bus at that particular stop every day.

An elderly woman who happened to be on the bus during the driver's questioning said the exact opposite. She was able to describe the girl in the photo and her sister, who was not in the photo. She claimed that the bus did indeed stop, that the girl got on, and that on that Thursday she was alone.

The investigators were baffled and asked the advice of a traffic expert to determine whether the bus stopped. Consultants determine this by using an onboard recorder that registers the top speed and the slowest speed continuously so that the length and timing of the bus journey can be calculated. These times are then compared with the witnesses' reports. Because the bus route is fixed, it can be calculated quickly from passenger reports at different stops whether the bus was late, at which stop the bus gained or lost time, and at which stops the bus did not stop at all.

In this case the report came back with the information that the bus had stopped at 13, 14, 16, and 19 minutes after 7 A.M. at Manuela's bus stop that week. It also implied that the bus driver was mistaken and that the old woman was right.

In the meantime, the investigative group had grown so large that police from other units were called in to look through the usual mass of accident reports, hospital admission records, and witness statements for the area. Everyone's shift was extended to 12 hours.

Still, there were no new clues by the night of the following Saturday. When reporters from the weekly magazine *Focus* asked the police whether there was anything to the rumor about a kidnapping in Essen, the police finally decided on Sunday evening to inform the public. At the same time, Manuela's parents were questioned again. Until then they had been spared so that her father could remain at home to answer the telephone in case there were more calls from the kidnappers. (In 1994, call forwarding was not easily available in Germany.) The parents' interrogation took all day Saturday.

Meanwhile, there were other developments. After the police had distributed missing person posters of Manuela and had driven through the streets making announcements over a loudspeaker, a neighbor told police that he saw a colorful opened umbrella lying in the street on the day of the kidnapping. There had been slight drizzle on that day. Manuela's sister said that the description fit one of her parents' umbrellas. Two more independent witnesses also came forward and said they had seen the same umbrella in the street. The umbrella was never found. Assuming that the child probably did not lose it or throw it away, did this mean that a struggle had taken place?

To everybody's relief, quite a few witnesses had other stories to tell. Once the police went public with the story on Sunday, May 8, the phone at the Essen police station began ringing every 10 minutes with calls from her former hometown, Iserlohn. All of the callers said they had recently seen Manuela. From the reports of the Iserlohn witnesses, it was plain what Manuela must have been up to. She probably ventured to stables near Iserlohn. This sounded convincing because the 12-year-old, like many girls her age, was an avid horse lover. From there she supposedly walked along a dirt road.

The only thing the police were unable to do was to actually find Manuela, although several unmarked and marked patrol cars were sent to look for her.

The following Monday, Manuela's girlfriend clarified her movements just before her disappearance. On Thursday, around 9 P.M., the day of Manuela's disappearance, the 13-year-old witness took a shortcut through a community garden. Because her parents had strictly forbidden her to walk there, she was startled when she ran into another person there. But she was relieved when the late evening stroller turned out to be Manuela. Manuela certainly would not tell her parents her little secret. In fact, Manuela herself told her that she had something on her conscience and said that she was on her way to see her aunt in Iserlohn. The two girls then said goodbye and continued on their way, each in her own direction.

Once her friend told the police this story, they searched the community garden. As expected, they did not find Manuela, and they assumed that she had already gone to Iserlohn. There were no traces of Manuela in the area.

The same Monday, a mother turned up at the police station and declared that while her daughter was on her way to school that morning, she saw the missing girl close to the community garden, which meant that Manuela must have returned.

The new witness, who knew her from former times in Iserlohn, described Manuela perfectly. "Manuela was exhausted when I saw her this morning," the schoolgirl told the police. "Her head kept flopping backwards and sideways, and her eyes were half closed. She sat in the grass by the path, and she looked disheveled and unkempt. When I tried to convince Manuela to come with me, and I took her by the hand, she threw her backpack at my head. That hurt a lot, because there was something very heavy in it. Then Manuela ran up the hill and called out several times, 'Alex!' "

It was clear from further questioning that the girl knew Manuela very well, giving many details of Manuela's childhood. She also mentioned that Manuela's parents once had a large shed or summer house in the community gardens.* Perhaps the runaway girl was returning to it. In the past, Manuela had often hidden in the small summer house when she was sad or angry, according to the young witness. In addition, she had a friend named Alex in Iserlohn.

The following picture emerged: Manuela must have slept the first night in the house in the community garden or gone directly to Iserlohn. There, she met her friend Alex and later returned to the garden house. The young witness's mother stressed that her daughter was not in the habit of inventing stories or imagining things.

The police then heard that Manuela was seen getting off a bus in Essen a short time earlier. Surely it would be only a matter of minutes before the wandering girl was returned to her parents.

Just to be on the safe side, the police examined the area where Manuela threw the backpack at her friend's head. She must have recovered her backpack, or Alex did, because all they found there was a very visible flattened area of grass where the exhausted Manuela must have sat down. They also found footprints in the grass running uphill. This corroborated the evidence the witness gave: that Manuela had run uphill toward Alex. So far, so good.

On Monday, May 9, the evening news on television had just ended when the phone rang at Manuela's parents' home, and a hesitant male voice said,

---

* It is common in Germany and other parts of Europe for city dwellers to rent or own a patch of land for recreational purposes elsewhere in the city, usually to grow vegetables or flowers. Very often there is a little house or shed on it in which the owner may sleep on occasion.

"Two million in unmarked bills, not in a numbered series. No later than, um, until, Friday." Then he put down the receiver. The investigators, who were becoming convinced that this was not a kidnapping case, froze.

Was this a prank? Perhaps. Consider this: Manuela's sister, Melanie, was certain that this caller's voice was not the same as the previous caller's. Perhaps the sister and her parents had concocted all this: Had they abused Manuela and then tried to mislead the investigators? But where was Manuela? Was she already dead? Or did she run away, only to be kidnapped upon her return?

At this point the police felt certain only that Manuela had been in the community garden and had then gone on to Iserlohn and finally had returned to the garden house. The only new clue on the evening of May 9 was that the caller had called from a phone booth in the Essen area. Could the family have paid him to do this?

Meanwhile, the police were looking through unsolved case files in Iserlohn. According to several witnesses, Manuela had been seen with a young man in a shopping area in Iserlohn. With their last remaining energy, the investigating team, who for 8 days had worked an average of 12- to 16-hour shifts, drove back to Iserlohn. Manuela's back-and-forth travels with Alex were beginning to get on their nerves. It seemed as if they were always just missing them.

The mysterious caller needed to be taught a lesson. On Friday, May 13, at 1:45 P.M., he called Manuela's parents again, asking whether they had the 2 million marks ($1,250,000) ready. It was the same person who had called on Monday. Following police instructions, the father told him that he could not get such a large sum so quickly, and asked for a sign that his daughter was still alive. The caller hesitated for a moment. Manuela's parents and the police held their breath. Then the voice said, "Okay," and hung up.

Everyone assumed that the caller was bluffing because he gave them no sign of Manuela. Again, the call was from a phone booth in Essen. The police guessed that Manuela was living on the street. The train stations in the Rhine Ruhr area provide many possible hiding places. With commuter trains constantly leaving in all directions, these stations provide an ideal opportunity for runaway kids to avoid detection in the most densely populated part of continental Europe.

The mysterious caller called again the next day and offered something: He played a noisy tape recorder held up to the phone. A voice that was unmistakably the missing girl's said, "Hello, this is Manuela. I am no longer afraid, but please do as the man is asking, so I can be with you again soon." The call then ended.

A new possibility arose in the minds of the investigators. Was it possible that Manuela and Alex were playing a cruel trick on her parents? Did they want money, which they were then going to make off with? If yes, where would they go? They would certainly have to be close by, at least until the money transfer had been worked out.

The detective leading the investigation did not believe this scenario. He gathered his team together and announced to officers that the search and the night shifts were back on. On Monday, May 15, at 9:30 P.M., the phone rang again, and this time it was Manuela herself: "Hello, this is Manuela, I love you all very much! Please take care of everything until Wednesday. Bye, Manu." Then, something unforeseen happened.

The next day, a call came in to the Essen police headquarters. Manuela's father told them that Manuela had just called him, and it had not been a tape. Then, a short time later, the frozen and distraught girl had arrived at the door.

Exactly what had happened?

During a engineering inspection of the Ruhr Valley Bridge, a construction foreman had found the girl hunched up in the second of eighteen bridge piers that support a 1.5-mile section of the road between Düsseldorf and Essen. The bridge has a hollow substructure, and Düsseldorf's inspectors had hired a private firm to check whether retrofit construction should be done in the hollow spaces to strengthen it. The girl had been hidden there by her abductors. She was lying on a mattress that lay diagonally on top of five metal supports of the bridge's interior.

So Manuela was not a runaway but had been hidden in the first bridge pier since Thursday, May 5, and had not left it. But where were the kidnappers?

The police concentrated on a smaller area and did not have to search the entire area between Essen and Iserlohn. Finally, the decisive clue came in: A witness told them that on the Thursday of the abduction, she saw a suspicious car in a parking lot favored for cruising by gay men. She described the car and provided its license plate number. Manuela confirmed the witness's account.

The police went directly to the car's owner. Many objects and clothes in his apartment were identical to things Manuela had mentioned. However, the owner of the car and the apartment clearly knew nothing about the crime. He was a doctor at a nearby hospital. Apparently he usually left the car for his 21-year-old boyfriend, Daniel, to use. Naturally, suspicion immediately settled on Daniel. Sure enough, Manuela's description of the kidnapper perfectly fit this young auto mechanic.

When confronted with the witnesses' testimony about the objects, the car, and the abductor, Daniel admitted the crime. He did not need the money; it was for his brother, who acted as his co-conspirator. His brother was HIV positive and wanted to have a nicer life in the short time left to him.

The kidnappers in this case made a monumental mistake. They did not do enough research; they simply went to a rich neighborhood and observed which children went to school and at what time. Because Manuela left a nice villa every morning, the kidnappers assumed that she was the child of wealthy parents.

On the day of the crime, the two amateur kidnappers talked to the child, asked for directions, and then offered to take her to school. When Manuela refused, they pulled her into the car. That was when she lost the open umbrella.

In the bridge pier, they tied Manuela to the interior brace and bound her feet and hands. Meanwhile, they gave her sandwiches, cola in a plastic bottle, chocolate, tea, and pasta salad.

The police probably would have done better had Daniel not gone on a vacation to the Netherlands immediately after the kidnapping with his partner, the doctor. Because he did not want the doctor to know about the crime, Daniel could not make any ransom demand calls in that period. He also could not cancel the trip without looking suspicious.

Considering the poor planning by the criminals, no one can say what would have happened had there not been a routine inspection of the bridge piers. Because the kidnappers never wore masks, it was unclear to all involved how they could have brought their plan to completion without being caught.

"Although it worked out well in the end," said detectives Wälter and Westphal, "there still remain questions that can never be answered."

Every expert criminal investigator is aware of the unreliability of witnesses, but in this case, many independent observations combined to produce an almost perfect puzzle that defies rational explanation. The interrogations were tainted by the mistaken accounts of witnesses and the outright fantasies of some media-seeking people who in reality had no idea about Manuela's movements. This was compounded by the fact that the information that was given to the public had been filtered and adapted using this erroneous information. This seemed to produce even more confusing accounts from the public.

But what can be done when all expert questioning and investigative experience cannot make sense of what the 13- and 14-year-old witnesses told them? Both girls remained steadfast in their accounts of what they saw, even after Manuela's return. How can all those sightings of Manuela in Iserlohn be explained? Maybe, as the detectives say, city people make better observers and more reliable witnesses than rural folk. Or was it simply that the people in Iserlohn got too wrapped up in finding out Manuela's fate and started imagining things? The police believe that because of the intense media attention, people's senses were dulled, and for the people in the town of Iserlohn, this stimulated their fantasies.

One thing is certain: On May 16, 1994, Manuela, her parents, and the Essen police had luck on their side. A matter of life and death turned out to have a happy ending.

The kidnappers were not so lucky. They were sentenced by the Essen District Court to jail terms of 8 and 10 years. Daniel tried to appeal to the Federal Supreme Court, but the appeal was thrown out on July 31, 1995. Thus ended a case the likes of which the police hope they will never encounter again. Two amateurs almost succeeded in carrying out a terrible crime.

A Deadly Case:
The Kidnapping of Charles Lindbergh Jr.

The Ruhr Valley Bridge case is not the only example of a failed and ill-conceived crime that excited public interest and curiosity. An extremely puzzling case started in the United States when flight pioneer Charles A. Lindbergh (1902–1974) realized one evening that his son was missing from his bed. It took 60 years to solve the crime, and neither criminal nor victim ever heard the full explanation of this mysterious crime.

When the case began, Lindbergh was one of the most famous men in the United States, if not the Western world. From May 20 to May 21, 1927, the tall, 25-year-old man flew in 33 and a half hours from New York to Paris. When he landed at Le Bourget Airfield, his reception was enormous. "I had just enrolled at the Sorbonne," remembers an American witness of that time, "when we heard on the radio that Lindbergh had been sighted over Scotland and would shortly land in Paris. A colleague and I took the bus to the airport. There we were squeezed with a great many other people, behind a wire fence barrier. When Lindbergh landed in his 'Spirit of St. Louis,' the crowd just ran the barrier and poured onto the field. The police had to save Lindbergh from the enthusiastic crowd." They brought him to the U.S. Embassy, where he spent the night.

"In the intermission of a theater performance it was announced that 'Lindy' had landed safely," another eyewitness recounted. "We cheered and ran out into the street, where people embraced and started a huge party. The next day was a parade in honor of Lindbergh the length of the Champs-Elysées. That was one of the best days of my life."

For Lindbergh, these days changed his life forever. The pilot had not had an easy life before, but now he was received by the French president. He was allowed to address the French Parliament, and later he was asked to visit King George V in England.

Americans wanted their flying ace back as soon as possible. President Coolidge sent a battleship, the *Memphis,* to Cherbourg to pick up Lindbergh and his *Spirit of St. Louis.* When he stepped onto his native land 3 weeks later, he was whisked off to a stage at the Washington Monument, in Washington, D.C. There, waiting for him, was the president, who gave a long oration. Lindbergh, on the other hand, gave an extremely short speech. In only seven sentences he conveyed that the Europeans felt solidarity with the American people. Then he thanked everyone again and sat down.

Although Lindbergh was not born to be a society hero, he soon received the highest order for bravery, which usually is given only during times of war. The military conferred on him the rank of colonel in the reserves. He was very proud of this military rank and asked to be addressed as Colonel from then on.

The tributes reached their climax when Lindbergh was the center of the biggest parade in New York City on June 13. "Colonel Lindbergh," the mayor at City Hall said emotionally, "New York is yours!"

After that, Lucky Lindy toured all forty-eight states with his airplane. He received $100,000 for his book about the flight across the Atlantic and received further tributes. He became a consultant for the oil industry, among other enterprises.

The Colonel was showered with gifts. When the ambassador to Mexico, Dwight Morrow, invited Lindbergh to spend Christmas with him at his country home in New Jersey and then later in Mexico, Lindbergh accepted. From Mexico, he started a promotional tour through Latin America. During his visit he met one of the ambassador's daughters. Anne was 27 years old, intelligent, and, like Lindbergh, quiet and shy. In late April 1929, Lindbergh and Anne returned to New Jersey from Mexico by train, and they married on May 27. The world seemed bright and carefree to them.

But trouble was on the horizon. Anne had two sisters, Constance and Elizabeth. The younger, Constance, was attending a fancy boarding school, but she came home for holidays. Shortly before Anne and Lindbergh took their train to New Jersey, Constance received a strange letter.

The local police still have this letter in their files: "April 24th, 1929 at 10:20 P.M. A. H. Weed, 150 School Street brought to station a letter received by Constance Morrow, Milton Academy, demanding money under threats of violence. Miss Morrow lives at Hathaway House. Sergeant Shields sent to detail Officer Lee to guard Hathaway House tonight."

A letter with exact instructions for the money transfer arrived at the Morrows' home after 2 weeks, an unusually long time. In the meantime, Lindbergh and Anne had arrived at her parents' house in Englewood, New Jersey.

According to the letter, $50,000 was to be put in a box. The box was then to be placed in a hole in a wall of a nearby property. The police were surprised about the strange way the transfer was proposed to take place. Did the criminals really think that they could blackmail a member of a diplomatic family, then choose their time to walk along the wall, expecting to find the box with the money? The police believed it might have something to do with Lindbergh. Why would anyone choose, of all people, the youngest daughter of the American ambassador to Mexico, while the famous Lindbergh was staying in the same house? To be on the safe side, an actress was asked to take an empty box of the specified size and shape and put it into the hole in the wall. After that, the police observed the area for days, but nothing happened.

In the meantime, Anne got to know her husband better. She realized that he was uncomfortable keeping up with her privileged upbringing and education. Lindbergh was anything but a well-read charmer. Despite his successful flying career, he was a solitary person. She found out that Lindbergh liked silly practical jokes. The man was plainly something of a nerd, socially awkward but highly knowledgeable about something few others understand or can do. For Lindbergh that thing was his daring flying.

Good People and Bad People

Lindbergh was also awkward in matters of love. "On May 27, 1929, I married Anne Spencer Morrow," he wrote in his autobiography. "From the standpoint of both individual and species, mating involves the most important choice of life, for it shapes our future as the past has shaped us. It impacts upon all values obviously and subtly in an infinite number of ways. One mates not only with an individual but also with that individual's environment and ancestry. These were concepts I comprehended before I was married and confirmed in my observations over the years that followed."

Such wooden references to "mating" and "environment and ancestry" are easier to understand if we remember that at this time there was a prevalent belief that certain groups of people could be genetically improved. The rules of classical genetics appeared to indicate that one could obtain better characteristics and qualities through selective breeding. This was correct in peas, chickens, and rabbits but only in very limited ways for people. However, Lindbergh believed in eugenics and believed that he had chosen the correct partner. He did not understand that from the point of view of genetics there is no absolute good or bad, healthy or unhealthy, only different types of adaptations to different environments.

HITLER AND GENETIC IMPROVEMENT:
NONSENSE MASQUERADING AS SCIENCE

Hitler had at least one genetics book in his prison cell, from which he pla-
giarized, often in error but without the slightest apology. This is how he
created the idea of *guten, züchtbaren Menschen* (good, breedable people).

This is all the more astonishing because, as he later admitted as "Füh-
rer," he knew from his own experience that a person is formed largely by his
environment: "It ends badly," he wrote in 1924–1925 in the first part of *Mein
Kampf,* "if the husband goes his own way from the beginning, and his wife,
for the sake of the children, opposes him. Then there is fighting and quar-
reling, and, as the man grows estranged from his wife, he becomes more
intimate with alcohol. He is drunk every Saturday, and, with her instinct of
self-preservation for herself and her children, the woman has to fight to get
even a few pennies out of him; to make matters worse, this usually occurs
on his way from the factory to the bar. When at length he comes home on
Sunday or even Monday night, drunk and violent, and always totally broke,
such scenes often occur that God have mercy! . . . These people are the unfortunate victims of bad circumstances."

The eleventh (and the most extensive) chapter of *Mein Kampf,* with the
heading *Volk und Rasse* (People [or Nation] and Race), begins with a new observation: "There are some truths that are so obvious that for this very reason they
are not seen or at least not recognized by ordinary people. They sometimes pass
by such truisms as though blind and are most astonished when someone suddenly discovers what everyone really ought to know. Columbus's eggs lie around
by the hundreds of thousands, but Columbuses are met with less often."

Hitler had been exactly that "blind," but the party leader became his
own Columbus. Even with his lack of schooling, as he would say, he picked
up one essential "truism": that of the improvement of the genetic makeup
by selective mating.

Hitler was a shrewd writer, and he wrapped everything in a logic that
seemed captivating to many readers at the time, even though this logic is
based on almost no scientific facts. "Every animal," he says in his chapter
11, "mates only with a member of the same species. The titmouse seeks the
titmouse, the finch the finch, the stork the stork, the field mouse the field
mouse, the dormouse the dormouse, the wolf the she-wolf, etc. . . . Any
crossing of two beings not at exactly the same level produces a medium
between the levels of the two parents.

"This means that the offspring will probably stand higher than the racially lower parent but not as high as the higher one. Consequently, it will succumb in the struggle against the higher level. . . .

"If the process were different, all further and higher development would cease and the opposite would occur. For, since the inferior always predominates numerically over the best, if both had the same possibility of preserving life and propagating, the inferior would multiply so much more rapidly that in the end the best would inevitably be driven into the background unless a correction of this state of affairs was undertaken."

Many people accepted this notion and understood it to be true. Despite its apparent "scientific logic," they were wrong. For one thing, in the natural sciences, there are no strictly defined human races. There are also no groups of people who are inherently stronger or weaker. What does it mean to be stronger or weaker in this context anyway? Second, there are different rules for the mating of people and the pairing of different kinds of animals. All humans belong to the same species. Hitler's comparison with finches and wolves is nonsense.

Third, one's genetic makeup is not visible. The genes are indeed transmitted, but they cannot be assessed simply by looking at what the parents look like; they are expressed in ways that are not all that predictable.

Fourth, in the course of 2 years of writing, Hitler failed to realize that many characteristics that race adherents would prefer to ascribe to genetic factors are determined largely by environmental or social factors and have no genetic basis. Honor, love, and belief cannot be developed by crossbreeding, for example. Therefore, the apparently logical tenets of eugenics collapse like a house of cards.

In the fall of 1929, Anne Lindbergh became pregnant. She still managed to join her husband on a demanding record flight between Los Angeles and New York; in May 1930, she moved to the home of her parents in Englewood. On June 22, 1930, her birthday, she gave birth to Charles Lindbergh Jr. Although the press waited anxiously for the news, the Lindberghs announced the birth of a happy and healthy child only 2 weeks later.

At that time, Lindbergh began to travel on business. He had enough money, time, and interest to speculate in stocks. He consulted for several companies in New York, and he planned new flying trips for himself. One of these was a flight crossing the Soviet Union and Japan to China. American businesspeople hoped that he could open up new transcontinental air routes for trade on this tour. For this reason, the tour with his new plane, the *Sirius,* was easily financed. He insisted that Anne accompany him. This adventure lasted from the end of July to the beginning of October 1931. When Anne's father died suddenly, Lindbergh reluctantly interrupted the tour. It was then that their problems began.

The Lindberghs spent their weekends in a house in the town of Hopewell, New Jersey. On Monday mornings, Charles drove to Manhattan to work, while Anne drove with the baby to their other house in Englewood. There, she met Charles again in the evening. Nanny Betty Gow had the weekends off and normally worked only in Englewood.

On Monday, February 29, 1932, Lindbergh changed the living arrangement for that week. He called his wife twice and asked her to remain in Hopewell. The weather was bad and the baby had a cold, so that the drive to Englewood would not be prudent. Anne did what he told her. Just this once, the nanny worked in Hopewell. However, Lindbergh himself did not stay with the family but stayed in Englewood. Maybe he thought Englewood cozier; certainly this house was easier to reach from Manhattan.

The rest of the family, including the nanny, remained 2 days longer in the new house at Hopewell, which still did not have curtains. This did not bother the Lindberghs because the house was remote. The windows of the new house could be locked with shutters, except for the one in the baby's room; because the bolt was bent, the shutters could be closed but not locked. In those days, paparazzi did not exist, and it was considered very bad form to invade the privacy of a hero.

It rained constantly on Tuesday, March 1. When the rain subsided in the evening, a wind came up. Betty began to get Charles Jr. ready for bed at 6 P.M. She fed him and then rubbed his chest with menthol ointment, used to this day, to clear his respiratory tract. Between 7 and 7:30 P.M. Anne and Betty put the boy to bed. Half an hour later, Betty looked in on him once more. Except for his cold, Charles Lindbergh Jr. was an extremely healthy child. He slept peacefully in his flannel shirt. His thumbs were put in a small metal tube, called a thumb guard, to keep him from sucking them.

Half an hour later, a car sounded its horn at the front door. Lindbergh arrived home, about 45 minutes later than usual. In the joy of seeing him again, nobody asked the Colonel why he was so late.

Although he had not seen his boy since Monday morning, he let him sleep and did not go to his room. By telephone, he had instructed the women not to enter the room once the boy was asleep so as not to disturb his recovery. The Colonel ate a leisurely dinner and then retired with his wife to the living room. The wind was getting strong, howling around the corners of the house and in the trees of this remote area. Suddenly Lindbergh asked his wife, "Did you hear that?" But Anne had heard nothing but the roaring of the storm.

In such weather, Lindbergh liked to take a hot bath before going to bed. The bathroom he used was next to the child's room. He kept his own rule and did not go into the sleeping child's bedroom. He then went to his study on the ground floor, while Anne was in her bedroom on the first floor.

Lindbergh's dog Wagoosh wandered peacefully through the house. He had been quiet all day and did not stir that evening. This was not surprising because he barked only at strangers, although he did so with great fervor. There were no strangers in the house; in addition to Lindbergh, Anne, and Betty, only Oliver and Elsie Whatley, the butler and cook, were present, and they stayed in their room.

At 10 P.M., Lindbergh's ban on disturbing little Charles expired, and Betty went to his room to take him to the bathroom. She did not turn on the light so that the child would not be startled. Instead, she closed the window and turned on the electric heater. Only then did she realize that the little boy was gone.

Betty Gow asked his mother whether she took Charles Jr. to her room. Anne had already changed into her pajamas and told her that the Colonel must have taken him. But he was not with his father. Lindbergh ran into the child's room, turned on the light, and saw that the bed was made but empty. Calmly he said to his wife, "Anne, they stole our baby."

At this point, things turned chaotic. The butler called the police, and Lindbergh loaded his gun and called out, "Don't touch anything!" and then ran out of the house. Meanwhile, the three women looked in every room despite the command not to touch anything. Finally, they all sat helplessly in the living room while the butler ran to Lindbergh's car and drove, together with the Colonel, down the unpaved driveway. With a flashlight they searched right and left but found no trace of the boy.

Again, Lindbergh searched the child's room. He found an envelope that the women had not seen. It had been placed under the window with the unlocked shutter. Lindbergh would not let anyone touch the envelope, even the two police officers who had just arrived. The envelope remained unexamined until the detectives arrived.

When the two police officers walked around the house, using their flashlight to search below the child's room, they found footprints in the mud and the impression of a ladder. The investigators followed the footprints, which led to a ladder lying on the ground. It was an unusual ladder clearly built by an amateur carpenter, just tall enough to the reach the child's room on the second floor.

The ladder was very portable and could be disassembled into three pieces. The end pieces were pushed into the central piece, and it was held together with wooden pegs so that the 18-foot ladder was secure and could not collapse. The builder had adequate carpentry skills but clearly did not know how to build a good, strong ladder.

The rungs showed signs of wear, were thin, and were only nailed to the vertical braces. Even stranger, the rungs were 19 inches apart. Whoever built the ladder must have had very long legs. Because the ladder was not attached anywhere, only a practiced climber could have used it. A typical person would not want to step on it, even if the ground had not been muddy and the wind had not been so strong.

An old chisel was lying in the mud next to the ladder. The kidnapper must have used it to get into the room from the outside. He must then have carried the child down the ladder, and while running away he must have thrown the chisel away. He probably put the baby in a backpack because he would have needed both his hands for climbing down and carrying the ladder away.

Charles Lindbergh remained remarkably calm. His entire life had been controlled and orderly, and as usual he had the situation under control. He exploited his heroic status to the fullest, and any police officer who could not accept his assumption of a leading role in the investigation was dismissed. In this way he kept the investigation under tight control to the end.

As soon as word of the kidnapping reached New York, the New York Police Department (NYPD) closed the George Washington Bridge to drivers from New Jersey, and all travelers were checked. At the same time, the New Jersey State Police went to Hopewell. When the state troopers arrived on their motorcycles, they again searched the entire house very carefully. In doing so, they left their own footprints all around the house. Whatever footprints had been there before were compromised by the many police footprints.

Soon, the press arrived. Lindbergh greeted each journalist personally, had sandwiches made for them, and ushered them into his living room. The last to arrive was Norman Schwarzkopf, head of the New Jersey State Police.

Like many police chiefs, he was a political appointee, and he wanted to be on good footing with the famous Colonel. When Lindbergh suggested that they open the envelope only after it was examined for fingerprints, he immediately agreed. But they did not find a single fingerprint on the envelope, on the letter itself, or anywhere in the boy's room. If that wasn't odd enough, the ransom note was written in scrawling handwriting, bristling with mistakes. It said

Dear Sir! Have 50000$ redy 25000$ in 20$ bills 15000$ in 10$ bills and 10000$ in 5$ bills After 2–4 days we will inform you were to deliver the Mony.

We warn you for making anyding public or for notify the Police the child is in gut care.

Indication for all letters are singnature and 3 holes.

The "singnature" mentioned in the letter consisted of two intertwined rings. The inner parts of the rings were colored: the two rings in blue, the overlapping inner ring in red. In the middle of each of the three colored fields was a hole in the paper. The letter reads like a parody of a German writing bad English. *Gut* is the German word for *good,* and Germans have difficulty pronouncing the English "th," so they often substitute "d" or "s."

The investigation went nowhere, despite great efforts. All clues and footprints near the house were trampled, the ransom note was strange, and somebody had taken great care in the bedroom wipe off all fingerprints. When exactly did the kidnapping take place? How could this happen in a house that had several people inside? On top of all this, there was a watchdog with a good nose and good ears.

The list of questions grew longer: Who would kidnap a sick child—an inconvenient hostage for the kidnapper? There also seemed to be no car: No tire marks were found. Why do it during such bad weather? How could the criminal have known that the Lindberghs were in the house on exactly that Tuesday, totally unplanned? Did someone watch the house? Did he follow the Lindberghs? If yes, since when and from where?

Even if the criminal had known and planned all this, he must surely have had an accomplice inside the house. How else could he have known that nobody would come into the child's room during the kidnapping? Even an accomplice could not know whether the Colonel or Anne Lindbergh might not follow a parental impulse and suddenly look in on the sleeping child. It would have been less risky if the criminal had known of Lindbergh's order not to disturb the child until 10 P.M. But which of the servants could have passed this information on? Most of them were not in the house but in their own homes.

Even assuming that the kidnapper had perfect information, it was still a highly risky affair: The child could have started screaming at any time. And why *didn't* the child scream during the kidnapping?

The odd construction of the ladder was also mysterious and inspired more questions. Not only was it extraordinary that someone was actually able to climb up such a wobbly ladder in such bad conditions, but the person must also have known that the window in question had a bent lock. Was the kidnapper clairvoyant, too?

Nobody wanted to speak of the most unsettling assumption: The criminal must have been to the window twice on that horrible night. When the women looked through the house the first time, they did not see the ransom letter. Only when Lindbergh and his butler came back from their first search outside did they find the note, dry and in good shape by the window. The perpetrator must have placed the letter near the window from the ladder. The perpetrator either was mad or had strong nerves. They could expect the worst.

On May 12, 2 months and 11 days after the kidnapping, the decomposed remains of Charles Lindbergh Jr. were found. They had been thrown into a small street almost 3 miles from the Lindbergh house. The coroner believed that the child died soon after his disappearance. A court-ordered autopsy was not performed because Lindbergh ordered an immediate cremation and funeral. With that, any remaining direct clues went up in smoke. There were now only three avenues open to the police: indirect evidence, a betrayal, or a lucky break.

As far as betrayal was concerned, Lindbergh had already thought of this; it occurred to him that New York gangsters could best help him to get his son back from the clutches of other criminals. This thinking was not so bizarre, but it obstructed the police investigation.

Lindbergh had one of the ransom notes leaked to the Manhattan underworld in a way that made it possible for his contact people to investigate leads. However, any freeloader also could view the formerly secret "singnature."

Some police officers asked themselves, and rightly so, why someone from New York would have kidnapped the boy. Whoever watched the house and had a connection with some of the people in the house probably could not drive each day from New York to Hopewell without attracting attention.

The connection between Lindbergh and Manhattan's underworld was made by a young attorney who worked at the same law firm as Lindbergh's attorney. Such contacts were easily made during Prohibition. Bootlegging had flourished and had brought attorneys together with the masters of that new trade.

Two days after the kidnapping, a shady character named Mickey Rossner sat in Lindbergh's living room and demanded an advance payment of $25,000 and the right to work independently, not hindered or observed by the police. A better deal had never been offered to someone from the underworld. What exactly Rossner did with this payment is left to the reader's imagination.

The next day, Lindbergh said he wanted direct contact with the kidnappers. In an open letter published in the national press he wrote, "Mrs. Lindbergh and I . . . urge those who have the child to select any representative that may desire to meet a representative of ours." He promised the kidnappers safe conduct, open negotiation free of conditions, and total confidentiality. By doing this Lindbergh destroyed for good any opportunity for useful police work. Norman Schwarzkopf took his time, and several days passed before he could regain control of the police investigation. But by then, it was too late. On March 5, the second ransom note reached the unhappy family:

Dear Sir: We have warned you note to make anyding Public also notify the Police now you have to take the consequences. ths means we will holt the baby untill everyding is quiet. . . . Dont by afraid about the baby. . . . We are interested to send him back in gut health. Ouer ranson was made aus for 50,000 $ but now we have to take another person to it and probable have to keep the baby for a longer time as we expected So the amount will by 70,000 $.

This letter, which Lindbergh's negotiator received as a photocopy, made the rounds in Manhattan, prompting a radio evangelist to denounce Lindbergh's choice of underworld "helpers." In this increasingly muddled situation, one man remembered forensic procedures. That man was Ed Mulrooney, chief of the NYPD. If there were no longer any useful clues, maybe they could make some useful observations.

Because the second letter was postmarked at 9 P.M. at a certain district in the Brooklyn area, Mulrooney logically assumed that the kidnappers lived in Brooklyn. If they sent another letter, they would do so under the watchful eyes of the NYPD. Every mail drop would be checked immediately by the police. If a letter was addressed to the Lindberghs, the sender would be arrested on the spot. This tactic would not further endanger the abducted child. If the letter writer or mailer happened to notice the police beforehand, at worst he would drop the letter into another mailbox. If he discarded it, he would be caught.

Lindbergh opposed this plan. In contrast to the diplomatic Schwarzkopf from the New Jersey police, Mulrooney didn't care what the amateur Lindbergh wanted. Lindbergh did not like being treated as a typical crime victim. He told Mulrooney that he would speak to every one of his political and business friends if Mulrooney did not comply with his requests. This was too much: Schwarzkopf backed down. However, the next day a third letter arrived bearing a postmark from the same Brooklyn district that Mulrooney had wanted watched. In retrospect, if Mulrooney had carried out his plan the case probably would have been solved, but the opportunity was lost.

A Butler, a Sailor, and a Nanny

While these arguments raged, the background investigation continued slowly in New Jersey. First, the house servants were questioned. The Whatleys were quickly ruled out as likely co-conspirators and informants of the abductors because they had no motive. Betty, the nanny, was a more likely subject. She was a poor immigrant from Scotland, and she was unmarried. She had called her boyfriend, Red Johnson, immediately after Lindbergh had changed his schedule on the night of the kidnapping. This seemed suspicious. Johnson was also an immigrant, but from Scandinavia. Where exactly he was from he would not say, and that in itself aroused further suspicion. It was learned that he had worked on a sailboat that belonged to a partner of Anne Lindbergh's recently deceased father. This was too much of a coincidence. Johnson was in deep trouble.

Betty Gow and Johnson had met when the Lindberghs, together with the Morrow family and their business friends, were at a summer resort. Johnson had had the nerve to sneak onto the Morrows' friends' boat and captured Betty's heart. Shortly before the kidnapping, he had moved to Englewood to be closer to Betty. The police were even more suspicious, and they kept him under close observation.

Shortly after this, Red Johnson was arrested for interrogation. At that time this could be done without an arrest warrant issued by a judge. They found an empty milk bottle in his car, perhaps to feed little Charles, the police thought. It looked very bad for Johnson.

"I love to drink milk," he said during his interrogation, "and I always throw all kinds of things on the back seat." The police did not believe him, and they kept him in custody for 17 more days and continued to question him. Things began to look worse for Johnson.

On the nineteenth day of his incarceration, he received both good and bad news. Johnson was released but was not allowed to see Betty. His papers showed that he was in the United States illegally. This, it turned out, is why he wanted to hide his place of origin. The authorities decided to deport him back to Scandinavia. It was a sad Atlantic crossing for Johnson, with only one advantage for him: The police could no longer arrest him for kidnapping.

Now it was Betty's turn. Maybe she alone had committed the crime, hiding the baby during all the commotion? If the nanny did it, it would explain why Charles Jr. did not cry: He knew and loved her. But why did she go back to the room half an hour later? Why did she not turn on the light when she entered the room at 10 P.M.? Why did she call Johnson after she heard of the change of plans? The nanny supposedly knew nothing. But was she really so innocent?

After further questioning, which Anne Lindbergh, in a letter, called "a grilling," one of the New Jersey State Police officers said Betty Gow was "a highly sensitive girl of good morals . . . above being in any way connected with the persons responsible for the kidnapping of the baby." This eliminated her and Johnson as suspects. Red Johnson could not have committed the crime without Betty's help. But because Betty was innocence personified, this path turned out to be a dead end.

There remained only the Whatleys. The two had lived in the United States for only a short time. They had arrived 2 years before from England. As it turned out, Mr. Whatley had lied during his job interview: He had never been part of a household staff. He had worked as a jeweler and a mechanic, and at one time he worked in a munition factory. Why had he lied? After gentle questioning, the police concluded that it was probably just to get the job. The Whatleys were presumed innocent. The same went for all twenty other household staff members. Many had small lies and irregularities in their lives, but nothing about them could be linked to the kidnapping.

Calls came in from clairvoyants, with the usual absurd predictions. For a time, nothing happened in the Lindbergh case.

Ransom

Another figure entered the scene: retired school principal John Condon. He was from the Bronx, and he offered himself as a negotiator after Lindbergh had advertised for one. Whether Condon was the victim of a misunderstanding, we will never know: Lindbergh had asked for a negotiator who had a criminal background, not a friendly fellow citizen who had no idea how the criminal mind works.

He maintained that he had received letters in which the criminals asked him to be their negotiator. This could well have been true because Condon wrote articles for the *Bronx Home News,* a small newspaper in the Bronx, and the criminals may have known him through his articles.

One of the letters specified the handing over of the money: $70,000 was to be put in a box the size and shape of a shoebox. Later, more instructions would follow. When Lindbergh heard on the telephone that the letters to Condon were signed with circles and indented holes, he allowed the educator and columnist to come to Hopewell in order to discuss things.

Once there, Condon made valuable observations right away. He carefully looked over the child's room. He was the first and only one to detect the trace of a fingerprint on the windowsill, in a spot where the criminal might have left a dirty fingerprint when he climbed the ladder a second time. "A prominent and well-defined mark left by the ball of the thumb," wrote Condon. "There is evidence of muscular development there. . . . The print might have been left by a painter, a carpenter, a mechanic." Condon did not mention that a thumbprint cannot indicate muscular development and that not even a detective can deduce from a print the occupation of the person who left it. He was the only one who saw this print, and he divulged his observation only years later.

Lindbergh decided that Condon should be in on the investigation. But he was a little suspicious. The Colonel sent his lawyer, Breckinridge, with Condon back to the Bronx to wait for further instructions from the kidnappers.

Then on March 12, they received two calls: one from a caller with an Italian accent and another from a caller with a German accent. Both voices asked, among other things, whether Dr. Condon was the one from the newspaper, which Condon confirmed.

At 8:30 P.M., a taxi driver rang the doorbell and delivered a letter. The driver had been asked by a tall man with a strong German accent to deliver the letter, and he had been paid $1.

This letter, finally, contained more specific instructions for the money transfer. Condon was to take the Jerome Avenue streetcar to the last stop. This stop was also in the Bronx, in the direction of Van Cortlandt Park. In front of a closed hotdog stand, beneath a stone, he would find another message.

Condon convinced Breckinridge, who was to be the lookout, to stay at home. Instead, he went with his friend Al Reich to the stand. The note in front of the hotdog stand directed them to the other side of the street. There they should drive straight ahead, following the fence of Woodlawn Cemetery. Fortunately, Condon got out of the car, despite the cold, and walked. This was lucky because otherwise he would have missed the hand with a white handkerchief, which appeared suddenly between the bars of the fence.

The man with the handkerchief climbed over the fence, and after some chatting, the man finally came to the point. Condon later reported that the man had told him that, of all things, he was a sailor from Scandinavia. But Condon also said that the man had an unmistakable German accent. To Condon's question, "Are you German?" he got no answer. Investigators later called him "Cemetery John."

"Cemetery John" then told Condon that the kidnapping team consisted of two women and four men. Condon tried to have the ransom amount reduced to the original $50,000. The man turned him down, arguing that his boss would not go for that. Today it seems astonishing that a retired educator with no experience of police work was able to chat pleasantly with kidnappers in icy cold weather.

The men agreed that Condon would get the money and then take out an advertisement in the *Bronx Home News*. At this point, the police had no control over the negotiations. They knew nothing. Apart from the friend who was waiting in the car, Condon was the only witness to all this.

If it had been up to Lindbergh, it would have stayed this way. But Norman Schwarzkopf had regained some of the initiative and had made sure that, at the very least, the serial numbers of the ransom money would be recorded. When a banker named by President Hoover also suggested recording the numbers, Lindbergh for once kept quiet and allowed the police to do their job. The prescribed wooden box could hold only $50,000 dollars, so 400 $50 bills, in the form of gold certificates, were put in a plain brown bag to accompany the box.

About a week later, on March 19, Condon, an amateur violinist, was at a flea market and had just sold some of his violins, with the proceeds going to the renovation of a chapel. Suddenly, an Italian woman stood in front of him and said, "Nothing can be done until the excitement is over. There is too much publicity. Meet me at the depot at Tuckahoe, Wednesday, at 5 in the afternoon. I will have a message for you." No one called the police to pursue the woman or follow up on this remarkable development. Lindbergh and Condon clearly did not want to run the risk of arousing Cemetery John's or the Italian woman's suspicions. However, no one appeared on Thursday at the Tuckahoe depot.

Two weeks passed, and it was April 2 before the last message reached Lindbergh. He had been forewarned and therefore waited with the money at Condon's place. The note told them to go by car to "3225 East Trement Ave." (actually Tremont Avenue) in the Bronx and then to pick up a letter from beneath a table close to a florist's shop. The police had politely asked several times whether they could observe the handing over of the money. The Colonel had refused and had also withheld the time of the transfer from the New Jersey police.

Lindbergh and Condon started on the route described in the latest note. Near St. Raymond's Cemetery was a flower shop. On the bench next to it, there was a stone with a message underneath: "Follow Whittemore Ave to the soud." As soon as they started going south, Cemetery John called out, "Hey, Doctor!" He was standing, as befitted his name, next to a gravestone in the cemetery. Because John did not have the baby with him, Lindbergh, in a short negotiation, told Cemetery John that he had only $50,000 because of the poor state of economy and their finances. Amazingly, he got a receipt for the money.

On the receipt was written, "The boy is on the Boad [boat] Nelly it is a small Boad 28 feet long, two person are on the Boad. the are innosent. you will find the Boad between Horseneck Beach and gay Head near Elizabeth Island."

There seemed no end to the incredible coincidences: The described place, off the coast of Massachusetts and close to Martha's Vineyard, where the child was supposed to be was very close to the place where the Lindberghs had stayed for their honeymoon. But nobody ever found the Nelly.

The Educator Under Suspicion

John Condon got into a lot of trouble. Lindbergh had mistrusted him from the start, and he was the only one who had witnessed all these crucial events. Nobody else had witnessed the first meeting at the cemetery, and nobody else had listened in on the first telephone conversation at his house, which his wife had answered. She recognized the Italian accent of the caller. Condon answered the second telephone call himself, and he said he detected a German accent. Again, there were no other witnesses. Only the taxi driver had met the elusive "Cemetery John," the tall blond man with a German accent. Maybe the cab driver was an accomplice of Condon?

Condon could also have overheard in Lindbergh's living room that the nanny's boyfriend, Red Johnson, was a sailor from Scandinavia and might have attributed this background to Cemetery John. But the fact that the boat was supposed to be at the exact spot where the Lindberghs had once spent happy days was an even odder coincidence. Condon could not have found out easily that the Lindberghs had spent their honeymoon there. On the other hand, perhaps he had seen a photograph of them on their honeymoon and had asked the servants in Hopewell about it.

Condon also had possible motives. Perhaps at first he wanted to make himself important and wanted the attention that being a negotiator would bring. Only later, when he realized what an opportunity was being presented to him, might he have opted to be the man who handed over the ransom and thereby pocket the money himself. For this, he would have needed only one or two accomplices.

Maybe Condon had planned it from the very beginning. The fact that he later managed to knock $20,000 off the kidnapper's demand made him seem more trustworthy to Lindbergh, but was this just a clever ploy?

Once Condon realized that Lindbergh did not want to involve the police, it might have been easy for him to falsify the letters and to have his accomplice pop up in different roles. There was no risk because Condon could have stopped at any time, maintaining that he had not received any further letters. He could stop his negotiating role anytime he liked. The fact that he never did and kept his primary role in the affair displayed either his shrewdness, his carelessness, or his innocence.

The police could not be faulted by anyone. Lindbergh had blocked all their attempts to investigate the crime by the book. He had made it so that he had to solve the puzzle himself.

Gold Certificates

There was worldwide grief and anger when truck driver William Allen found the dead body of the child on May 12. Allen expressed what most people felt when he said, "I just hope they get the man that did it. Nothing would be too bad to do to him."

There was some consolation in this development. Police Chief Norman Schwarzkopf finally could work without interference from Lindbergh. The Colonel's argument that the life of his child might be in danger if his orders were not followed was now moot.

Charles and Anne Lindbergh moved permanently to Englewood, and at last the police were free to try to reconstruct the crime scene in Hopewell unhindered by Lindbergh's interference. The police reconstructed the crime using the ladder. A police officer climbed it to the second floor, took a 30-pound dummy out of the child's bed, and climbed back down again. He carried the dummy in a linen bag that had been found near the corpse. After a week's work with various alternative ascents and descents, it began to dawn on the investigators that it was almost impossible to climb down the ladder with the bag. The weight of the bundle caused it to bang repeatedly against the braces of the wooden structure, and the rungs could barely hold the weight of the kidnapper and the child. One of the rungs on the ladder broke when an 185-pound man with a package the size and weight of Charles Jr. stepped on it. The child probably had died while being carried down the ladder, either from being banged against the rungs or from falling from the ladder, perhaps along with the kidnapper. The kidnapper had then thrown the lifeless body, which was no longer of any value to him, from the car, not far from the house. The fact that he did not bury the body or even cover it with branches proved that he was in a great hurry.

From the criminal's point of view, this new discovery was hard to explain. Why did the kidnapper run the risk of asking for a ransom when a kidnap victim usually is returned during the transfer? Also, the criminal would have to contend with the possibility that the corpse would be found and that the negotiations would then be broken off.

Even a foolish criminal would know that after the body was found, he would have to expect a murder charge. At that time in the United States, a murder was much more serious than a simple kidnapping, which had a much lighter sentence. Only after the Lindbergh case did kidnapping become a capital offense. It also became a case for the federal authorities and the FBI (as specified in the Lindbergh Law, passed by Congress after the kidnapping).

The real kidnapper would have known that the corpse was very inadequately buried. So why did he take his time and ask for a ransom? Surely he would be worried that the corpse would soon be found, making a ransom out of the question. Or did he just play along with the charade, despite knowing the child was dead, planning that if the body was found he would just stop his demands? How did this fit with Cemetery John's coolness as he negotiated for an hour with Condon? Knowing that the child was already dead and could be found at any time must have added to the time pressure on him, and this should have made him accelerate the payment of the ransom. Or did he convince Condon to become his accomplice? Maybe Condon was innocent after all and was drawn into the whole mess by the kidnapper's letter. Whichever way the investigation turned, the possible explanations did not fit.

The years 1932 and 1933 passed. Several families offered their own children to the Lindberghs as a substitute for their lost son. But in August 1932, their second son, Jon, was born. The Lindberghs could gratefully turn down the generous offers of other parents.

Two and a half years after the kidnapping, the case was on the police back burner with no new clues. This changed abruptly on September 16, 1934, when a man drove up to a gas station in Harlem, in Manhattan, to get some gasoline. He paid Walter Lyle, the gas station attendant, with a strange bill, a gold certificate. These certificates, looking quite similar to today's dollar bills, were given to everyone who brought gold to the bank. For silver, one received silver certificates. The U.S. Federal Bank guaranteed to exchange the precious metal for every gold certificate, knowing full well that almost nobody would do that. It was much easier for people to stash money in a safe or a bank as notes rather than as ingots or coins.

In the spring of 1932, when Lindbergh's private bank made the ransom payments available, such gold certificates were still a normal means of payment, available at many different face values. The ransom payment consisted almost entirely of those certificates.

In 1933, a year after the kidnapping of Charles Lindbergh Jr., the continuing economic and banking crisis in the United States and the world made people prefer the gold over the notes. The Reserve Bank no longer had enough gold reserves. The government did what any government would do this situation: On May 1, 1933, it forbade the banks to redeem gold certificates. People tried to get rid of their gold certificates, starting a black market.

The next year, all state and federal banks that still had precious metal in their safe deposit boxes had to hand it over to the Treasury in order to fight the ongoing economic crisis, so within 2 years gold certificates lost their usefulness because no bank could redeem them.

"You don't see many of these around anymore," growled the Harlem station attendant when his client tried to pay with a $10 gold certificate.

"I still have a hundred of them," responded the well-dressed customer, who had a German accent. The attendant, Lyle, took the bill. But because he did not know whether his bank would honor the certificate, he wrote the license number of the client's car on the note. The license number was 4U13-41.

Lyle's sixth sense bore fruit just 2 days later. The registered numbers on the certificate were among those of the ransom money. The car belonged to a 34-year-old carpenter who lived in the Bronx at 1279 222nd Street. This was the residence of German immigrant Bruno Richard Hauptmann. One day later, he was arrested while sitting in his car. "What is the matter?" he asked the police officer; "What is this all about?"

He still professed ignorance when a second gold certificate was extracted from his pants pocket. At the police station on the lower West Side, Norman Schwarzkopf, his team from New Jersey, and some police officers from New York explained to him what it was all about.

Hauptmann, who was 6 feet, 1 inch, was taller than most Americans. He had light brown hair and resembled Condon's description of Cemetery John.

Hauptmann and his wife stated that they had never been to Hopewell and that they listened to music rather than wandering about New Jersey on rainy nights. The carpenter denied having had anything to do with the kidnapping. He had saved the money to protect himself against inflation, and now he meant to spend it. When he was asked to give a handwriting sample, he immediately agreed. "I would like to do that," said Hauptmann. "It will prove my innocence."

Tilting at Windmills

However, Hauptmann lied during the interrogation. When his living and work quarters were searched on September 20, it turned out that instead of finding the alleged savings of $300, police found forty-six times this amount, neatly tucked into holes, cracks, and clefts in the wood. Without exception, these were bills from the Lindbergh ransom money. Now, Hauptmann was clearly in trouble.

He gave a very interesting explanation for the origin of the money. He said that it was not his money. It belonged to a colleague, Isidor Fisch, who deposited a package with him. Fisch left on December 6, 1933, for Germany, and had not yet returned. One day, Fisch's package got wet, and Hauptmann opened it. Because Fisch owed him money anyway, he used some of it and kept the rest hidden. Fisch died of tuberculosis in Leipzig in March 1934, and Hauptmann did not want to send the rest of the money to his relatives. Hauptmann was proven to have stolen the money, and he even admitted this during his trial. He talked also about being the son of an abusive, alcoholic father.

But it was not only the hidden money. Further searches revealed a small pistol. Information from the German police said that Hauptmann had been in prison for armed assault and that at one time he had even burglarized the mayor's house in the town of Kamenz.

Hauptmann was born in Kamenz in Saxony, Germany. He lived alone with his mother after his father died of alcohol abuse, his two brothers were killed in World War I, and his only sister emigrated to the United States. His mother loved him, but he was a difficult child. Soon he became known as the bandit of Kamenz because of his frequent burglaries. He was sentenced to 2 years and 6 months in prison on June 3, 1919, by the high court in Bautzen for burglary and 14 days later for another 2 years and 6 months for street robbery.

After 4 years, he was released on good behavior. He immediately went to a nearby forest, where he dug up the hidden money from his earlier burglaries. Meanwhile, however, the rampant inflation of the time had destroyed its value.

He dug up nine 100-mark bills and fifty back-drawn bills (not real money) for 1 mark each. When he went to a butcher with the 950 marks, the butcher asked him for 11,600 marks for half a pound of cheap sausage. His money was useless, so he returned to live with his mother. He continued his criminal career. Soon he was charged with being the lookout while others burglarized. Back in prison again, he threw pepper in the eyes of the guard and managed to escape. He boarded the liner *Hannover* by pretending to be a blind passenger and also by acting as a stevedore carrying coal. He was caught later in the third-class area but was punished for being a stowaway only by being given minor jobs while on board.

Returned by the U.S. authorities, he managed to befriend some U.S. sailors, who smuggled him on board the *U.S.S. Washington*. He jumped into New York Harbor but was sent back to Hamburg after being rescued.

Finally he managed to enter the United States after he stole a U.S. passport from an American visiting Germany. The passport was canceled by the U.S. consul in Hamburg, but it was too late; the *Porta* reached the United States before the letter, and Hauptmann realized his dream of entering the United States. He spoke no English at all, and soon "his" passport was stolen by another thief. It eventually reappeared in Chinatown during a police search.

While sitting around in Central Park in New York City, he was noticed by a rich woman, who gave him a job in a hotel working as a dishwasher. By October 1925 he had earned enough money from several jobs to move in with a German female immigrant.

Despite all this incriminating evidence and his criminal background, Hauptmann's lawyer, James Fawcett, was convinced of his innocence. When asked whether he believed Hauptmann was guilty of the kidnapping, the federal prosecutor said he knew of no one who was not convinced that he was guilty.

Opinions are of not much use in a criminal case, of course. There was little direct evidence of his guilt. One thing the police had measured, albeit late in the game, was Cemetery John's shoeprint after he walked in the cemetery. Two handwriting experts were enlisted to compare Hauptmann's handwriting with the scrawling writing on the ransom notes, even though the writing was obviously disguised. The experts were Albert Osborn and his son. The two Osborns made little headway, even when they asked the right-handed Hauptmann to write with his left hand. In his final testimony, Albert Osborn said he believed Hauptmann to be the writer, but his son had the opposite opinion. He thought that although there were some similarities, there were also distinct differences.

So far nobody had thought of showing the first blackmail note to a German reader. It is very apparent to me, a German who speaks pretty good English, that in the letters some English words were replaced with German words, such as *gut* for *good* and *aus* for *out*. Also, there was the replacement of "th" with the similar-sounding "d": Instead of *anything*, the writer of the kidnapping notes wrote *anyding*. Anybody studying English would write these simple words correctly from the start. Therefore, it is strange that these words, which any American would naturally pick up in Germany, are the ones being Germanized. Other words such as *ransom* were written correctly, even though they are less common and easier to write incorrectly. This suggests that somebody was trying to imitate a German writing English. The author seemed to know only a few partially distorted German words and could write only a bad imitation of simple words. On the other hand, Hauptmann had had to learn English purely phonetically, so it is possible that he wrote such a crude note, almost a parody of a German writing English.

The handwriting experts could not agree in court. But because they needed a ruling, it was eventually pronounced that the letters were written by Hauptmann. Thus the problem was "solved" for the court's purposes.

On September 25, Lindbergh was asked whether he was sure he could recognize the voice that, at a distance of 230 feet, had called out, "Hey Doctor." The Colonel was not sure but undertook the test the next day. Hauptmann had to call out several times, "Hey Doctor," and after a few tries, Lindbergh appeared to be sure. In October, he testified that the voice of Cemetery John was identical with that of Hauptmann. Just try this test yourself: Take a person whose voice you have never heard, stand 230 feet away from him in a forest, and let him call out, "Hey Doctor." Then wait 3 years and repeat the experiment with five people, one of whom is the original person. Would you be able to recognize that voice again? Condon, who was also asked to identify the voice, kept quiet, perhaps because it would mean the death penalty if he got it wrong or perhaps because he was not sure.

Hauptmann and his lawyer were delighted by all this uncertain evidence. But their confidence did not last long. The decisive evidence appeared: a missing piece of wood.

A Gap in the Floor

Among the very few useful crime scene traces, the homemade ladder certainly was the most conspicuous one. It also turned out to be the best one. The ladder was investigated by Arthur Koehler.

Koehler was working for the Wood Research Laboratory in Madison, Wisconsin. He immediately offered his help to Norman Schwarzkopf when he heard that wood was part of the evidence. Only after Charles Jr.'s body was found did the police send him a piece of the ladder for examination. Indeed, the ladder produced numerous fingerprints, but, as shown much later, not a single one belonged to Bruno Hauptmann.

In February 1933, Koehler examined the entire ladder, having already examined several pieces. He stated that the wood was cut up by hand with a badly sharpened and clogged blade. The corners were cut with a dull and notched blade. It was not a very professional piece of work.

One piece of the ladder, which had earlier received evidence number 16 or rail 16 (specifically, "piece of wood from disassembled ladder #16"), was interesting. In this piece of wood there were holes made by four old nails that had been removed.

The distinctive feature of the holes was their square shape. These holes must have been made with square nails. These nails were rare in the 1930s because they were handmade. The new, industrially manufactured nails, which we still use today, have a round cross-section, and they were already on the market at the time. Furthermore, the old type of nails rusted when used outdoors. They were made of iron that was not nickel plated, and they were not protected from the effects of the environment.

But the nail holes in rail 16 of the ladder showed no trace of rust. That meant that they must have been made of wood from an interior room.

Koehler told Schwarzkopf that when they found a suspect and searched his home, they should look to see whether any floorboards or other wooden planks contained square nail holes. Perhaps, Koehler suggested, they could even find some floorboards made of the same wood as the ladder.

Koehler took the ladder apart and looked at all the pieces under a magnifying glass. He found that two pieces, the bottom two rails (#12 and #13), were new pieces of yellow pine sapwood, and they had the same planing patterns that matched end to end, having been cut from a single strip of wood at least 14 feet long, and Koehler calculated that the original strip had been 3 3/4 inches wide. It was wood from a California pine, and it showed a characteristic scrape and saw pattern. These sawing patterns are produced by an industrial wood saw with six vertical blades and eight horizontal blades. From the scrapes, Koehler calculated that the wood must have been run through the machine at a speed of 2.5 miles an hour. The only problem with this clue was that there were some 1,600 sawmills on the Atlantic coast of the United States alone.

Koehler did not give up. He wrote to all the sawmills and asked about their cutting machines. He also asked for wood-cutting samples from a few of them. In South Carolina, he found the blade he was looking for. This firm furnished wood to a lumber outlet in the Bronx. This evidence began to point toward Hauptmann.

So did another piece of the puzzle when, on September 19, 1934, Koehler found a gap in a floorboard in Hauptmann's apartment (figures 11 and 12). The grain in this floorboard looked familiar. It was similar to the wood seen in rail 16, containing the square nail holes. When he took that piece and placed it in the gap in the floor, he was certain: This piece of the ladder had been part of Hauptmann's floor. The pattern of the grain did not exactly align with the piece left on the floor, nor did it connect to the neighboring strip of wood; it was a bit smaller (figures 11 and 12). This could well be because the carpenter had sawed off some of the length in order to make it fit the ladder. In addition, the floorboard showed a distinctive notch made by the saw that had cut it, and this notch exactly fit the one seen on the cut edge of rail 16. It again indicated that someone had sawed rail 16 so as to make it fit the width of the ladder.

"So many different things could be observed on this ladder," Koehler later wrote in a scientific article, "that it was almost certain that if one thing did not yield important clues another or several others would."

The third strike against Hauptmann was that the police found a note with the telephone number of negotiator John Condon in his apartment, on the side of a cupboard. The number was written in pencil and left in a hidden place. As the evidence against her husband increased, Hauptmann's wife moved out, on the police's advice. The trial proceeded and concluded quickly.

Hauptmann was executed in the electric chair. On April 3, 1936, his corpse—that of prisoner number 17400—was driven out of the state prison in a black shiny hearse, and a curious crowd had gathered outside to say goodbye. A photograph shows a spectator waving his hat in the direction of the hearse and another leaning against an upper tree branch in order to get a better look. The case was closed.

Gaps in the Evidence

The public was content with the result of the investigation, but there were dissenters. According to Eleanor Roosevelt, "The whole trial left a big question mark."

Even the American Bar Association thought that the prosecutor and the defense counsel were prejudiced and conceited. It announced, "Life becomes, unnecessarily, a cheap commodity when a simple trial becomes a public circus."

There were still quite a few discrepancies. Hauptmann always claimed that on the day of the kidnapping he been working on the construction site of the Majestic Housing Development. The only witness who placed him at the scene was an 87-year-old man with bad eyesight who said he saw Hauptmann that morning near the Lindbergh house. The defendant maintained to the last that he was innocent, and he appeared so relaxed during the trial that he would lean back in his chair and smile, apparently in all innocence. He seemed to be unable to believe what was going on in the courtroom and that he really was on trial for his life. The piece of wood apparently sawn out from the floor in Hauptmann's apartment was a good 1/16 inch (1.5 mm) thicker than the planks on either side. How could that be? Also, the direct connecting pieces that would have linked the rung to the surrounding floorboards were missing. For that reason, a claim that the wood in Hauptmann's floor had without doubt yielded the piece used to build the ladder could not possibly be made. Finally, all of the people concerned were so convinced of Hauptmann's guilt that it was possible that someone had placed Condon's address inside the cupboard in order to incriminate him more strongly. (Such planting of evidence was not uncommon in those days.) Moreover, it was true that the gold certificates Hauptmann had used before his arrest smelled musty. This supported his testimony that the certificates got wet and that he then spent some and hid the rest. Next, the new governor of New Jersey, Harold Hoffman, visited Hauptmann on death row. He left the prison convinced that the German was innocent. Hoffman was not reelected in 1938, partly because he had intervened in favor of the German immigrant. Then there was Isidor Fisch, who according to Hauptmann had originally owned the money. He had been involved in money laundering and the black market. Finally, Fisch had a Polish accent, which few Americans could differentiate from a German accent. Then, to top it all off, Charles Lindbergh Sr. and his entire family left the country.

Lindbergh's Travels

Governor Hoffman was very attentive to the Lindbergh case and at one point almost overturned the verdict. When he visited Hauptmann in the summer of 1935, the condemned man asked to take a lie detector test or be injected with a truth serum. To Hoffman he seemed totally innocent, and unlike many guilty criminals, Hauptmann made useful suggestions to try to prove his innocence.

But the public and the police were not interested in the idea that Hauptmann might be innocent. Lindbergh the hero had identified Hauptmann's voice as that of Cemetery John. It seemed that whoever doubted that Hauptmann was the kidnapper also doubted Lindbergh's abilities. For most Americans at the time, this was unimaginable—almost like saying that Einstein is not a genius. It could not be true!

Hoffman went even further. He met with the detectives and also looked at the piece of wood that supposedly had come from the floor of Hauptmann's apartment. Hoffman then did something that took more courage than most politicians in this situation would have shown. He informed the press that as a member of the clemency commission of New Jersey, he would put into action a deferment of the death sentence. At that time, the governor was not the only one who had the power to grant clemency, as is the case today. The Supreme Court could also get involved. Hoffman committed himself politically to this case. Both Hauptmann and Hauptmann's wife had convinced him that the court and the jury had committed a judicial error.

As soon as Hoffman announced his plans to forward a clemency plea on December 5, Lindbergh ordered Anne to pack everything for an immediate departure of the family to Europe. He leaked to the press that the media circus was too much for him, and on December 22 he left the country. The New York Times published an article on page 1, and the journalist who wrote it got the Pulitzer Prize for the best newspaper story of the year.

To lawyer Gregory Ahlgren and police officer Stephen Monier, authors of the book Crime of the Century, Lindbergh's explanation is suspicious. They are certain that Charles Lindbergh was fleeing.

According to their analysis it was not a coincidence that Lindbergh fled the country shortly before Hauptmann's execution, which was originally planned for January 1936 but was postponed to April, while Governor Hoffman investigated and expressed skepticism at the guilty verdict. During these ongoing investigations, Lindbergh did not want to be in the country. But he was able to manipulate the press. The New York Times wrote about his departure exactly the way Lindbergh wanted it to be published: According to him, he had to leave the country because his family was no longer safe.

But what exactly was Lindbergh fleeing from? Perhaps, in the end, it would be found out who exactly had little Charles on his conscience—might it be Lindbergh himself?

Lindbergh clearly was not out to get the ransom. He had plenty of money. Perhaps the whole money business was initiated by someone else. What about Condon; might he not have tried to make some money for himself?

But there is nothing to prevent us from thinking that Lindbergh pocketed the money himself. When he left the house of his in-laws, the first ransom note arrived, demanding exactly $50,000—the same amount as the ransom demand in the actual kidnapping. The first ransom paid by Anne's parents was never collected, possibly because Lindbergh and Anne were already on the train, on their way to a happy future.

But if Lindbergh wasn't interested in the ransom, what was this all about?

"We know that Colonel Lindbergh enjoyed playing very sick and cruel pranks on people," Ahlgren and Monier explain in their book. They recount some of the practical jokes that, according to several biographers, our hero liked to play. "There is no humor in putting kerosene in a man's water pitcher, causing the victim to be hospitalized after gulping it. . . . There is no humor in putting a venomous snake into the bed clothes of a fellow military officer known to be deathly afraid of snakes. That victim could have died, if not from the snake bite then certainly from a heart attack. . . . There was no humor when the Colonel, during a dinner engagement with Amelia Earhart, suddenly, and without provocation, dumped a glass of water over Anne's head, spoiling her new silk dress." The authors continue, "As bad as that incident was, it did not mark the nadir of the Colonel's 'jokes' towards his family. A few months prior to the baby's disappearance [Lindbergh] had taken the baby from its crib and hidden him in a closet. The house had been thrown into an uproar as the family panicked that the baby had been kidnapped. Lindbergh let the ruse last for twenty minutes before the infant was discovered."

In comparison, the blackmail note to his parents-in-law would be only a mild joke. Perhaps Lindbergh, who all his life felt controlled and organized, wanted to play a truly great joke on March 1, 1932. Maybe he felt inspired by Houdini, the world's most famous magician, who died 6 years before. Houdini was also a flight pioneer. He was the first person to perform acrobatic feats while flying a biplane. Maybe Lindbergh only wanted to play a joke—the perfect, unexpected joke. This time, after plunging the house into panic and despair and even worse than the first time because Charles Jr. would not even be found in the closet, his father would then coolly walk in through the front door happily whistling, with his son on his arm. Now this was a joke that Charles Sr. would find amusing.

So perhaps he made the ladder and told the family by phone to remain in the old house. Only in this house could he get the child out of his bed from behind closed shutters, without being seen. The child's room was on a corner of the house that could not be seen from the main entrance area (figure 9). Then he planned to dismantle the ladder and later appear with Charles Jr. in triumph.

Seen in this context, the fact that the dog did not bark and the child did not cry is not surprising. It was only the master roaming around the house. The blackmail note, which suddenly appeared close to the window, had been placed there by Lindbergh himself. Nobody climbed the ladder a second time, and Lindbergh himself later "found" the letter during all the commotion. The fact that he did not immediately open it, as any other person in that situation would have done, but strictly ordered everyone to wait for the arrival of the forensic scientists also speaks in favor of his plan: He knew there would be no fingerprints on the envelope and in the child's room because he wiped the smooth areas clean. The fingerprint that Condon claimed to see was almost certainly not there. No police officer saw a print. Condon must have fabricated the entire testimony.

It is therefore understandable why Lindbergh delayed and blocked the investigation whenever possible. He wanted the most misleading clues possible, presenting an inextricable tangle.

But what about the corpse? The spot where the body was found may be the strongest clue that Lindbergh might have been the culprit. Lindbergh slipped from the ill-conceived ladder, and the child was unintentionally killed in the fall. Lindbergh then had to get rid of the body quickly. He was able to get less than 3 miles away from the house before throwing it in the bushes. He had no time to bury it because he had to get back home quickly. Anne had already noticed that her husband was unusually late, for unknown reasons.

The discovery site of the child's corpse also cleared Bruno Hauptmann as a possible culprit in some people's eyes: The Bronx is north of Hopewell, and the body was found several kilometers south. Why would a kidnapper choose a location that would make it more likely that he would encounter a roadblock on his way home? The fact that even the George Washington Bridge to New York was closed off, after Lindbergh's alarm, makes that fear plausible.

A last clue hinting at the culpability of Lindbergh, as seen by Ahlgren and Monier, is the fact that one of Charles Jr.'s thumb guards was found near the main road to the house. Could anybody seriously think that the kidnapper would have carried the child, with his thumb guards, along the main driveway leading to the house, to his car?

The two authors wrote in *The Crime of the Century* that no kidnapper would have driven into the driveway in order to carry out the crime. The winding single-lane driveway was half a mile long. The only place to turn the car around was directly in front of the house. If a kidnapper were to park there, he would have to expect to be caught or at the very least be seen by someone in the house or by someone leaving the house to drive away. Even worse, a visitor might arrive at the house, blocking his escape. Whatever happened, all these scenarios suggest that those in the house or visitors in their car would witness the crime—at the very least the loading of the child into the car.

But this was not all. Having watched the house for days, a criminal would have noticed that Lindbergh had not yet arrived home on that evening. For this reason alone a kidnapper would not park close to the house. The possibility of being caught by Lindbergh would have been suicidal. Yet the thumb guard was near the driveway by the house's main entrance.

A logical explanation is that Lindbergh himself put the dead child into his car and lost the child's thumb guard in the process. He was the only person who could drive at that time on his own road without having to give an explanation.

Skeptical? Consider what Lindbergh had to say in court about his actions and whereabouts on the day of the kidnapping:

REILLY (*defense counsel*): Would you please relate to us what you did the day of the kidnapping?
LINDBERGH: I was in New York all day on that Tuesday.
REILLY: Where?
LINDBERGH: I can't remember in detail where I was. I think I was in the Pan Am office building, maybe also in the cargo office of Trans Continental. Part of the day I was at the Rockefeller Institute, and if I am not mistaken, I was at my dentist's in the afternoon.

That was it. One would expect him to have a clearer memory of the worst day of his life.

In 1941, Lindbergh asked the president whether he could enter active service as an Air Force pilot. Roosevelt declined. Instead, he was allowed to fly missions against Japan as a private citizen and as a consultant to the Ford Motor Company and to the United Aircraft Corporation. Lindbergh had a certain admiration for the Nazi Party in Germany. He had received Germany's highest civil medal from the supreme commander of the German Luftwaffe, Hermann Göring.

After the war, both the Americans and the Germans tried to put the past behind them. When Lindbergh died in 1974 in Hawaii, he was again the "Lone Eagle," an honorary title Lucky Lindy had received after his flight across the Atlantic. The jokester and self-appointed investigator was 72 years old when he died. After the death of Charles Jr., he and his wife gave the Hopewell house to a charity that opened a kindergarten there on June 23, 1933. They had five more children: Jon (who was born in Englewood), Land, Anne, Scott, and Reeve.

Bruno Hauptmann's widow, Anne, lived with relatives in Philadelphia until her death in October 1994. Her husband's defense lawyer died in 1940, and Governor Hoffman lost his governorship in 1938.

In 2003, another Lindbergh bombshell appeared in the news. Twenty-nine years after Lindbergh's death, his children had their say, but these were his *German* children, who had not been listed in any biography. That summer, the hottest in centuries, Astrid Boutenie, whose maiden name had been Hesshaimer, stated that she and her brothers, Dyrk and David, were the issue of a romance between Lindbergh and German milliner Brigitte Hesshaimer. The often prickly loner fell in love with the young woman. When he saw her for the first time in Munich, on the Odeonsplatz in front of the Feldherrnhalle, where there are two large lion statues, he asked her, "Why aren't the lions roaring?" Naturally, Brigitte did not understand, and so the older man explained, "Somebody once told me that when you hear lions roar, you fall in love— and I just fell in love with you!"

Lindbergh was very careful to keep the liaison secret. He assumed an alias: Caren Kent, the name his three children also used when speaking to him. In 1974, when Lindbergh died, his daughter Astrid began to look for photos. She found some negatives in an old chocolate box. Astrid's investigative zeal was awakened. She lived in France at that time, but she searched in her mother's house in Germany on the banks of Lake Ammersee. In the attic, she found a pile of letters, most of them handwritten and tied together with a red ribbon. When her mother realized that Astrid had taken the letters, she warned, "You don't know what you are starting with this, you don't know what you are doing." Astrid did not give back the letters, but she did not pass on the secret until her mother died. The first letter dated from 1957.

"When he was with us," remembers his son Dyrk, "he looked after us. Other fathers just sat in front of a beer glass, but we went on excursions." He seemed to truly love his children. "Give Astrid a hug from me and Dyrk an extra push on the swing," wrote Lindbergh in one of his letters. Lindbergh was at the house on the Ammersee for the last time in 1972. He paid for private schools for his children, and he left each of them an investment portfolio (not at all common in Germany at that time). During his last visit the flying hero was already so weak that he was unable even to change a flat tire. In his last letter, dated August 1974, he mentioned that his health was very poor and that he could hardly write: "My love to you and the children is all I can send."

Brigitte Hesshaimer learned about Lindbergh's death through the newspapers. Not a soul knew anything about his second family in Bavaria. This was just the way he had wanted it.

Facts

Was Lindbergh innocent? Was Bruno Hauptmann the kidnapper? How would you decide? It would have been you who had to decide if you had been on the jury. If you found the culprit guilty, you could be sure that he would get the death penalty.

Imagine you are one of the jurors in the Lindbergh case. The case has unfolded in front of you, and you have reached the last day of the trial. Soon it progresses to jury deliberation. You leaf through your notes and remember that a wood expert found out something important. A wood expert? What was that all about?

The ladder was made of four different kinds of wood: the common pine, the yellow pine, the Douglas pine, and the birch. One year after the disappearance of Charles Lindbergh Jr. in March 1933, wood expert Arthur Koehler had been asked to go to the police station in Trenton, New Jersey. He studied the entire ladder, not just a few samples of its wood.

Wood can provide useful evidence, partly because it does not rot when stored in a dry place. When Koehler arrived in Trenton, he was able to do three things. First, he carefully looked over the ladder. As described before, the ladder consisted of three parts and had a total weight of only 38 pounds, not enough for great stability. The fact that the ladder could be dismantled could have several explanations. One reason might be so that it could be used both inside and outside the house. Another reason might be that it had to be stored someplace where there was little space, such as in a small apartment. The parts also fit easily into a car.

The construction of the ladder was careless. The steps were nailed onto the side rails, as an amateur probably would have done. They were fitted into crudely chiseled notches. This could mean different things. Either the builder knew nothing about carpentry or he had very little time. Maybe he wanted to use the ladder only once. To the expert, the effect of the findings on the case is unimportant. His or her job is to find the truth, not provide justice. The expert can concentrate on the investigation and leave the interpretation to the police and lawyers.

Koehler measured the pieces of the ladder to a hundredth of an inch. The ladder was made of seventeen pieces, plus the dowels that were used to put it together. Piece #16 (rail 16, discussed earlier) is very conspicuous. It is made from a piece of inferior pine that obviously had been used before. Whereas all the other long parts of the ladder originated from planks of wood usually used in roofing that were generally available on the market, rail 16 had different

JUSTICE VERSUS TRUTH

Continental Europeans often are bemused by the U.S. jury system. It is not the basis of the justice that seems strange to them but the process of jury selection, the often Hollywood-like courtroom antics of the lawyers, and the media circus associated with some trials. It is well known that people are easily influenced in the courtroom. As someone who has testified in criminal cases in the United States, I also believe that these doubts are somewhat justified. Appeals to the jury's prejudices and emotional state and the often theatrical approach of the defense counsel and prosecutor have played major roles in many U.S. criminal cases. I do not believe that this approach to justice has any value in uncovering the truth. But as a professional forensic scientist, I am interested only in truth.

The fact that justice, the judiciary, and truth are not always the same is known by every political decision maker. They often have to accept untruths in order to pursue a political goal; the goal can even be a very worthy one. In a courtroom, however, there should be no room for tactical maneuvers and speculations. The question is how to find the truth of what, when, and why something happened. If that is not accomplished, any judgment can only accidentally be just.

This is why in recent decades more and more factual evidence has entered the courts. The most important type is fingerprints, which have been used since 1900, followed by the discovery of genetic fingerprinting in 1985. These two forensic techniques connect not only the criminal and the crime scene but also different crime scenes. Even if a criminal is caught years later, it is possible to prove that he or she committed a much earlier crime or series of crimes.

The main advantage of this kind of evidence over witnesses' testimony is that it is objective, independent of prevailing trends and opinions. If evidence is missing, the case is wide open for all sorts of assumptions and speculations.

If there is evidence, it must be correctly understood and interpreted. Any further haggling and analysis is fruitless: There is only one possibility that combines the evidence with the crime. However, only a good criminalist can remove all doubt that there might be another explanation. Good criminalists may be police detectives, lawyers, crime scene technicians, or natural scientists. As Sherlock Holmes says, "When all other contingencies fail, whatever remains, however improbable, must be the truth."

measurements. It was hand-sawn on the side and in front. In other words, rail 16 certainly did not come from an attic brace but from a piece of a sawn-off floorboard.

Its sides were smoothed by a blade that was obviously notched. Its notches can be seen when the light falls on it from an oblique angle.

What about the holes for the square nails in rail 16? They indicate that the piece of wood was nailed inside a dry building for quite some time; otherwise the nails would have rusted. There was no rust on the edges of the square holes. Because the piece of wood had very prominent grain and a few ugly knots, it was probably used to build closets or attics, where the wood's aesthetic short-comings are not so visible.

The report also showed that ladder pieces 12 and 13 were cut from a single plank. One end of the plank was 1/16 inch (half a millimeter) wider than the other end. How is such a difference possible with a board that was machine sawn?

The answer is that when the board came out of the machine, it was equally thick all over. The piece was cut from a living tree trunk, so it grew differently at each end of the tree. One end grew closer to the ground; the other end was soaring upward. The end close to the ground was more tightly compressed wood and had a tighter grain. The upper end had more air and water and was less compressed because it bore less weight. Therefore the end at the top shrank more than that taken from closer to the base of the tree. This shrinkage becomes visible only weeks after sawing, when the wood has dried out.

Koehler calculated that the lower end of the wooden plank could not shrink much because it was already very dense. He measured this as being 3 11/16 inches (94 mm) thick; the other end was 3 5/8 inches (92 mm) thick.

This was unusual because at the time most machines sawed fresh wood to a thickness of exactly 3 5/8 inches. After cutting, the wood then dries and shrinks. In this case, after drying out the wood of the ladder was at least as thick as the fresh wood and even thicker at one end. Industrial wood-sawing machines found in sawmills are adjusted to a certain thickness. Only one explanation remains: The wood came from a machine that sawed planks and boards 3 3/4 inch (95 mm) thick.

This was the most important point Koehler could present to the jury. Per-haps surprisingly, there were only a few dozen machines on the entire East Coast that could have sawed the wood that went into pieces 12 and 13.

Koehler returned to his lab in Madison. After the police sent him the lad-der for further analysis, he realized that under sharply oblique light the strips showed small marks on the side that was planed flat by the machine at the sawmill. These marks arose from small notches on the planing machine's cutting blades. He counted and measured the notches and calculated that the plane roller used to plane the wide sides of the plank had eight blades. (The roller used on the narrow sides of the plank had only six blades.) This was the second important point.

Each blade leaves an impression with each turn of the roller. These impressions can be regarded as nothing more than spacing marks. These rollers normally revolved fifty times per second, so Koehler was able to calculate how fast the wood went through the machine. The notches repeated on the wood every 0.93 inch (24 mm). That means that the wood had to move 0.93 inch until once again it reached the first (notched) blade out of the eight on the roller.

If a rotation of the roller takes 1/50 second and the wood moves 0.93 inch in that time, the strip in the machine moves at 230 feet per minute, or roughly 2.5 miles an hour (4 km/hr). Most machines at that time cut wood at only half this speed.

Sherlock Holmes himself would have been impressed with Koehler's rigorous detective work. Koehler wrote to the 1,600 lumber companies on the East Coast, looking for a sawmill with six blades on the edges and eight on the top and bottom, an unusual cutting thickness of 3 3/4 inch, and the ability to cut wood at 230 feet per minute. On the day of the kidnapping, only twenty-three had such equipment with the same number of blades and the same cutting thickness; only one had, in addition, the cutting speed of 230 feet per minute. In September 1929, engineers of the Dorn family lumber company in McCormick, South Carolina, had worked on the machine and doubled its speed.

They provided details that were even more useful: Because clients had complained about the notches, the Dorns had their machine's blades sharpened in the same year. After that, their blades made no more notches. This proved that the ladder in the Lindbergh case was built from wood cut at the Dorns' lumber company between September and December 1929. One look in their dispatch book showed that only forty-six trucks with the requisite notched wood had left the company during these 4 months.

At this point one of the most incredible investigations in the history of criminology began: Koehler and police officer Lewis Bornman checked out all the lumber companies close to Lindbergh's house for wood that came from the Dorn lumber company. At the end of 1933, the two inseparable sleuths struck gold. At the National Lumber & Millwork Company, they found piles of this wood from the Dorn machine. Not only was this lumber company located in the Bronx, but a shipment was received there on December 1, 1931, 3 months before the kidnapping of the Lindbergh baby.

The ransom money was given to Cemetery John in the Bronx, so it seemed very likely that the criminal came from this area. The investigation had gone nowhere in the beginning because they had no Bronx suspect in their sights.

Only 9 months later, carpenter Bruno Hauptmann was arrested. After his wife moved out of the Bronx apartment, two New York police officers and Bornman, Koehler's partner, searched Hauptmann's attic. The remaining ransom money was still missing. Perhaps it was hidden under the floorboards?

It was then that the police noticed that one board had been sawed off, leaving a gap. This made no sense, but it made the police suspicious and reinforced their desire to look for the ransom money at that spot. They did not find it, but they looked to see whether rail 16 fitted the gap. It did not fit; it was too small. Luckily, there were four square nail holes for orientation. They happened to exactly fit the four holes of the crossbeam below. The grain of rail 16 also could be copied on paper and plausibly matched to Hauptmann's floorboard. Even the annual rings in the wood matched each other. Also, the blade in the wood plane found in Hauptmann's workshop left the exact notch imprint that had been noticed on the poorly sanded areas of the ladder.

Conclusion: Ladder piece number 16, found on a stormy night in Hopewell, New Jersey, originated from the attic of the Hauptmann house in the Bronx.

The evidence was too incriminating for the defense not to try to cast doubt on both it and the experts. When on the fifth day of the trial Koehler reported his irrefutable evidence that was inexplicable without Hauptmann's involvement in the crime, the defense lawyer tried to create doubt about the expert's credibility.

Hauptmann's lawyer, Edward Reilly, said that there was no such thing as a "wood expert" and that Koehler was just a forester at the U.S. Forest Products Laboratory in Madison, Wisconsin. He could "probably" identify different types of wood by visual inspection. However, the fact that he could tell pine from oak and birch was the "extent of his expertise" and in no way qualified him to testify in court as a "wood expert."

The more lawyers attack an expert witness, the less important his or her evidence is. The aim is to distract the jury from the actual facts. Hauptmann's defense lawyer clearly wanted to win the jury over; that is what he was paid to do. But he twisted the facts when he said that the jury could decide just as well as the expert. Edward Reilly pulled out all the stops. Outside the courtroom, he said things that he could not get away with in front of a judge. "What a witness," he cried, "one they got out of the forest!"

But all this was of little help. Hauptmann, who had a good explanation for the origin of the money (it came from Isidor Fisch) and who knew that the handwriting evidence was inconclusive, began to worry. Hauptmann not only denied having sawed out the board from his attic but also denied that the ladder was a ladder at all. "It looks like a musical instrument," he said in court.

It is clear why Bruno Hauptmann was the only person who could have committed the crime, according to the forensic evidence and after the judicial assessment. Who other than he could have built the ladder, using his tools, out of a board from his attic floor? Who else could have built that ladder out of used wood, which had been delivered to a lumber company only ten blocks from his house only 3 months before the crime?

Not even the defense claim that the piece of wood sawn out of the attic floor was 1.5 millimeter thicker than the other boards was correct. The board was uneven, but only because it was not totally dry when it was nailed to the planks.

"Scientific methods," Arthur Koehler wrote in a 1948 report to his superior, "should, in the light of this case, be used more often in criminal cases." This kind of scientific evidence, as well as expert testimony on plant material, commonly appears in courtrooms, often to the dismay of the defense attorneys.

We don't know why Lindbergh's dog did not bark in Hopewell. Maybe it did not smell or hear Hauptmann because of the wind and the closed windows. It is also understandable that the women in the house did not at first see the ransom note. They were looking for the child, not for a letter. Lindbergh traveled to Europe before Hauptmann's execution because he really did want to find peace from the press and the public. The fact that he arrived at home late that evening was explained by the simple observation that sometimes one does get home later than usual; it is not proof of wrongdoing.

He wanted to do the investigation himself to save his child at any cost. He both overestimated himself and underestimated the police. Many people believe that they can do things better than the experts. Many people, if given the possibility, might also unwisely take over the leadership of a police investigations or dispense their own form of justice. Lindbergh could do this because he was a celebrated hero. What about Condon's telephone number? It was not hidden in Hauptmann's apartment because the police put it there, as has been suggested. No, the explanation was as the police say: The criminal wrote it and put it there himself.

Surely you would tell all this to your fellow jurors. In this case, the jury correctly understood that evidence has more weight than a thousand legal arguments. Hauptmann built the ladder and hid the money.

If Hauptmann had not been a German immigrant and Lindbergh had not been the idol of an entire generation, the case could indeed have gone in a different direction. Had Hauptmann been rich and famous and Lindbergh a poor devil, maybe the pilot instead of the carpenter would have ended up in the electric chair in front of twenty-five witnesses.

My conclusion is that no one should pass judgment about the culpability of a person before an expert has intelligibly explained the case evidence. When scientific evidence is consistent and relevant to the case, any court in the world should be eager to hear it, as should the jury. It is not worth considering elaborate guesswork if the objective evidence does not fit; that would be unjust and irresponsible.

CHAPTER 4

FATAL CRIMES, SOMETIMES
FATAL PUNISHMENTS

CAN YOU TELL A MURDERER BY HIS LOOKS?

It is not just in life-or-death cases that we need to base our decisions on solid evidence. Simple accusations or a criminal investigation can ruin a person's reputation.

This became evident when, in late 1980, a wave of child abuse accusations against fathers swept across Germany. As soon as suspicion is aroused, most fathers are vulnerable. Rumors spread quickly. The first question people ask is always, "Would he be capable of such a thing?"

Can you imagine a case in which a lovely little girl freely invents such a story, tells the police about it, and then sticks with it even after the case has been cleared up? What about a man who had sexually abused his young step-daughter for years and is strongly suspected of having subsequently murdered his entire stepfamily? (This happened in a case of mine in 2000.) Can we suspect a reliable laboratory scientist of inventing genetic fingerprints that will lead to severe penalties for an accused person who had nothing to do with the crime?

Quick presumptions of guilt or innocence are dangerous. There are two sides to most human beings. Emotional depths often remain hidden, imperceptible even to a person's parents or spouse, who cannot understand what is happening or why. For example, consider the case of multiple murderer Jeffrey Dahmer, who discussed with his father in public and on television what might have gone wrong in his life that made him the way he was. No really useful information came from this discussion except that Jeffrey was the child of divorced parents, that he had started drinking seriously as a youngster, and that he enjoyed playing with dead animals in his childhood. His father, a chemist, later wrote a very interesting book (Lionel Dahmer, *A Father's Story: One Man's Anguish at Confronting the Evil in His Son*) in which he tries to explain that, among other similarities, he recognizes several of his son's characteristics in himself, such as a longing for a controllable personal environment.

If you look at photographs of the young Jeffrey Dahmer, you can see that evil is not always evident in the human face. You might never find more innocent or friendlier images in a family album. (Even my wife, coming across a picture of Jeffrey by chance, remarked, "He does look pretty nice.") Contrary to popular stereotypes, a serial killer does not necessarily walk stiffly, speak without emotion, or lack normal human feelings and impressions. Even in personal meetings, a brutal killer can be friendly, as I found out from talking to Luis Alfredo Garavito, a Colombian serial killer who is thought to have killed more than 300 boys. Jeffrey Dahmer himself stressed time and again that he alone was responsible for what he did—not society, not his upbringing. He did not ask for leniency; he actually asked to be prosecuted. Just before the judge sentenced him to 957 years in prison, he said, "I hoped to find out in these proceedings what made me such an evil person."

The wife of serial killer Peter Kürten, known as the Düsseldorf Vampire, who was executed in the Cologne penitentiary on July 2, 1931, never had the slightest notion of her husband's other side. They did not have a loving, close relationship, but they lived together in the closest physical proximity.

PETER KÜRTEN: THE DÜSSELDORF VAMPIRE

In the entire history of crime, no single killer has caused such widespread fear and indignation as Peter Kürten in Düsseldorf in the interwar period. It may be said without exaggeration that the epidemic of sexual outrages and murders occurring between February and November 1929 provoked a wave of sheer horror and contempt not only in Germany but throughout the entire world. Through extensive examination, the judicial system has sought not only to punish the killer for his crimes but also to probe the mind and soul of this extraordinarily enigmatic man. A clinical study of Kürten has rewarded diligent and patient analysis with an enlargement of our understanding of abnormal and pathological crime.

The killer committed his first murder in the city of Cologne on May 25, 1913. Kürten had been stealing throughout the spring, specializing in pubs or inns where the owners lived in an apartment above the premises. On this particular evening, he was surveying an inn in Cologne. Here, he takes up the story: "I broke into a house in the Wolfstrasse—an inn owned by [Peter] Klein—and went up to the first floor. I opened different doors and found nothing worth stealing, but in the bed I saw a sleeping girl of about 10, covered with a thick feather bed."

Kürten seized the girl by the neck and with both hands throttled her. The child struggled for some time before losing consciousness, and Kürten then drew her head over the edge of the bed and penetrated her vagina with his fingers.

"I had a small but sharp pocket knife with me, and I held the child's head and cut her throat. I heard the blood spurt and drip on the mat beside the bed. It spurted in an arch, right over my hand. The whole thing lasted about 3 minutes. Then I locked the door again and went back home to Düsseldorf."

The child's corpse was pallid. There was hardly any postmortem lividity, and her tongue was severely bitten. On her throat there were two wounds separated from each other: one shallow (only 1–2 mm); the other deep (9 cm). The upper wound suggested a single stroke; the lower wound had been made by four movements.

Kürten's first victim had been Christine Klein, a 10-year-old schoolgirl. Her father, Peter Klein, ran the tavern, and suspicion immediately fell on his brother Otto. On the previous evening, Otto Klein had asked his brother for a loan and had been refused; in a violent rage, he had threatened to do something his brother "would remember all his life." In the room in which the child had been killed, the police found a handkerchief with the initials "P.K.," and it seemed conceivable that Otto had borrowed it from his brother Peter.

Suspicion of Otto was deepened by the fact that the murder seemed otherwise motiveless; the child had been throttled unconscious, and her throat had been cut with a sharp knife. There were signs of some sexual molestation but not rape, and again it seemed possible that Otto Klein had penetrated the child's vagina in order to provide an apparent motive. He was charged with Christine's murder, but the jury, although partly convinced of his guilt, felt that the evidence was not sufficiently strong, and he was acquitted.

The next day, Kürten went back to Mülheim, sat in a café opposite the Kleins' inn, and drank a glass of beer. The killer later remarked that all around him people were talking about the murder, and "all the horror and indignation did [him] good." Kürten was safe from capture, and his sadistic impulse had been awakened. With his appetite whetted, Kürten soon began a series of axe and strangulation attacks on the people of Düsseldorf.

He was arrested for robbery and spent the period from 1913 to 1921 in prison. He then moved to the city of Altenburg in central Germany and got married, and for a time Kürten seems to have lived a perfectly normal and respectable life. He found permanent work in a factory and became very active in trade union circles. With his new guise as a political activist, he lived in peace for 4 years.

In 1925, Peter found his way to Düsseldorf, and once again the town proved to be a catalyst for his criminal inclinations. Kürten saw Düsseldorf again in the evening light and rejoiced that "the sunset was blood-red on my return," interpreting this as an omen of his destiny. Four years of arson attacks and petty crime seemed to have controlled the murderous streak, but these proved to be only a prelude to the horrors Düsseldorf witnessed in 1929.

The Düsseldorf police first became aware of his presence on February 9, 1929, when the body of an 8-year-old girl, Rosa Ohliger, was found under a hedge. She had been stabbed thirteen times, and an attempt had been made to burn the body with gasoline. The murderer had also stabbed her in the vagina, and semen stains on her underwear indicated that he had ejaculated.

The essential factors to be considered in diagnosis of the cause and time of death and the murderer's motive were the characteristic stabs, the congestion of blood in the head, and the injury to the genitals. From the evidence it appears that Kürten's objective was not coitus but that he must have inserted a finger smeared with semen under the intact underwear of the child and then inserted it into the vagina.

Six days earlier, a man overtook a woman named Kühn, grabbed her lapels, and stabbed her repeatedly. Appolonia Kühn suffered twenty-four wounds before the man ran off. Kürten's sadistic appetite was not yet satisfied, and he had discovered a new sexual stimulant by returning to the scenes of his crimes.

"The place where I attacked Frau Kühn I visited again that same evening twice and later several times. In doing so, I sometimes had an orgasm. When that morning I poured petrol over the Ohliger child and set fire to her, I had an orgasm at the height of the fire."

Only 5 days after the murder of Rosa Ohliger, a 45-year-old mechanic named Scheer was found stabbed to death on a road in Flingern; he had twenty knife wounds, including several in the head. The next day Kürten returned to the scene of his attack and even had the audacity to strike up a conversation with a detective at the site. Although suspicious, the detective had no reason for concern and so spoke frankly about the crime; this fantastic episode was confirmed during the trial by the detective in question.

Shortly after this spate of attacks, a mentally retarded man named Stausberg was arrested for assaulting two women with a noose. Naturally, the police accused Stausberg of the February attacks, and for some reason, unknown to this day, he confessed to all the crimes and was committed to a mental asylum. Because Stausberg was arrested for assaults so similar to Kürten's, the Vampire continued to avoid detection.

In August, however, a series of strangulation and stabbing incidents showed the police that a madman was once again on the prowl. On the 21st of the month, in the western suburb of Lierenfeld, three people were stabbed while walking home at night. The three random victims were all bidden "good evening" before being subjected to deep knife wounds in their ribs and back.

As the lights went out on the night of August 23, 1929, hundreds of people were enjoying the annual fair in the ancient town of Flehe. At around 10:30 P.M., two foster sisters, 5-year-old Gertrude Hamacher and 14-year-old Louise Lenzen, left the fair and started walking through the adjoining allotments to their home. As they did so, a shadow broke away from among the trees and followed them along a footpath. The shadow stopped the children and asked whether Louise "would be very kind and get some cigarettes for me? I'll look after the little girl." Louise took the man's money and ran back toward the fairground. Quietly, the man picked up Gertrude in his arms and strangled her before slowly cutting her throat with a clasp knife. Louise returned a few moments later and was dragged off the footpath before being strangled and decapitated.

The next afternoon, a servant girl named Gertrude Schulte was accosted by a man who tried to persuade her to have sexual intercourse. When she said, "I'd rather die," he answered, "Die then," and stabbed her. Fortunately, though, Schulte survived and was able to give a good description of her assailant, a pleasant-looking, nondescript man of about 40.

Kürten had reached a state of sexual overdrive, and the increasing frequency and ferocity of the attacks convinced medical experts that the Vampire had lost all control of his sadistic impulses. A young girl named Ida Reuter was raped and battered to death in September, and on October 12, another servant girl named Elizabeth Dorrier was beaten to death. This was followed by hammer attacks on Frau Meurer and Frau Wanders, both on October 25.

Düsseldorf was thrown into a panic comparable to that caused by Jack the Ripper as the murder toll continued to mount. On November 7, 5-year-old Gertrude Albermann disappeared, and 2 days later the newspaper *Freedom* received a letter with a map enclosed, stating that the child's body would be found near a factory wall. The body was indeed found where the killer had described, among a mass of bricks and rubble. She had been strangled and stabbed thirty-five times.

The period between February and May 1930 saw a continued spate of strangulation and hammer attacks, none fatal. Despite the enormous manhunt under way, the killer had still not been apprehended and Düsseldorf was at the point of public outcry. Although his motives were similar, the means used by the elusive Kürten were constantly changing, giving detectives no clear pattern to investigate. By May 1930, sheer terror had gripped Düsseldorf, and the Vampire was still on the loose.

Capture

As is invariably the case with serial crime, the killer was captured almost by chance. On May 14, 1930, an unemployed domestic servant named Maria Budlick left the city of Cologne in search of work in nearby Düsseldorf. On the platform at Düsseldorf station she was accosted by a man who offered to show her the way to a girls' hostel. They followed the brightly lit streets for a while, but when he started leading her toward the park she suddenly remembered the newspaper stories of the murderer and refused to go any farther. The man insisted, and as they argued a second man appeared and asked whether everything was all right. Clearly both upset and intimidated by the newcomer's arrival, the man from the railway station soon slunk away, and Budlick was left alone with her rescuer: Peter Kürten.

"The girl told me that she was out of work and had nowhere to go. She agreed to come with me to my room on the Mettmanner Strasse, and then she suddenly said she did not want sexual intercourse and asked me whether I could find her somewhere else to sleep."

The pair went by tram to Worringerplatz and walked deep into the Grafenberger Woods. Here Kürten seized Budlick with one hand by the neck and asked whether he could have sex with her.

"I thought that under the circumstances she would agree, and I was right. Afterwards I took her back to the tram, but I did not accompany her right to it because I was afraid she might inform the police officer who was standing there. I had no intention of killing Budlick as she had offered no resistance."

Kürten was remarkably calm and collected throughout the incident and made sure that no one on the tram saw him deposit the young girl at the station.

"I did not think that Budlick would be able to find her way back to my apartment in the rather obscure Mettmanner Strasse. So much the more was I surprised when on Wednesday, the 21st of May, I saw her again at my house."

Contrary to Kürten's expectations, Budlick had indeed remembered the address, vividly recalling the nameplate "Mettmanner Strasse" under the flickering gaslight. Most crucially, however, Maria wrote of her encounter in a letter of May 17 to one Frau Bruckner. The letter never reached its intended recipient. It was misdirected and opened by a Frau Brugmann, who took one look at the contents and called the police.

Maria Budlick was immediately located and questioned extensively. After a long time and much hesitation she led Chief Inspector Gennat into the hallway of number 71 Mettmanner Street. The landlady showed them into an empty room, which Budlick immediately recognized, and it was soon established that a man by the name of Peter Kürten occupied the premises. While at the house, Budlick found even more conclusive proof when her attacker entered the house and began climbing the stairs toward her. He looked briefly startled but continued to his room and shut the door behind him. A few moments later he left the house with his hat pulled down over his eyes, passed the two plain-clothes officers standing in the street, and disappeared around a corner.

Realizing that capture was inevitable, Kürten explained the Budlick case to his wife, Auguste. Because the incident could be prosecuted as rape, Kürten realized that along with his previous convictions it could be enough to ensure 15 years of penal servitude.

"Throughout the night I walked about. On Thursday, May 22, I saw my wife in the morning in the flat and so fetched my things away in a bag and rented a room in the Adlerstrasse. I slept quietly until Friday morning."

Up to this point, nothing linked Kürten with the earlier attacks. His only known crime was rape, but he knew that there was no longer any hope of concealing his identity. Peter Kürten described the consequent events of Friday, May 23, in writing.

"Today, the 23rd, in the morning, I told my wife that I was also responsible for the Schulte affair, adding my usual remark that it would mean ten years' or more separation for us—probably forever. At that, my wife was inconsolable. She spoke of unemployment, lack of means, and starvation in old age. She raved that I should take my life, then she would do the same, since her future was completely without hope. Then, in the late afternoon, I told my wife that I could help her."

Peter told his wife that he was the infamous Düsseldorf Vampire and disclosed every murder to her. Kürten then hinted that a high reward had been offered for the discovery of the criminal and that she could get that prize if she would report the confession and denounce him to the police.

"Of course, it wasn't easy for me to convince her that this ought not to be considered a betrayal but that, on the contrary, she was doing a good deed for humanity and for justice. It was not until late in the evening that she promised to carry out my request and that she would not commit suicide. It was 11 o'clock when we separated. Back in my lodging, I went to bed and fell asleep at once."

On May 24, 1930, Auguste Kürten told the story to the police, adding that she had arranged to meet her husband outside St. Rochus church at 3 o'clock that afternoon. By that time the whole area had been surrounded, and four officers rushed forward with loaded revolvers the moment Peter Kürten appeared. The man smiled and offered no resistance.

"There is no need to be afraid," he said.

The Making of a Killer

Unquestionably the victim of a vicious background, Kürten was born in Köln-Mülheim on May 26, 1883. His childhood was spent in a poverty-stricken, one-room apartment, one of a family of thirteen whose father was a brutal drunkard. There was a long history of alcoholism and mental trouble on the paternal side of the family, and his father often came home drunk, assaulting the children and forcing intercourse on the mother.

"If they hadn't been married, it would have been rape," Kürten once remarked.

Irascible and self-possessed, Kürten's father was sexually uncontrolled and was later jailed for 3 years for committing incest with Peter's 13-year-old sister. Kürten's mother seems to have originated from a fairly respectable background. The daughter of an affluent proprietor, Mrs. Kürten had five brothers and sisters, all of whom lived to a ripe old age. She separated from her husband after his imprisonment, and in 1911 she remarried. She died in 1927.

Kürten's sadistic impulses were awakened by the violent scenes in his own home.

"The whole family suffered through his drinking, for when he was drunk, my father was terrible. I, being the eldest, suffered the most. As you may well imagine, we suffered terrible poverty, because his wages went for drink. We all lived in one room, and you will appreciate what effect that had on me sexually."

At the age of 9, Kürten befriended a dogcatcher who lived in the same house. This man was a sadist who showed him how to masturbate and torture dogs. Whereas a normal child would have recoiled from his influence, the boy welcomed his friendship, and a powerful and significant bond developed. Around the same time, Kürten drowned a fellow schoolboy while playing on a raft in the Rhine. When the boy's friend dived in to rescue him, he too was pushed under the raft and held down until he suffocated.

His sexual urges were developing rapidly, and Kürten was soon committing bestiality on sheep and goats in the nearby stables. He quickly discovered that he had his most powerful sensation when he stabbed a sheep as he had intercourse, an act that he performed with increasing frequency.

By the age of 16, Peter was stealing and had run away from home. He was soon to receive the first of twenty-seven prison sentences that occupied 24 years of his life. The crimes were at first petty, mostly thieving for food and clothing, often earning short sentences in Düsseldorf prisons. Upon release from detention in 1899, Kürten began living with an ill-treated masochistic prostitute twice his age. His "education" was complete, and his sadistic impulses were transferred from animals to human beings.

The first lengthy period of incarceration left Kürten bitter and angry at human penal conditions. "I do not condemn those sentences in themselves, but I do condemn the way they are carried out on young people."

Internment also introduced Kürten to yet another perverse refinement, a fantasy world where he could achieve orgasm by imagining brutal sexual acts. He became so obsessed with these fantasies that he deliberately broke minor prison rules so that he could be sentenced to solitary confinement. This proved to be the ideal atmosphere for sadistic daydreaming.

Shortly after a release from prison, Kürten made his first murderous attack on a girl during sexual intercourse, leaving her for dead in the Grafenberg Woods. No body was ever found, and the girl probably crawled away, keeping the terrible secret to herself. Inevitably, more confinement followed, and after each jail term Kürten's feelings of injustice were strengthened. Unfortunately for the people of Düsseldorf, his sexual and sadistic fantasies now involved revenge on society.

Confession and Trial

Once under arrest, Kürten spoke with remarkable frankness to Professor Karl Berg, an eminent German psychologist who later wrote the most comprehensive guide to the career of Peter Kürten in a book titled *The Sadist*. Berg was supremely successful in winning the prisoner's confidence and provided a fascinating insight into the mind of a killer. Kürten's memory functioned with extraordinary clarity, and the vividness with which he preserved the details of each crime indicates the gratification of the acts. When Kürten dealt with matters that had no emotional value for him, his memory often was highly flawed.

The manner in which Kürten enumerated all his offenses is astounding. He was not accused of these crimes one by one but reeled off his own account, beginning with No. 1 and ending with No. 79. He dictated every single case to the stenographer, and Kürten even enjoyed the horrified looks on the faces of the many police officers who listened to his shocking recital.

Such is the so-called great confession attributed to Kürten after his arrest. The fullness and detail of the disclosure naturally awoke doubts as to its veracity, and yet, aside from the occasional and perhaps understandable error, he reiterated most of his salient statements in discussions with the examining magistrate and later with Professor Berg. Kürten himself recognized the obvious skepticism regarding his confession and consequently took time to describe each crime as precisely as possible to Berg.

"It is very easy to describe crimes one has not committed. One could scarcely doubt that a confession could be founded on very full newspaper reports and yet be simply an invention. To that extent, I quite understand your doubts, Professor."

Kürten's overriding motivation to explain his wrongs was not a feeling of guilt or repentance but simply the desire to secure a lucrative future for his wife. The consistently high regard paid to Auguste Kürten throughout the ordeal is one of the most fascinating aspects of the account and contradicts much of what we know about Kürten. Though unfaithful throughout his marriage, Kürten was still exceptionally fond of his wife and was desperate to ensure a substantial reward for her future years.

"I had already finished with my life when I first knew the police were on my track. I wanted to fix up for my wife a carefree old age, for she is entitled to at least a part of the reward. That is why I entered a plea of guilty to all the crimes."

The trial of the Düsseldorf Vampire, charged with a total of nine murders and seven attempted murders, opened on April 13, 1931. A special shoulder-high cage had been built inside the courtroom to prevent his escape, and behind it were arranged some of the grisly exhibits of the Kürten museum. There lay skulls of his victims and body parts displaying the injuries inflicted by the killer, each meticulously presented in a chronological fashion. Knives, rope, scissors, and a hammer were on display, along with many articles of clothing and a spade he had used to bury a woman. It was indeed a gruesome exhibition.

However, the initial shock to the crowd was the physical appearance of the Vampire. Dressed in an immaculate suit and with sleek, neatly parted hair, Kürten had the look of a prim and proper businessperson. Speaking in a quiet, matter-of-fact voice, he initially denied his earlier confession and presented a not-guilty plea to the examining magistrate. He had confessed to the crimes on the first occasion only to secure the reward for his wife, he said. Although persistent at first, Kürten was eventually broken down by the examining magistrate and, after a trying 2 months, reverted to his original and full confession.

His description of his crimes was more monstrous than anyone had imagined, yet the most brilliant doctors in Germany testified that Kürten had been "perfectly responsible for his actions at all times." His motive was made clear from the start: He wanted revenge on society for the wrongs he had suffered in prison. In answer to the judge's question as to whether he had a conscience, Kürten replied, "I have none. Never have I felt any misgiving in my soul; never did I think to myself that what I did was bad, even though human society condemns it. My blood and the blood of my victims will be on the heads of my torturers. There must be a Higher Being who gave in the first place the first vital spark to life. That Higher Being would deem my actions good since I revenged injustice. The punishments I have suffered have destroyed all my feelings as a human being. That was why I had no pity for my victims."

In his trademark flat, unemotional voice, Kürten described a life in which a luckless combination of factors—heredity, environment, the faults of the German penal system—had conspired to bring out and foster the latent sadistic streak with which Kürten believed he had been born. The court was hypnotized by the dramatic extent of the revelations, with the killer at one point describing his thoughts on how to cause accidents involving thousands of people with no modicum of self-restraint: "I derived the sort of pleasure from these visions that other people would get from thinking about a naked woman."

Kürten went on to narrate the details of his crimes, presenting each incident with exemplary logic and clarity. The confession was so damning that the prosecution barely bothered to present any evidence. The defendant's counsel, Dr. Wehner, had the hopeless task of trying to prove insanity in the face of insurmountable evidence from the many distinguished psychiatrists: "The man Kürten is a riddle to me. I can not solve it. The criminal Haarman only killed men, Landru and Grossman only women, but Peter killed men, women, children, and animals; killed anything he found."

The jury took only one and half hours to reach a unanimous verdict: guilty on all counts. The presiding judge, Dr. Rose, interrupted the continuing self-righteous ramblings of the defendant to sentence him to death nine times. Kürten behaved in a dignified fashion and did not challenge the judgment or feign remorse. However, he did note every discrepancy in the accounts of the witnesses and protested against the observations of the experts, which were not, in his opinion, wholly accurate.

On July 2, 1932, the Düsseldorf Vampire was put to death at a guillotine erected in the yard of the Klingelputz Prison. Kürten expressed his last earthly desire on the way to the yard: "Tell me," he asked the prison psychiatrist, "after my head has been chopped off, will I still be able to hear, at least for a moment, the sound of my own blood gushing from the stump of my neck?" He savored this thought for a while, then added, "That would be the pleasure to end all pleasures."

Inside the Mind of a Psychopath

It has long been accepted that there is no single reason for serial crime, but the same contributing factors rear their evil heads in the case of nearly all killers of this type. Peter Kürten is no different and exhibits many characteristics of the so-called lust killer. Essentially, he was a pathologically oversexed psychopath, a person so self-centered that, in his eyes, no other human being mattered.

Kürten admitted to a feeling of tension before and after the crime, a condition that convinced the experts of the sexual character of the motive. The attacks were planned and carried out in order to achieve a sexual satisfaction that could be obtained only through acts of violence. This is the ultimate operation of a monstrous and unique egotism: the satisfaction of one's sexual urges at all costs. "I committed my acts of arson for the same reasons: sadistic propensity. I got pleasure from the glow of the fire, the cries for help."

In personal appearance Peter Kürten was well built, clean shaven, and fresh complexioned. In all his personal habits he was meticulous, and this narcissistic tendency truly reflected the self-satisfaction of the inner man. Kürten dearly loved himself, and it was the kernel of his tragedy that he was unable to love any other human being.

Throughout his examination, Kürten constantly came back to the miseries of his childhood and his time in prison. He always spoke of them with great bitterness and often blamed them for turning him into the person he became. Perhaps more than any other killer of his type, Kürten seemed to understand exactly where his life went wrong. As George Godwin, an analyst of Kürten, once remarked, "If he did become a victimizer of the innocent, it must be remembered that he began life as an innocent victimized."

Inevitably the question of his sanity, and hence his legal responsibility, became a major issue of the trial. It was decided that Kürten was suffering from no organic mental disease or from any functional mental disease and that he was therefore legally responsible for his crimes.

Psychoanalysts say that the criminal differs from the person who adjusts to society in that he or she fails to sublimate the aggressive primitive urges. These actions are motivated by the wounds inflicted by injustice. There can be no doubt that Kürten suffered harshly in prison, and in this way he obtained the subject matter for an easy later rationalization. "So I said to myself in my youthful way, 'You just wait, you pack of scoundrels!' That was more or less the kind of retaliation or revenge idea. For example, I kill someone who is innocent and not responsible for the fact that I had been badly treated, but if there really is such a thing on this earth as compensating justice, then my tormentors must feel it, even if they do not know that I have done it."

In Kürten's case, this idea of vengeance and atonement is rooted in sadism and is a mask for sexual feeling. Even though he was studied by analysts in prison, these factors never seemed to come to the forefront of the evaluation. A basic prison diagnosis of sadism in the patient would have saved many lives, but Kürten was instead free to see his crimes as justification for the brutality witnessed throughout his life. He expressed regret for the innocent victims but never showed any remorse for his actions. "How could I do so? After all, I had to fulfill my mission."

Kürten thought a lot about himself and achieved a fair degree of self-insight. He was aware of his fatal sadistic propensity but always attributed it to heredity and his upbringing. However, on a number of occasions Kürten seems to have recognized his evil nature and made it clear to a victim, almost apologizing for his "unnecessary" actions. This is highly unusual for lust killers of Kürten's type, who are normally entirely convinced of their motives for atonement.

Also interesting, considering Kürten's psychopathic tendencies, is that his inclination to lie and deceive was supremely cultivated, and the mask of a respectable citizen was difficult to penetrate. His calm assurance allowed him to time his attacks perfectly and then to move off swiftly into the night.

Yet the most puzzling characteristic of Kürten is the immense loyalty he showed his wife. For this killer, the infidelity of the assaults weighed more heavily than the bloody murder. A baffling character, Auguste Kürten exhibited great humility throughout her married life and saw the bad times with Peter as punishment for her sinful former existence: She had worked as a prostitute and later shot a man who reneged on his promise to marry her. As much as Kürten disrespected women, he seems to have understood this devotion and once commented, "My relations with my wife were always good. I did not love her in the sensual way but because of my admiration for her fine character."

Was it perhaps that Kürten loved his wife for her preoccupation with the concept of redemption, an emotion that he seems incapable of displaying? Maybe if others had provided him with more than crude sexual gratification— a selfless and self-effacing love—Peter Kürten would not have turned out quite the way he did.

A WELL-ADJUSTED CITIZEN

Jeffrey Dahmer, seventeen times a killer, managed to remain unknown through his apparently well-adjusted behavior and his truly average looks. In addition, he was completely callous—easily enough to mislead two very experienced cops.

In late May 1991, one of his victims managed to flee for a brief time. Jeffrey lived in a run-down apartment in the western part of Milwaukee, close to Lake Michigan. As 14-year-old Konerak Sinthasomphone went to join a soccer game close to Jeffrey's apartment, he was sidetracked by one of Jeffrey's well-tried tricks. The serial killer promised money if he posed nude for a photograph. This was a clever ruse because the victim would disrobe voluntarily before noticing what danger he was exposing himself to.

In the case of little Konerak, Jeffrey behaved in a particularly bold fashion. He had already been sentenced for sexual misconduct with a minor: Konerak's older brother.

In court, Jeffrey said he took only two pictures of the boy and then made himself comfortable in front of the television with Konerak. But just before that, he had dissolved a sleeping pill into the drink he gave to the boy. While watching videos, Konerak fell asleep.

Jeffrey performed some oral intercourse before he noticed he had run out of beer. He was addicted to alcohol and needed even more when he had sex; he had more plans for his victim, so he went out to get more beer and left the passed-out young boy alone in the apartment.

On his way back, he was stopped by the police. Two women had seen a naked, bleeding, babbling boy stumbling across the street and had called 911. Konerak had awakened and was looking for help. Jeffrey reacted quickly. He claimed that Konerak was his homosexual friend and partner, who was of age and loved making a scene. This was by no means the first time, and he was drunk to boot.

That explanation made sense to the officers. They brought Jeffrey and the boy "home" with a few exhortations. Jeffrey produced a few pictures from his apartment, showing him and "his friend," and promised to take care of Konerak. When the police left, he strangled the boy, had some more oral intercourse, then photographed the corpse before getting rid of it by cutting it up and boiling some pieces. He kept the skull for himself but didn't cover it with lacquer, as he had done with other skulls. He had also eaten roasted body parts of previous victims, usually the liver, heart, and muscles.

It may appear extremely odd that nobody noticed the vile odors that must have issued from Jeffrey's apartment, which eventually held the rotting body parts of eleven different corpses. Jeffrey stated later that he had not wanted his victims to leave him. Only once, in 1991, had a police officer been called to the house to follow up on the vile smells. He knocked on the wrong door and, of course, found nothing extraordinary.

Oddly enough, Jeffrey was unable to kill an Irish setter he brought home for butchering and skinning after the dog looked at him with its big eyes. The dog must have reminded him of Frisky, his childhood pet. His father stated that the dog had been "Jeff's greatest love."

"Oh my God!" was the vocal reaction of journalists Robert Dvorchak and Lisa Holewa in the year after the Dahmer trial. "You wouldn't believe such disgusting imagery, if a specialist in a horror scene were to tell you this." In a novel, Dahmer's acts would be described as vastly exaggerated—so much so as to reduce them to banality. Thinking of real life, we exclude such acts from any real possibility. After all, what would happen if we had to suspect a serial killer behind every well-dressed man?

Jeffrey himself stated during the court proceedings, "Out there, I never felt any sense of real life. I am sure that here in court I will not find the sense of life either. This is just the grand finale of a wasted life and the end result is totally depressing. . . . This is simply a sick, pitiful, wretched, miserable life story, nothing else. How that is useful to anybody at all, I wouldn't know."

we all share. Let me quote a few newspaper reports. The *Rheinische Zeitung,* a paper that favored trade unions and catered to prejudices against the establishment, reported these incidents between 1900 and 1902:

Pastor Daniel Carcano from Milan, Italy, had committed several sex crimes. He fled to Lugano, in the Swiss canton of Ticino, and was sentenced in absentia to 11 years in the penitentiary. For months he lived a normal life in Lugano. He said he was a victim of the Milan uprising against the authorities. When the Italian government requested extradition of the criminal cleric, he protested that the request was nothing but an attempt by his political adversaries to punish him for his activities during the uprising in Milan in 1898. The Swiss Federal Court did not consider his arguments to be well founded and unanimously granted the Italian request.

Next Tuesday in Granada, Spain, Father Julian Anguita, who killed his father and his uncle, Candido Garcia, will be executed inside the penitentiary. To avoid any scandal, the Bishop of Jaen will first declare him no longer a member of the priesthood.

A Superior Court at Strasbourg, Alsace, had to deal with a case that received much attention. The Catholic parish priest, Louis Buhr, in the town of Otterstal was accused of arson. He had entertained forbidden relations with a woman, Elise Horter, but later split up with her because she had told everybody in her village about her affair with the priest. To get back at her, he transported a large vat of gasoline to a shed belonging to Elise and her husband, Eugene, that was located near the parish house. He intended to have the suspicion of setting the fire fall on Elise. His devilish design succeeded.

Still, the fire was quickly extinguished, and there was no major damage. Elise escaped the suspicion of arson because she spent the night in question not in Otterstal but in a psychiatric clinic in Strasbourg.

Suspicion soon settled on Pastor Buhr after a gasoline canister belonging to him was found in the shed. The priest originally denied any implication, but soon admitted his guilt.

His confession was prompted by a letter written to him by the bishop's office in Strasbourg that was found by an examining judge. The letter said that Buhr, given what was known and what he had admitted about his sexual escapades, could no longer be an active priest. He might join a monastery to avoid being prosecuted by a church court. When the investigative judge showed Buhr a copy of this letter, the priest collapsed and admitted his deed.

A while later, he retracted part of his confession and said that, in fact, he had asked someone else to set the fire. When the matter came to trial, he again denied guilt and stated that he had made his confession while being temporarily out of his mind. He had confessed only so that he would not be harassed further by the investigative judge. A court-appointed psychiatrist from Kaiser Wilhelm University ascertained that the defendant was mentally accountable, although his mother was insane, and that his passing dementia was only a subterfuge.

The jury acquitted him of having set the fire but found him guilty of a lesser charge of having caused material damage. He did not intend to burn down the shed because he had called his uncle and his aunt in order to have the fire extinguished. He was sentenced to 1 year in jail.

Today's media still enjoy reporting criminal cases when a priest is involved. Add elements of sex and insects, and the case is perfect. Here is an example.

The Case of Pastor Geyer

"I will ask the court to bring this nightmare to an end." These were the closing words of defendant Klaus Geyer as he addressed the court, for the last time, on April 16, 1998. Many in the audience of 140 people had not appreciated his sermon-like defense arguments and hissed "Amen."

Since early February of that year, the Braunschweig Criminal Court had dealt with a murder case that did not appear on its face to be significant. All the same, the media were in attendance for weeks, and the case made the evening news on television.

The defendant was sentenced to 8 years in jail. The audience had made up their minds: Geyer was an immoral and stubborn man. When the judge read the reasoning for the verdict, the priest became angry about a remark about his private life. "Impertinence!" he muttered, "and I have to listen to this!"

Waiting for Mrs. Geyer-Iwand

The trouble started on Friday, July 25, 1997, when a letter arrived at the parish house of the Geyer family. Veronika Geyer-Iwand, who was a teacher and also the mayor of the little town of Beienrode, was informed that her husband was having an affair. The letter, sent by the pastor's lover, was quite detailed.

On that morning the couple exchanged some serious words. To this day it is not clear exactly what happened. Pastor Geyer said that his crying wife addressed him as he sat in his study. After reading the letter, he admitted that he was in love with another woman. Veronika then tried to console him by putting her arms around him.

This sounds like a touching story—at least if it were true. Both of the Geyers had had extramarital affairs and had even talked about them to others. But over the years, witnesses noticed that the situation had become dangerous.

For instance, the housekeeper mentioned that there had been a lot of fighting in the house for months. "The first years I was there, it appeared to be a good and loving atmosphere. More recently, Mrs. Geyer has been raising her voice a lot," she said. The pastor confirmed that. He said, "My wife shows the greatest kindness and largesse toward other people, but she is also capable of getting quite grumpy and getting into people's faces."

Geyer mentioned his wife's grumpiness again later. He said, "My wife can get also quite aggressive, and she exaggerates beyond measure." He did not mention the reasons for this aggressiveness and the vocal volume in his house. The Geyers' adopted daughter witnessed her father's infidelity. She was the one who noticed, with great distress, that another woman was sleeping in her parents' bed after her mother disappeared.

We know from a colleague of Geyer-Iwand, who also worked as a teacher, that the pastor's wife was severely shaken and hurt by her husband's extramarital escapades. He said, "She indicated to me how important her relationship with her husband was to her. They had a lot in common." Geyer-Iwand, whom her husband described in court as "the woman whom I know as wearing only sneakers and pants," one evening put this question to her colleague during a class excursion: "What is it that men need in order to feel well? Do I have to put on makeup?" She objected to the notion that women who dress in typically feminine ways should be particularly attractive to men.

On the other hand, a friend of the pastor said that the Geyers' marriage had been contentious but certainly was not beyond repair. "Maybe there have been extramarital relationships, but doesn't that stabilize the marriage?" he said to a reporter of a Berlin daily as the trial began. The difficulties in the Geyers' relationship tainted the whole case. This witness predicted what the pastor would call insufferable when the final decision was read in court: "If Klaus Geyer has to explain such material stuff in his own defense in order to put the right slant on the structure of his marriage, isn't that incredibly embarrassing in front of this petty bourgeois assembly?" There were many "petty bourgeois" people with traditional views in Braunschweig at the time, and the Geyers, political activists of the late 1960s, clearly offended them.

The couple's loose marriage philosophy is not hard to understand. This does not mean that it is psychologically sound, but it is none of the public's business. Pastor Geyer openly stated, "During our marriage, both my wife and I have fallen in love with other partners. We knew a little about it, but not everything. We told each other about it when such relationships became very intense, when we really had fallen in love. Then we stopped. We did not openly talk about our affairs any more. But we knew each other well enough to get the vibes from the other person, so we knew." But is this kind of open partnership sustainable in a pastor's household with four children, living next to a retirement home, in a village environment, or must it end in disaster?

Despite their troubles, on the Friday in question the Geyers agreed to meet in the city that afternoon. Around noon, Veronika drove to Koenigslutter and then on to Braunschweig to a travel agency. There, she picked up airline tickets for a joint trip to the United States. They were to stay with friends in Salt Lake City before touring across the country.

She wanted to get some presents for their hosts in the United States, so she visited a boutique and a shop for household articles. She was last seen at 2 P.M. Klaus Geyer maintained that he had made an appointment with his wife at 3:30 P.M. But nobody saw either of them between 2 P.M. and 3:30 P.M. Where was Veronika? Where was the pastor?

Geyer stated that his wife did not show up for the agreed-upon meeting. He added that this was the first time in their 30-year marriage that she was late. He also said that he waited for a full hour, until 4:30 P.M., in front of a restaurant. But nobody recalled seeing him there. "She would never have waited that long for me," the pastor said in court, to the astonishment of everyone there.

A Telephone Call in the Afternoon

When Klaus Geyer grew tired of waiting around, he called home from the meeting place in the city. But nobody knew where Veronika was. "I kept running around Braunschweig, without direction, anxious and frightened. I ran around like a headless chicken. This kind of thing, you know, was not like my wife. She sometimes would lose track of time while out chatting, but I could go to bed knowing she would come home."

This little description contains at least one big lie. The phone call to his house was not initiated in Braunschweig but rather from a phone booth located halfway between Braunschweig and Beienrode, very close to where Veronika's corpse was found later. The telephone company database substantiates this.

Later, on Friday evening, Geyer called his wife's brother—a senior district attorney—and two other acquaintances. Also, he notified first the Helmstedt police and then the Braunschweig police department. His wife's car, a red Volkswagen Passat, was registered in Helmstedt. Upon later interrogation, nobody (not even the pastor himself) had any idea what the Helmstedt police might do to help find the pastor's wife. The pastor's nervousness appeared odd. He kept talking about a crime, but wasn't it possible that it was just a misunderstanding and that his wife was simply someplace else? This is what many people concerned were asking. But the pastor didn't think so. He had prepared a flyer and called the Braunschweig newspaper to have it published.

At about 2 A.M., a female pastor and friend of the Geyers arrived at the parish house. And soon, she and the pastor crawled into bed, as reported by *Der Spiegel* (a German weekly magazine). In the later court proceedings, this witness appeared in a black suit with a miniskirt. She testified that Geyer called her at 10 P.M. on the Friday in question and told her, "I miss Veronika." That is all the public found out about this particular extramarital relationship; for once, the public was excluded from the court proceedings. The female pastor's testimony went on for more than 2 hours. The technical criminal report included data on fresh sperm traces.

Shortly thereafter, this scene was repeated in the parish house, but this time with another woman. "I needed somebody close to me all the time," said Pastor Geyer in court. "I needed somebody who understands me. I needed on these days two people who would support me, and to whom I could cling. I thought I would drown, it was an absolute catastrophe. In situations like that, we have always been able to defy conventions. I felt I had the right to go beyond conventions on that night. My wife would have understood that."

Nine days after the disappearance of Veronika Geyer-Iwand, on August 3, 1997, *Bild am Sonntag* (a German version of *The National Enquirer*) mentioned the pastor's extramarital escapades; black clouds soon loomed over him. What Geyer found perfectly normal the public found highly suspicious. When the local court in Wolfenbüttel issued an arrest warrant for him on July 30, the public still believed there was some misunderstanding. But when the amorous escapades become known, they began to forget about all his pastoral activities, his work in senior residences, and his youth camps. The public could not accept the idea that a person whose position signifies virtue did not practice what he preached. However, life is not that simple; marital infidelity does not necessarily lead to murder.

A Reputation Destroyed

On Saturday, the day after his wife disappeared, Pastor Geyer canceled their flight reservations to the United States. "I wanted to inform the travel agency before they closed," Geyer explained. "I cannot see why anybody would reproach me for that." At this point, he also showed the poster he put together the night before, a missing-person flyer for his wife. It said, "A person is missing—we cannot exclude a criminal act."

Given the newly revealed circumstances of his bizarre family life, the flyer and the canceled airline tickets were immediately seen as a sign of guilt rather than concern. The people of Beienrode, the police, and most journalists thought that somebody who knew nothing about the whereabouts of his wife could not possibly act in such a calm and controlled fashion. How could the pastor know that she wasn't going to return home? And if she did, how would he explain to her that he had canceled the flight? On the other hand, if she was usually very punctual, doesn't his assumption of a major mishap make sense?

Very suspicious, some journalists wrote, eliciting Geyer's complaint of "media character assassination." "My wife's murder took my life partner away from me as if I were struck by lightning. . . . The persistent public suspicion of me eats away at me like a cancerous growth. It is destroying my integrity and makes me insecure. I am being morally judged. The only thing I can say is, 'Judge not, lest you be judged yourselves.'"

On Sunday, the first useful clue appeared. Geyer-Iwand's car, still filled with shopping bags, was found near the Braunschweig railroad station. Had she simply left? Probably not, because her credit cards and checkbook were still in her car. The police were at a loss.

When it turned out that Geyer-Iwand had purchased a lot of candy on Friday, the police became alert. They recalled that Pastor Geyer had assumed that a box of chocolate must be in one of the bags. The box, it turned out, contained ice cream spoons. What made the pastor think that his wife, on the spur of the moment, had bought a certain type of candy? Doesn't that imply that he talked to her after her shopping?

On Monday, Geyer-Iwand's body was found, with a fractured skull, in the forest south of Braunschweig. The hunter who discovered the corpse immediately noticed that the face had been severely bashed in. Criminalists call such facial mutilation overkill. It usually signifies a hate-motivated murder, so much that the perpetrator wants to extinguish the victim's most important features. Of course, this is only a generalization. There was no hint of sexual assault or robbery.

Even more telling was a puddle of blood found some 700 yards from the corpse. Clearly, the body must have been carried from this location (which, by sheer coincidence, is called the Pastor's Camp) to the place where it was found. The prosecution deduced from these facts that the murderer had beaten the woman unconscious with a crowbar on a country lane but actually killed her later at the place where her body was found. The head of the corpse was so badly beaten that even the court's medical advisors could not tell whether the final mortal injury came from a kick or a blow. They could say only that there were at least seven blows to the victim's head. A crowbar was then found in Geyer-Iwand's car. However, there was no trace of blood or other biological material (just as there were no blood traces near the body). Pastor Geyer was unable to help; he had never seen the crowbar and could not imagine what his wife meant to do with it.

Assume that the pastor was the killer. What motivated the couple to go to the Pastor's Camp? Head prosecutor Ulrich Hennecke assumed in his argument in court that the couple had met at the prearranged time and place but were upset enough to walk over to this somewhat isolated spot in order to have it out. Furthermore, he assumed that Geyer-Iwand did not offer any consolation to her husband but rather threatened that she would finally leave him for good.

Given that the pastor had made a socially advantageous marriage into the wealthy Iwand family, his world started to crumble before him. "What was he going to lose?" asked the prosecutor. "His honorary position, his appointment as the local pastor! He would have to accept an inferior position, and, what is more, he would no longer be the son-in-law of famous theologian Hans Joachim Iwand."

This desire to be superior to others asserted itself several times during the court proceedings; Pastor Geyer often mentioned his successes in life. "So, let me tell you about my life," he began on the first day of the trial. "My father and my mother were both mathematicians. In elementary school, I skipped a year. In high school, unfortunately, I was sick for most of the year. I graduated in 1959, but I was still undecided between two professional goals. That is due to my two gifts—as a mathematician and as a musician. My brother had already started studying mathematics. I was vacillating between going to a music conservatory as a pianist or majoring in mathematics."

He continued to enumerate honors and successes that came his way and his work for different professional associations. The elite National Studies Association provided funding for Geyer, who began as a student of mathematics but then opted to major in theology. He also founded an orchestra, studied classical languages, and married Veronika Iwand while still a student. When they had two children, the young couple moved into Veronika's father's castle. He founded a political action group and then organized meetings that were held in the castle estate's park. When he married, he was marrying not just an intelligent woman but also the daughter of a famous theologian, one of the very few German Protestant theologians who had resisted the Nazis and refused to collaborate with them.

In addition, he became the pastor for the village of Beienrode (with some 600 residents) and for the smaller hamlets of Ochsendorf, Uhry, and Kleinsteimke. It was a small community without too much work, so he had time and energy for international meetings and contacts with East Germany.

While he was in initial custody, he had to share a modest cell, and he tried to collect letters and other documents that would keep him mentally alert. He wrote to his pastoral flock at Christmas of 1997, "In my cell I have four well-filled binders with greetings and letters."

Geyer also got encouraging messages from well-known theologian Dorothee Soelle, a friend and colleague in his social work. "For the first time I understand what it means to be the subject of character assassination," she wrote. "Stay strong. The 'cruel one' also has another side. I am praying for you. Yours, Dorothee."

Most of his colleagues started to keep their distance from him. Deeply hurt, the pastor wrote to his flock about "diplomatic small-talk, which may keep up brotherly appearances but which in reality is devoid of all solidarity."

The Muddy Boots

So the pastor was not the kind of man his flock wanted him to be. So he had lied about the phone booth. Still, his contradictions and illogical statements did not add up to evidence supporting an indictment for killing his wife.

But there were no other suspects. Klaus Geyer clearly was not honest with the police or the judge. He therefore remained the focus of the investigation and remained in custody.

The pastor's story became even more suspicious. A witness said he had seen Geyer-Iwand 2 weeks before her disappearance, taking a walk past the Pastor's Camp with someone else; Pastor Geyer knew nothing about this. He surmised that his wife might have taken a walk there with a colleague. He was certain that he could not have been the person who accompanied his wife because he had not been there for years.

This statement, harmless as it might seem when first uttered, turned out to be another, even more serious lie. When the court technicians thoroughly in-

CARNIVAL GLITTER AND OTHER TRACES

Whether a suspect's lifestyle makes sense to others and whether that suspect has been leading a good life are of no concern to an expert. The only things he or she worries about are the traces themselves, not how they fit into the overall case. Others will have to determine the social or legal consequences of the expert's findings.

This is a narrow perspective, and it may make the prosecution, the defense, or the media unhappy with an expert. Such dissatisfaction is particularly common when statistical arguments are involved. But whatever these other parties would like, whatever they expect, does not interest the court expert. He or she lives in a world of facts and calculable probabilities.

In the Geyer case, there were several instances in which parties to the case wanted more precisely defined or formulated statements. Consider the implications of the soil samples on the yellow rubber boots: What was the probability that these samples had come from the location where the corpse was found? Soil experts stated that the samples could not possibly have come from the park around the castle. The soil there had a different composition. This contradicted the pastor's claim that he had walked only in that park in those boots.

The experts were also able to rule out the possibility that those samples could not have come from the place where the body was found. This double negation sounds a bit artificial, but the experts followed Sherlock Holmes's rule. To the forensic scientist, proving a correct assumption is as important as disproving the incorrect ones. In the Geyer case, it meant that the soil samples found on the boots were highly unlikely to have come from a different place that happened to have the same characteristics.

Natural scientists can make statements that are 100 percent certain only if they can exclude all alternatives. In this case, a soil sample cannot come from the place where it was found if an important soil component is missing. A thumbprint cannot be that of a suspect if an important skin characteristic is absent. An ant that lives in tropical heat has no likelihood of coming from a winter landscape in Germany.

There is a different way to demonstrate connections and identities that does not use exclusion and negative evidence. In this case, however, there is no mathematical tool that can make a statement with 100 percent certainty. Here, we have only probability. We don't need formulas if we can understand a relevant experiment.

Ask a friend to step behind a curtain with two cocktail shakers. Let him or her put a small amount of glittering crystals into one of them, then fill both of them with sand and shake them thoroughly. We now have one with pure sand and one that has a slightly glittering mix.

Now let your friend pour half of the pure sand on the table. Consider yourself a court expert who has to compare three samples of sand: the one that has been poured on the table, the one that is left in the first shaker, and the one in the second shaker. The judge asks you to decide from which shaker the sand on the table has been poured.

"Very easy," you will say. "The sample on the table has no glitter; it must come from the shaker with pure sand."

The defense attorney asks how certain you are of your statement. Couldn't there be other shakers somewhere in the world that contain the same sand we find on the table? Couldn't that sand come from any old sandbox, any old playground?

Because you are an honest expert, you will have to answer, "You are right, I cannot be sure whether the sand comes from that shaker or from some playground. I can only say that it probably comes from the shaker because there is no playground within 100 yards around us. Our friend cannot have produced some other sand so rapidly. So if you ask me how likely it is that the sand on the table is from the glitter-free shaker, I have to answer that the sand on the table comes with almost 100 percent probability from the shaker without the glitter because I see no glitter at all in this sand. But I cannot say so with 100 percent certainty because I cannot exclude your sandbox assumption by scientific means. But if you want me to make a statement that is 100 percent certain, I will say that the sand on the table contains no glitter. It most certainly does not come from the shaker with the glitter."

So why not say so right away? Aren't those two statements precisely the same thing? Maybe so. But the expert must tell the court only what he or she really knows. The court has no interest in common sense or general assumptions. The expert is not an attorney or judge; only the attorneys have the right to try to convince the court of a view that projects a world beyond proven facts.

In the case of the Geyers, the prosecutor was entitled to the conjecture that the pastor's wife had threatened to divorce him. Nobody except the pastor knows whether that is true. The letter from the pastor's lover, which was in the hands of the court, put the prosecutor's statement into the realm of probability. On the other hand, Pastor Geyer said that he and his wife had engaged in amorous dalliances outside their marriage. However, because there is no way to state a precise probability that Geyer-Iwand threatened divorce, no scientifically trained expert will take a stand on this topic. More precisely, he or she might want to but cannot give an opinion because that opinion is not derived from expert knowledge.

Let's take another example. Even an undeniably positive paternity test gives a result that has no more than 99.9999 percent likelihood. This means that among 1 million people, not one has the same genetic fingerprint as the presumed father. The agreement of the genetic fingerprints of a man and child implies that the child issues from the man (the child inherits one-half of his or her genetic fingerprint from the mother, the other half from the father). But only a judge, not an expert, can decide what importance this finding has in the proceedings at hand (e.g., what the father will have to pay in child support or where the child will live).

The soil experts in the Geyer case did not want to get involved in possibly misleading discussions about numerical values and probabilities, and so they stated only this: It can be ruled out that the soil sample is not from the place where the body was found. The double negative makes an absolute statement; a simple positive statement with the same meaning would not convey a full certainty that the court could accept.

spected his yellow rubber boots, they found soil samples from that very area that were quite fresh. They even contained an ant that must have lived in the very location where the corpse was found (as discussed in detail later in this chapter).

The investigators asked themselves, "Why would the pastor lie unless he had something to hide?" But the accused stuck to his testimony: "Those boots are not mine!" If they had been in that location, maybe some stranger or possibly even his wife had worn them. He had put them on only once, to walk in the park where they lived. He could not explain why boots not belonging to them had been kept in their home or why Veronika or the children would have put on boots that were several sizes larger than their own shoes.

Naturally, the court formed its own opinion about those boots. The jurors were convinced that the rubber boots found in the defendant's car had certainly been worn in the location where the corpse was found. The soil samples found sticking to the boots could not have been there before July 24, the day before Veronika's disappearance. These boots were known to have been worn only by Pastor Geyer and his wife, and at the time of her murder it must have been the pastor who wore them because his wife was found wearing her own shoes.

The soil sample and some logical thinking helped to form a more believable picture of what must had happened. Despite this evidence, the pastor insisted to the very last that there was only one possible explanation for the findings: His wife must have worn the boots in the place where they were found, and she must have put them in her husband's car.

Six-Legged Traces

The media paid particular attention to the investigation of insects in the Geyer case. I was an expert witness and investigator in this case and therefore cannot divulge any details of my investigation. However, I will describe the work of my colleague Bernd Seifert, who has also worked on cases in which insects were used as evidence. The main difference between his case and ours was that one expert was to find out from fly larvae data how long a corpse had been out in the open air, whereas the other used adult ants to find the location that had been visited by somebody wearing yellow rubber boots.

The use of ants is based on the same forensic principles as the use of fibers that might come from the sweater of the murderer and are detected on or next to the corpse. The obvious connection is the assumption that the sweater must have been in contact with the corpse.

You can say the same about the ants on the pastor's rubber boots. If the defendant was wearing these boots, and if the ants probably came from the place where the corpse was found, it is obviously possible that the defendant may well have been at the location. In other words, the ants tie up evidence in a way that can become important in court.

Seifert recalls, "In the final phase of the 20-day court proceedings discussing our evidence, those rubber boots with the soil samples sticking to them were the key evidence." The soil experts had already noted that the soil samples on the bottom of the boots could not be from the pastor's home. They could make that statement by microscopically studying the particles of minerals, rotten plant matter, and pollen that were found on the boots. The pastor's lawyer wanted to find out more. "Defendant's counsel questioned on April 8, 1998, the statement that it was likely that these boots had been used on the grounds where the corpse was found. We ask for proof of the identity of the ants in question." Seifert, who works at the State Museum for Natural Science in Goerlitz and is regarded as one of the most knowledgeable ant specialists in Germany, was asked for his opinion. "The court expects answers to the following questions. (a) Are the ants found in the victim's blouse and those seen in the earth samples of the boots the very same kind? (b) How frequently is this species of ant to be found in eastern Lower Saxony, should species identification be identical?"

Seifert went to his lab to identify the ant species that had been secured at the location where the corpse was found. "Some five to nine yards from the corpse, I found entrance channels to where the ant species *Lasius fuliginosus* (shiny black wood ants) were nesting at the bottom of hollow trunks of a silver birch. Also, it was seen that, notwithstanding the low air temperature of 46°F, many insects moved around." From the size of the colony of ants and from the amount of debris the animals had left behind, Seifert concluded that their colony must have lived in the hollow trunks for more than 2 years. A rotted piece of wood on the chest of the corpse could be traced to a location where the ants had entered the trunks. In other words, samples of the wood and ants had both been moved together with the corpse when it was found.

The ants found on the blouse of the dead woman and those found on the rubber boots were of precisely the same species. "The certainty of determining the species of the ants is 100 percent," says Seifert. "These ants are the only members of this subspecies called *Dendrolasius* that exist in Central Europe, and the ant specimens in both cases are very good. All of these ants operate locally; they cannot fly, and they don't move more than 25 yards away from their nest where they were born. The likelihood that they could be moved by strong winds or passively in other ways is negligible."

And this is where the forensic circle closes. The animals found in the soil samples sticking to the rubber boots were of the kind that function only in close proximity to their nest. This was close to where the corpse was found, and the inference that the boots must have been close to the dead woman is undeniable.

This sounds quite convincing. Still, there is one loophole. In court proceedings, the following questions must also be considered: How often is this ant species found in other places? What if the same boots were worn by somebody else who, by sheer coincidence, wandered about a different landscape where he or she trod on soil with the same shiny black wood ant?

Seifert now quoted numbers he himself had put together during a 20-year career in this field: Countless excursions over a hundred different areas had been used to find more samples of anthills or habitats and to investigate the ants living there. Seifert knew all about this particular species, and he was able to calculate that this shiny black wood ant exists in most regions of Germany; however, it builds nests very rarely. On a 100-square-yard site he found almost 140 ant nests, but he calculated that only 2.6 percent of them held the *Lasius* species. "The likelihood that somebody steps by sheer happenstance on a sample of *Lasius fuliginosus* while walking somewhat randomly in various diverse built-up or natural habitats of the cultured landscape in eastern Lower Saxony, and that this specimen actually sticks to the boot, is negligible on a statistical basis" was Seifert's opinion. He added, "Given that the suspect or corpse was close to the entrance tunnels of a densely inhabited colony of *Lasius fuliginosus,* where in the midsummer thousands of worker ants are on the move, the chances that this might happen are clearly stronger. This would increase the likelihood of stepping on a *Lasius fuliginosus* by a factor of 10^2 to 10^4, compared with chance patterns of walking through that neighborhood."

In other words, first, the same insect species found on the bottom of the rubber boots was found on the corpse and in the area where it was found. Second, only one in 100 casual wanderers in this region will step on one of the very ants and carry it away as it clings to the sole of his or her boots. Third, the boots were found in the pastor's car. Fourth, these boots were way too big for his wife. Fifth, the couple had not lent the boots to anyone. Sixth, the soil found on the boots was still quite fresh.

One person may consider this a convincing chain of arguments; another may not agree, particularly if the conclusion is likely to determine whether a defendant goes to jail. Therefore it was incumbent on the court to look at the pros and cons as best it could. True, the media covered the entomology expert's evidence in great detail, but the judge found it equally important to consider the phone calls made by Pastor Geyer. Then there were the contradictions in his testimony regarding his whereabouts and of the other witnesses who had seen him not in the city, as he had said, but close to the place the corpse was found. Moreover, the pastor's attempt to have an old member of his church congregation make statements in his favor left a negative impression on the court. In late April 1998, he was sentenced to 8 years in prison for second-degree murder.

CAPITAL PUNISHMENT

Sentences imposed by the courts differ from judge to judge and also depend on the point in history and on the country that has jurisdiction. Taken as a whole, they are hardly predictable. This is no wonder, because absolute justice doesn't exist.

Still, one particular sentence elicits strong feelings after hundreds of years: the death penalty. This is simply because it touches on the very basis of human existence: death or survival. It seems odd that we still have proponents of capital punishment. Not only is it irrevocable, but it also puts people in a position where they have no right to be, as masters over the life of other humans.

To this day, many people in Europe, where life imprisonment is the norm for first-degree murders, ask themselves whether it would make sense to execute those responsible for particularly vile crimes, such as the murder of a child. The United States and China cite very different reasons for retaining capital punishment.

In the United States, a largely Christian country, this unchristian procedure is motivated by the practical consideration that one villain less means just that: one villain less. Vengeance is also a common justification. And many people argue that the death penalty acts as a deterrent, although this is difficult to prove.

In China, the death penalty is used both as an expression of state power and as a radical deterrent against all kinds of crimes, not just murder or treason. A group of Chinese people was put to death as recently as 2001 for counterfeiting.

Attorney Kurt Rossa—former mayor of my hometown, Cologne—studied questions of capital punishment from an interesting angle in 1966. "A study of which crimes are seen as motivating capital punishment," he wrote, "tells us about the social and cultural standards of a given country. To this day, more than twenty types of crimes may be punished by death: murder, homicide in a duel, lynching, abortion resulting in the death of the mother, manslaughter or physical injury by a prisoner, perjury when it results in a death verdict, rape, kidnapping of minors for ransom, train robbery or derailment, assassination by dynamite, arson that leads to death, armed robbery, treason, manslaughter during civil unrest, and attempts to kill the president of the United States or a state governor."

"It is perhaps easy to criticize this obviously dated enumeration," continues Rossa. "Some of the felonies mentioned should be seen as inherited from pioneering times, some may have been motivated by a need to protect the state against criminal terror—say, at the time of prohibition. There are some oddities remaining on this list. In many instances we can only shake our heads. For example, rape remains a death penalty verdict only in Russia and a few African nations: Zimbabwe, South Africa, the Central African Republic, Dahomey (also called Benin), and the Ivory Coast. Rape with fatal consequences is on the list in Japan, Taiwan, and the Philippines. It is hard to understand that rape is still a death penalty crime in eighteen U.S. states."

So where does the problem lie? What is wrong when capital punishment can be administered for crimes that a given society will not tolerate, such as infanticide? There is a simple answer.

As early as 1867, Victor Hugo predicted that Europeans would not tolerate the use of the guillotine beyond the twentieth century: "Cutting a man's head off will be unthinkable." Maybe this statement by the French writer (who is venerated as a saint by some Vietnamese sects) will be universally accepted in the twenty-first century. While considering these social issues, it makes sense to ask whether capital punishment can provide, at least biologically, what it promises: the pain-free elimination of undesired fellow citizens.

A Blinking Head

Does capital punishment lead to immediate death? Ever since the guillotine was first used, this question has been asked. This may not be obvious because the guillotine has been seen as a humane death machine, which is why the revolutionaries with their "new world order" started to use this ingenious invention. There is a vague rumor that a severed head can still feel or see. Is that possible?

Detlev Linke, a neurosurgeon in Bonn, is convinced that a head still maintains some awareness for about half a minute. Similarly, a headless body can still run a few steps. This is what was reported to have happened to Klaus Störtebeker, who was executed in 1402. When a French criminal was decapitated in Lyon in 1875, a gasping crowd saw the headless body rise from its coffin, fall down sideways, and then try a second time to step out of the coffin. That was the last public decapitation in France. The intended moral lesson for the crowd had been usurped by the autonomic nervous system's reflexes.

Kurt Rossa, whom I mentioned before, described this mixture of fear, superstition, and medical assumptions in a very graphic way:

> In the gossip columns of world history, we find tales of the execution of royalist agent Charlotte Corday, who had stabbed Jean-Paul Marat, the president of the Jacobin club who during the French Revolution was responsible for the "September killings." She was decapitated on July 17, 1793, in Paris. When the executioner lifted her severed head by its hair to show it to the howling crowd, one of his helpers slapped its cheek sideways. The court reporter left the following description of what happened next. "A long time after Charlotte Corday's head had been severed from her body, her face kept an unmistakable expression of indignation . . . both her cheeks had turned red . . . and nobody can tell me that this was not due to the slap. You can hit the cheek of a dead person without any effect—they never change color. In addition, she had been slapped on only one cheek, but both of her cheeks changed their color."

Is this a legend? Listen to these two doctors who witnessed a decapitation:

"If you permit us to tell you our own opinion on this matter, we will start out by now describing what we think is a gruesome act to observe. All blood leaves the veins to the rhythm of the severed arteries, and then it starts clotting. The muscles cramp up, and these last motions put the fear of God into you. The guts are moved by some last impulse, and the heart contracts in irregular, strange last movements. The mouth is distorted for brief moments such that it creates an awful grimace. In the head that has been severed from the rest of the body, it is true that the eyes with their dilated pupils remain immobile. Fortunately, they are expressionless. Even if they show no opalescence (the clouding of the eyes in dead people), they no longer move. Their transparency might give them an appearance of living, but their terminally fixed rigidity is that of death. To get to this point can last minutes; for a completely healthy person, it may take hours. Death does not take hold immediately; all vital parts survive the decapitation proper. For the medical professional it gives the impression of a grisly experiment, a murderous vivisection followed by a speedy interment."

This report dates not from the French Revolution but from 1956. It was written by French doctors Piedelievre and Fournier for the French Medical Academy, which had asked them to research the matter using the corpses of decapitated criminals.

If we look at other reports, we find some astonishing details. There are tales of running corpses, even though their heads had been severed by swords. Before their decapitation, they had uttered their intent to prove by doing this that they were innocent, so that their accomplices would be freed or their families would be given the land that their headless body ran through. An old chronicle tells us that in 1337, the knight Dietz von Schaumberg, who had been given a death sentence for a breach of peace, petitioned the judge to free his four innocent followers who had acted only on his order if, after his own beheading, his rump were to get up from the floor and walk past these four men. "Right after his head had hit the floor, his rump got up, walked by his retinue, only then to drop down dead."

We are told that some executioners knew how to take advantage of the brief survival of beheaded people. In the book *Voigtland Myth* (written by Robert Eisel in 1871), we are told about an executioner who accompanied a decapitated woman across 9 acres, thereby acquiring the farmland. Similarly, Eise Angstmann reports the case of another executioner called Mr. 30-Acres, who had been given a title of nobility with this name by Duke Johann Georg I in Dresden in 1647 after having managed to walk with a decapitated corpse, whose blood flow he had stopped by placing a patch of lawn grass on his neck, across 30 acres of land.

The idea that the muscles of a corpse in a coffin keep twitching for hours (which is incorrect) is a disgusting play on our imagination. There is the awful idea that the severed head, now lying in some pail, might still have some feeling, some consciousness.

In 1803, a doctor named Wendt, together with a group of colleagues in Breslau, was sufficiently cold-blooded to run an experiment on what they called the "short autonomous life" of a severed head. To do so, they observed the execution of a man named Troer. Dr. Wendt reports,

"The wound specialists, Drs. Illing and Hanisch, were kind enough to take turns in holding the severed head, making things easier for me. I kept focusing on the face of that head and was not able to see even the slightest distortion. The face remained at rest, with bright open eyes and a closed mouth. There was no facial feature that would have given away the state into which the head of this unfortunate man had been transformed by his head being severed from the rump. I touched his eyes with the tips of my fingers, and indeed, that poor head actually closed its eyelids in order to protect the eyes from any danger they might be exposed to. . . . Dr. Illing lifted the head to point the face into the direction of the sun. In that moment the head closed the eye that was pointing directly toward the sun. Just to test whether the hearing organs continued functioning along with the visual organs, I called out twice loudly the name 'Troer' into the ear of the severed head. The result may have been influenced by my own feeling and imagination, but it produced the most unexpected result you could imagine: After every call, the head reopened its eyes, directed them toward the origin of the sound, and, while so doing, opened its mouth. In the process, some observers insisted that it attempted to speak. This experiment appeared to give some support to reports of a man named Soemmering who maintained that a severed head would talk if it could be outfitted with an artificial lung.

"When I tested the hearing, an assistant named Otto Kaufmann, who was taking notes of the time elapsing, told me that one-and-one-half minutes had already passed. I touched the spinal cord with a needle and, would you believe it, the face of the executed person changed so obviously that several observers called out, 'There is life,' and I couldn't help saying, 'If this is not a sign of life and of feeling, what is?' After all, when I touched his spinal cord with the needle, he closed the eye convulsively, clenched his teeth, and the cheek pouches twitched as they approached the lower eyelids."

Such experiments on executed corpses appear to have been performed repeatedly at that time because a report on Prussian criminal procedures dated March 3rd, 1804, specifically forbade "galvanic and mechanical stimulation attempts on the bodies of decapitated persons or on parts thereof." An expert from the State College of Medical and Sanitary Matters (Ober-Collegii-Medici et Sanitatis), had convinced King Friedrich Wilhelm III of Prussia that "this kind of stimulation could reawaken the brain and its functions and thereby also feelings and consciousness, if only for a few moments, after the executed criminal had lost them at the instant of decapitation."

That order relieved the king of a preoccupation he had alluded to in an order previously given to the cabinet and the chancellor: "Tales of the results of recent experiments do not contain anything precise about how long consciousness remains. Were this not so, we would have to change the laws about how to perform execution by the sword."

The lively interest from scientists of that time resulted largely from a dispute on the question of where the human soul is located. Famous German scholar Samuel Thomas Soemmering argued vehemently against using the guillotine; he hypothesized that it might be possible that the human brain could continue to function, notwithstanding interrupted circulation of the blood. This means that it could continue to live for a while after the head has been severed. This argument was strongly attacked by French scholars. Needless to say, the theories that followed, based on what was seen as experimental evidence at the time, have no value today. Still, modern medicine has not provided a reasonable explanation of the bases of their observations.

On June 4, 1932, psychiatrist Alfred Erich Hoche addressed a neurologists' meeting as follows: "The act of execution does not inflict any suffering. Seen from this angle, a dentist is worse than a guillotine. Decapitation leads to an easier death than most illnesses. It is more humane than any other form of execution. Even in the absence of any report from somebody who went through it, it must be seen as painless. We arrive at this opinion as a consequence of observations that are simple and understandable to every layman. There can be no consciousness if there is no blood pressure in the brain vesicle. We do know that a small lowering of this pressure, while not yet life-threatening, leads to a complete loss of consciousness. This loss occurs at the very moment where the guillotine's hatchet cuts up the blood vessels of the neck. The sensation due to this blow does not come instantaneously; the nerves need a given time, measurable by methods known today, to get a message to the brain. Consciousness stops before the message about the severing of body tissue has arrived in the brain." Medical experts today will tell you the same thing. However, if you inquire about the experimental results, the answers are not as straightforward.

Consider the work of Dr. Beaurieux, who certainly understood the "simple observations" understandable to every layperson regarding the loss of consciousness concomitant with diminishing blood pressure. Nonetheless, some 100 years after Dr. Wendt, he investigated what happened to the head of a man named Languille, who was beheaded on June 18, 1905. He reports in the *Archives d'Anthropologie Criminelle*,

"The head dropped down on the severed plane of the neck, so I did not have to take it in my hand, as was reported by all the newspapers. I did not even have to touch it to keep it upright. This was lucky for the observation I was planning.

"I shall now tell you what I saw right after the beheading. The eyelids and the lips of the decapitated man moved rhythmically but irregularly for about five or six seconds. This phenomenon was observed by all those present, reactions following the severing of the neck. I waited for a few more seconds. The spasmodic motions then stopped; the face relaxed; the eyelids closed halfway over the eyeballs, so only the white part remained visible—just like we see it every day on our jobs, when we minister to dying or very recently deceased patients. At this point, I cried out with a sharp tone of voice: 'Languille!' I saw his eyelids open slowly, without any spasmodic contraction—a fact I want to stress—but with a clear, quiet, normal motion just as we see every day when people are awakened from their sleep or from a train of thought. Then Languille's eyes focused intently on mine, his pupils narrowing. This was not a vague, expressionless look we often see in dying people when we talk to them. Here, the eyes that looked at me were full of life.

"A few seconds later, the lids closed again, slowly and with even motion. The face reassumed the expression it had held before I called his name.

"When I called him again, his eyelids opened again—slowly, without contractions; and two eyes—obviously alive—looked at me firmly and more piercingly than the first time. And again they closed, but not all the way. I made a third attempt, but this time there was no reaction. His eyes had a glazed expression which is known in dead people. The entire experiment lasted 25 to 30 seconds."

Are these simple reflexes? Despite well-established research methods, Beaurieux concluded from his observations that the brain remains alive in all its elements after the decapitation. "Believe me, I am not planning to write a fantastic story," he resumed his tale, "when I follow up on physiological problems. Nonetheless, I have to admit that the cerebral cortex can keep functioning when we have to acknowledge that the visual apparatus still works and that there is no reason to deny its continued functioning. Only the dying person could tell us whether there is a conscious perception. And that is the reason why the problem is not scientifically soluble. Still, the fact remains that conscious perception cannot be negated a priori. This question deserves further discussion."

Graven reports a contribution to the discussion in which a Dr. Bentham says he found, by means of experiments he conducted, that decapitated warm-blooded creatures remain sensitive along their extended spinal cord all the way to the brain.

"Most modern physiologists who approach this problem are very reserved about an idea so bizarre and so disgusting as to have a head looking at its awful state after it has been severed from its body," says Kershaw. "And still, they rule out this possibility. There is that possibility staring us in the face like a satanic grimace."

Nevertheless, today's medical understanding reduces this possibility to a gruesome nightmare. Although the capillaries might widen by reflex, the over-all blood pressure in a severed head is diminished by the lack of incoming blood. That makes a reddening difficult to imagine.

Furthermore, a reaction by the head itself is barely believable with or without blood, given that people often lose consciousness after no more than a hard hit on the head or during strangulation. Even more important, a noose tightening around the neck will cause immediate unconsciousness, simply because the blood vessels to and from the brain are constricted. As the noose tightens—unlike in the case of a beheading—the blood remains in the brain. But the oxygen supply to the red blood cells is stopped in both cases.

The action of a guillotine therefore does everything necessary to cause unconsciousness. It stops the blood flow and the oxygen supply, and there is a violent blow by the falling hatchet. The original account of Troer's execution, as described by Rossa, includes another observation. It says that the medical investigator held a silver plate against one end of the muscles in question and a zinc plate against the other. The resulting small amount of electric current caused the muscles to contract. This effect can be created even in dead bodies without a brain. The muscles of the upper arms of a decapitated human may contract even a few hours after death. That means we have to admit the possibility that the observed head movement could be induced in this fashion.

However, animal experiments also appear to confirm that some life remains in a severed head. The eyes of rats that have been decapitated will keep moving for a while, and the brain functions of sheep that have been knocked unconscious show measurable activity up to 14 seconds after the carotid arteries are severed. Experiments on dogs show similar results: After an electrical current makes the heart stop beating, it takes 12 seconds before the brain sends out waves that look different from those emitted by an animal that is awake or in light sleep.

We still do not know whether a severed head can perceive itself; after all, muscle movements do occur in bodies without consciousness (as can be observed during hen slaughtering). We cannot rule out the possibility that an executed person still feels the pain induced by the cutting tool or that he or she might perceive sensations a few seconds later.

The only explanation that is consistent with current medical understanding (immediate unconsciousness with a slackening of the muscles) to account for the eye motions and brain currents of electrocuted or beheaded people is this: The brain could use the remaining oxygen or whatever stored energy still exists in facial or neck muscles to function for another 7 seconds. However, whether the energy used in this process is still sufficient to get to the brain must remain an open question. There is nobody who can tell us about his or her own beheading from personal experience.

Who Deserves the Death Penalty? The Bernardo and Homolka Case

Alan Wallace, a Canadian colleague of mine, recalls the crimes of Karla Homolka and Paul Bernardo: "The Bernardo case was a full blown media frenzy from the abductions, to the discoveries of the bodies, to the arrests, the deal with the devil and the trials. I was working in news in those days and it seemed to dominate the agenda forever. What lingers the most of course is the sick realization that it should not have happened—that Mahaffy, French and Tammy Homolka (and likely a few others) should have been safe because Bernardo should have been caught when he was 'the Scarborough rapist,' but the investigators . . . did not share information. . . . The dots were never connected until it was far too late. . . . I hope [your book] does its part to ensure that this manner of obscenity is never repeated."

To this day, the Canadian public's horror has not worn off. Karla Homolka was sentenced in 1993, her ex-husband in 1995. From the media reaction it is obvious that Canadians felt betrayed not only by the criminals but also by the authorities.

A local Web master even went to the trouble of starting a Web page on which people could place bets about how long it would take before Karla Homolka was killed. This site reflects the grim reality that child killers sometimes are murdered while still in jail and sometimes even after having been set free.

Therefore, it made sense that Karla Homolka feared for her life. Unlike Dahmer, Karla contributed to the public fury directed against her. It was exacerbated by the fact that she made a deal with the district attorney and was sentenced to only 12 years in jail, a term the public considered unbelievably lenient. In the summer of 2000, she was working on trying to get an earlier release by July 2001 for "good behavior." "I have fulfilled all conditions that were imposed," she stated, which is essentially correct given her sentence and the normal parole process. She later waived her application for early release, and her prison term ends on July 5, 2005.

She did not know that one of her former fellow prisoners had quite legally taken pictures of her during a prison party in July 1998. She sold these pictures

Jeffrey Dahmer's Death

The prison warden may have made sure that Jeffrey Dahmer had to work alongside particularly aggressive inmates, who finally killed him.

This process started when Dahmer found he could no longer tolerate living in his windowless, 8-square-yard cell, where he listened to Gregorian chants, whales' songs, and the compositions of Johann Sebastian Bach. He also studied the Bible alone or with Pastor Roy Ratcliff and was christened in the prison swimming pool. Beyond that, he had nothing to do. As a consequence, even a haircut became a major event, as he told his attorney.

There was no change in his situation on the horizon; going anyplace else in the prison was too dangerous. In any country, when a felon convicted of killing children enters prison, his life is in danger. Even the tiny prison chapel was not a safe place for Dahmer. In July 1994, another inmate almost succeeding in cutting Dahmer's throat. Still, he was so lonely that he wanted to interact with other people. (By comparison, Colombian serial killer Louis Alfredo Garavito has been living in the administration wing of the prison so he can safely catch some air.)

Four months later, the prison administration finally permitted Dahmer to join a cleanup crew. That netted him a small amount of mobility, plus 24 cents an hour. But his happiness was short-lived. On November 28, 1994, after only a few weeks of his new life, another member of the cleanup crew, Christopher Scarves, beat him to death with an iron rod as Dahmer was cleaning a toilet door in the prison gymnasium. Including presentence custody, he survived for only 3 years in prison.

2 years later—this time illegally—to the *Montreal Gazette*. In these pictures, the public caught a glimpse of an exuberant celebration of a small circle surrounding the happily beaming Karla. This party would have been sufficient in itself to justify its appearance on page 1 of the newspaper and thereby to excite popular uproar. With the photographer's added comments, the outrage boiled over. The woman who took the photo was quoted as saying, "The women's prison in Joliette is a kind of 'playroom for adults,' where the inmates are being spoiled."

The Canadian felt that criminals should suffer, not celebrate. All talk of an early release was shelved. When it became known that the prison cell of her ex-husband was supplied with a copy of the men's magazine *Maxim*, which features pictures of barely clad women, Bernardo's warden was fired, and the Web page betting on Karla's death appeared on the Internet. Another prison warden told the *Toronto Post* that it was as though somebody had put gasoline on a fire.

What crimes had Karla Homolka and Paul Bernardo committed that would motivate a ban on prison parties and the delivery of magazines for them? What had happened in this liberal country? And what happened to the happy young couple in the carefree wedding pictures taken next to the swimming pool (figure 15)?

Killing a Soul

The lead actor in the tragedy that follows is Karla Homolka's ex-husband, Paul Bernardo. His childhood had been a fiasco. He had wished his mother were dead, and he hated his stepfather, not least because of his sexual transgressions against Paul's older sister, Debbie. When Debbie started to talk about it, her mother did not believe a word. She scolded, "How on Earth can you invent such disgusting stories?" When Debbie's mother finally confronted him 8 years later, it was too late; by then Debbie had grown up and moved out.

From then on, Paul's stepfather became more and more silent. His mother neglected the housework and became a tremendous nag. Paul stayed at home simply because he could not afford anything else. He applied himself to his school work, never cut classes, and did fairly well in mathematics and the sciences. To make some money of his own, he became a newspaper boy, then a waiter, and finally a cleaning product salesperson. In the summer he organized YMCA holiday camps and enjoyed, so it seems, a few summer loves. He knew what he wanted; he gave his first girlfriend, Lisa, a T-shirt that said "Hands off" on the front and "Property of Paul" on the back.

The first shadows of his darker side appeared when Paul made friends with Steve, Van, and Alex Smirnis. These three were the sons of a restaurant owner who lived on the same street as he did. Given this restaurant connection, the four boys had no trouble getting alcohol. The more they drank, the more macho they felt, and they acted on it. This included peddling stolen low-cost items, such as pizzas from the restaurant's kitchen, in exchange for gasoline. They used to go on excursions by car, and they were caught trying to pay for their meals with a credit card stolen from a restaurant patron.

About this time, Paul began trying to impose his will on the others. He told his friends, time and time again, that he enjoyed anal intercourse with his girlfriend, and he stuck with this practice for years. Later, the police thought that this was evidence of homosexual tendencies.

He continued to act out, but nobody took him seriously. In 1980, while he was a high school senior, crime investigators gave a presentation at his school. This led to an odd scene that should have sounded an alarm.

The officers showed the students slides of a corpse that had been hacked to pieces. Its parts had been wrapped in a green plastic bag and were in good shape. An inspection of the bones and the still recognizable soft tissue parts led the medical examiners to believe that the body was that of a woman of Southeast Asian origin who had given birth at least once. More importantly, one of her legs was found close by in a coffee bag made of linen. According to the lab report, samples of soil found in the bag could be traced to Kenya and also to Montreal—a pretty strange combination. The investigators located a coffee importer in Montreal whose merchandise came from Kenya. This merchant gave its empty coffee bags to a woodshop, which used them as wrapping material. The employees were closely screened; two of them looked suspicious, and they turned out to be the murderers. One old coffee bag containing soil samples from two different parts of the world had given them away.

After this presentation on forensic technology, a round of questions by the students followed. Paul Bernardo did not ask about biological traces or soil samples but asked, "If two people commit anal intercourse inside their own four walls, how would the police find out about it? Would policemen sneak in the house and arrest the two?" Obviously, the investigators were stunned.

Paul Bernardo Grows Up

In 1980, Paul finished high school. His parents were divorced, and the boy hooked up with a new girlfriend named Jennifer. From the very start he beat her, poured water over her when she was feeling cold, and almost strangled her with a rope when he drove her home after the high school prom. One day he took degrading pictures of her and threatened to hang them on the church walls should she ever think of leaving him. His frightened girlfriend let it all happen.

Amazingly, even after Jennifer found photographs of a young woman from the Philippines under their bed, and when the woman threw fits of jealousy outside the door, Paul managed to make peace with Jennifer. When he wanted, Paul was able to act like a caring partner in an instant, throwing kisses and promising eternal love. Not that this kept him from producing videotapes that showed him having sex with the Philippine woman.

He attended the Toronto University Business School, which was located in Scarborough, Ontario. On the side, he worked for a company that employed him mostly in the immediate area but sometimes sent him to customers in nearby Niagara Falls. In 1986, he graduated with a bachelor of arts degree and continued to work for the same company.

Despite his meager income, Paul had taken to dressing quite expensively. He was known to be extravagant. Together with a few colleagues, he soon became known as an MCP (male chauvinist pig). It was not alcohol that made Bernardo uncouth and conceited. Only rarely did he drink strong cocktails, for example.

Fateful Meeting

On October 17, 1986, Bernardo met Karla Homolka in a restaurant. He was 23 years old, worked at Price Waterhouse, and was taking advanced management courses. He betrayed his girlfriends often enough to make them all hate him. Karla was 17 at that time, and she was different from the others. Right away, she invited him for the next weekend to her parents' house in the little town of St. Catharines, where she had planned a party.

Karla and Paul met as planned, but instead of joining the party they went to see John Carpenter's new movie, *The Prince of Darkness*. When they got back from the movie, the party had started without the hostess.

For privacy, the two new lovebirds locked themselves in Karla's room. There she pulled a pair of handcuffs from a drawer. To Paul this meant the beginning of a soul kinship because he also loved to use handcuffs whenever he had sex. A few minutes later, he put the cuffs around Karla's wrists and asked her what she would say if he turned out to be a real rapist. Karla answered, "That would be cool." Paul was enraptured!

To St. Catharines and Back

From then on, every Thursday Paul drove to St. Catharines to see his new love. The drive took him 2 hours. Karla's parents felt that the nice boy, who soon also visited on Saturdays and Sundays, should save on gas expenses and driving time, and they offered to let him spend the night on a sofa, supposedly in front of Karla's door.

Karla began to write letters and notes to Paul as frequently as possible. (These daily communications were important evidence later on, but that was when the romance was already beyond repair.) In November, Karla, who still considered herself newly in love, tried to put her thoughts into verse, poking gentle fun at a famous piece of doggerel:

> Roses are red,
> violets are blue;
> there's nothing more fun
> than a pervert like you.

In the meantime, Paul Bernardo's relations with his friends in Scarborough became worse and worse. When they held a farewell party for him in November, he insulted his girlfriend Jennifer by calling her a whore. On the way home in his car, he held a knife to her throat: "All you gave me for my graduation was a goddamn sweatshirt" was one of his reproaches. When the knife slipped between the front seats of the car, Jennifer managed to run away.

As the love between Karla and Paul intensified, Paul's psyche started running wild. On December 16, 1987, at 10:30 P.M. he attacked a young woman named Libby Ketchum in the middle of Scarborough. First he shut her mouth forcibly, then he put a cable around her throat. "If you're smart, you won't make a noise," he ordered. "Not a word! I won't harm you; I just want to talk to you. If you want to stay alive until Christmas, just shut up. And what's your name?"

He then raped her brutally, not far from the road. It took him more than an hour to get up and leave. His victim later told the police that her assailant told her repeatedly, between the tortures he inflicted on her, how smart she was not to resist him, which is why he did not kill her.

Useless Profiles of Suspects

Detective Steve Irwin of Scarborough police's homicide department thought the rape of Libby was strange. For one thing, in May and July, three women in the district had been snatched when getting off the bus by a man who groped and abused them brutally. Also, a female jogger in Warden Woods Park, outside Scarborough, had been pulled into the bushes, where she had been raped and killed.

The three surviving women agreed in their description of the perpetrator as somebody who appeared clean-cut, with good teeth and no disagreeable odor. He kept talking to his victims, asking them their names and whether they had boyfriends. He was meticulous about their answers and checked their names against the IDs in their bags.

Although Irwin argued that the similarities of the attacks tied the rapes to the murder, a special investigator in this case thought that the same observations did not suggest that this was a series of crimes. The sexual attacks had happened inside the city limits, but the murder happened outside the city limits. A serial criminal usually sticks with the same place and circumstance for his crimes.

A week later, on December 23, Mary Both was attacked in the street and subsequently raped. The women who had previously been attacked had long, dark hair and looked dainty. Mary Both, on the other hand, was blonde, was a bit taller, and weighed almost 150 pounds, another indication that this was not a serial criminal.

Still, Mary's rape occurred along the same lines as the previous attacks. The rapist became ever more urgent in his need to be taken seriously. He forced Mary Both to repeat, "I am a whore, Merry Christmas, I love you, I do what I am doing because I loathe my boyfriend, I am here as my gift to you."

Before the perpetrator let her go, he threatened, "I have your identification card; if I see anything about this in the local paper, I'll come after you and kill you." It became more and more obvious that this man, like all serial rapists, wanted only one thing: power. The sexual assault was only a means to achieve power.

Paul Bernardo, obsessed with control, made a serious mistake in the process. Mary Both had been able to get a good look at him in the light of a streetlamp. Her description should have been sufficient, in any small town in the world, to put an end to this series of rapes.

She described him as having a birthmark just below his slightly aquiline nose, with no scars or tattoos. His hair was light colored, and so was his skin. He was well-shaven, about 6 feet tall, slender, and circumcised. He also smelled good and wore a gold ring with three diamonds on one hand and a high school graduation ring with a red stone on the other hand. The knife he used in his attack was a stiletto, which he pulled from a black leather cover. And, last but not least, he drove a white Capri sedan.

Merry Christmas

The day right after this rape was Christmas Eve. For Karla and Paul, this was the time to exchange gifts. Bernardo showered his girlfriend in St. Catharines with jewelry, clothes, and an expensive teddy bear. Karla had thought up a special gift for Paul: She gave him a handwritten gift certificate for "sick, perverted acts which Karla Leanne Homolka will perform on Paul Kenneth Bernardo upon passing of this certificate. The precise kind of these perversions can be chosen by the receiver. This certificate expires January 2nd, 1988. Love, Karla."

But luck was no longer on their side. For one thing, Mary Both's testimony and description of her assailant were very precise. And just as the certificate was about to expire, Paul's ex-girlfriend Jennifer was picked up by the police. To be more precise, police commissioner Kevin McNiff had had to take Jennifer away from a McDonald's because he couldn't stand her sobbing any longer.

Bernardo's girlfriend then told him, both there and at the police station later on, details that sounded much worse than a simple lovers' quarrel at Christmas. In fact, it was a great deal worse. Paul had again come very close to raping and killing Jennifer. She had survived only because she ran away from him into a thicket outside town. When Jennifer finally made it home in desperate condition, maltreated and filthy, barely making sense in what she said, she told her parents that she had had a vision of the Virgin Mary while she was escaping, and that gave her the strength to run on. Nonetheless, her parents did not call the police. The abused, exhausted woman fell asleep immediately. Her parents were sufficiently worried to veto any further visits to their house by Paul Bernardo. A few days later, Paul knocked on the door with an innocent mien and told them he was bringing a diamond ring for his betrothal to Jennifer.

Upon hearing the story, Commissioner McNiff pulled out his notebook to write down these unbelievable happenings. But Jennifer refused to testify. The only thing she said she wanted was that Paul should pay her back the money he had borrowed from her. McNiff felt he had to comply with her wish, but he still wrote an internal note for the department and passed it on to the officers who were working on the rape case. Now, his colleagues had a name, an address, and witnesses from the party who viewed his treatment of

Jennifer, in addition to a physical description of the aggressor by the surviving rape victims, for their report.

McNiff's colleagues were stunned when they read the report. Jennifer had twice before reported being assaulted by Bernardo. But despite these very clear clues, McNiff was the first to put two and two together. Jennifer's assailant, just like the rapist of the day before Christmas, drove a white Capri sedan. This coincidence was the last straw. On January 5, 1988, McNiff wrote a five-page report in which he clearly stated his findings. But he made a mistake and dated the report January 5, 1987, instead of 1988. McNiff's report was stashed away in the previous year's paperwork and was promptly forgotten.

A Never-Ending Series

The next rape victim also was able to describe her assailant and the clothes he was wearing. By the late 1980s, the technique of creating Identikit pictures had been developed, so the Scarborough police were able to create a facial portrait of the criminal. The result was excellent: The Identikit clearly was an image of Paul Bernardo. Too bad that Paul had so far not been considered a suspect—at least not by the police department.

Upon further investigation, the police found a messenger who looked very much like the man in the police sketch. However, this messenger had no trouble convincing them that he had no involvement in the deeds they were investigating.

The criminal in the most recent case had again forced his victim to repeat some sentences and compliments. But this time, the rape scene was way outside town, halfway to St. Catharines. Another place, another criminal, the investigators concluded. Paul Bernardo was left unhindered, and the series of rapes continued.

On the night of August 14 to 15, 1989, Cathy Thompson was attacked at a bus stop and raped. The perpetrator chose the same pattern of behavior, but like all serial felons, he became more and more vicious. When he sent Cathy on her way, he not only threatened her in the usual fashion but also told her exactly what she had been doing the night before and what she was wearing when she read a book after going to bed. To her horror, he even knew the title of the book.

This time, however, Paul Bernardo was seen. A colleague at Price Waterhouse had passed by the bus stop in question and noticed her colleague sitting in his white Capri sedan. She tried to get his attention by waving, but Bernardo was staring with great concentration in the direction of the bus stop, so he did not notice her friendly gesture.

When this colleague heard about the rape of the night before, she easily came to her conclusion. "I saw you last night at the bus stop," she told Bernardo to his face. "You must be the rapist." Paul had no trouble answering her: "Oh, really?" he said. "One should never accuse anybody of such a disgraceful deed." And that was that.

Wedding Bells at Niagara Falls

In 1989, Karla finished high school. She started working in a veterinary office because she had no inclination to go to college. In October, she sent a puppy's tail to a girlfriend. "I just cut this off with a pair of nail scissors. Isn't it cool?" she wrote on the accompanying note.

In the same year, the technique for genetic fingerprinting was developed. In Canada, it took another year before an appropriate lab was built, although a few biological traces were picked up in crime locations and sent to labs in the United States. That is why, during the next rape victim's investigation in Scarborough on November 21, 1989, Detective Irwin sent not only all clothing but also traces of fingernails and anything that was likely to have come in contact with the criminal's penis to the department of criminal biology of the coroner's office, setting an important precedent in the case. Biological traces from different locations can be connected by matching DNA samples. In this way, the police can prove that various crimes were committed by the same person, even if they do not have a suspect. Suppose that at each crime scene there is the same genetic fingerprint. Once they have a suspect, they can attribute a number of different crimes to him or her. But for this case nothing happened with the materials Irwin sent because the lab in Canada had not opened yet.

The newly created Identikit came as no surprise; it just looked like the perpetrator of the previous rapes. Still, it established that this twelfth attack was part of a rape series in Scarborough.

Toward the end of 1989, both Karla and Paul gave notice to their employers. Karla moved to a larger veterinary office, where she was permitted to assist during operations. Paul started "independent work" by smuggling cigarettes on a grand scale. He bought cigarette cartons in the United States and transported them into Canada in his car; he then sold them at a hefty profit by avoiding the high tax in his country.

After his first smuggling expedition, he proposed marriage to Karla. For this occasion, he invited her to join him in romantic Victoria Village, next to Niagara Falls. Karla wrote in her diary about this day, December 9, 1989: "This was a love paradise. Red and green lights shone over the Falls; snow flakes descended in the moonlight. . . . Paul pulled out a musical clock with a glass unicorn. And around its horn he had put a beautiful diamond ring. . . . To warm me up, he held me very close and whispered words of love into my ear. In the end we were all alone outside in front of the Church of the Elves." Karla did not suspect that this diamond ring originally had been destined for Jennifer.

Less than 2 weeks later, the night before December 22, Deneen Chenier was the next victim of the Scarborough rapist. Her report made the police take notice. The aggressor had talked volubly, just as he always did while playing his sexual power games. In the background, Deneen had noticed a second person who did not participate in the act but pointed a video camera at them.

The police had their doubts about Deneen's testimony because she was clearly on the edge of despair and showed signs of having been cruelly beaten. In previous cases, there had never been a mention of an additional person. But the police were wrong. The second person did indeed exist; it was Karla Homolka.

The next night, under incredible stress, Deneen was asked to pick the criminal out of a lineup. She pointed at a man named Sylvester, who was innocent. Paul Bernardo was not among the men chosen for this lineup by the police. Why? Because nobody thought of him as a suspect.

The Press and a Few Witnesses Have a Premonition

In January 1990, serial rapist Paul Bernardo was still happily living at home. He spent his plentiful money right and left. He accepted several accounting jobs but stayed there for a short time only, although he was being offered steadily increasing salaries. To pay for the very elegant wedding ceremony he was planning, a year's salary would not have been sufficient. Smuggling cigarettes provided him with a better income.

His next rape happened in May. He told his victim that he was on his way back from a party (which happened to be Karla's twentieth birthday party). He tied his victim up and returned to her only minutes later. Both of these features were new behavioral elements. Having reappeared, he bit into the breast of the tied-up woman, telling her, "I need something that will remind me of you." In previous incidents, he had appropriated ID papers and purses, but now he wanted something more personal. So he pulled a clump of pubic hair from her and also took her makeup kit.

Gradually, the Scarborough police became frustrated. A public search had to be started, but to prevent media intrusion the police had told the media about only six cases out of a total of fifteen rapes. To avoid public

GENETIC FINGERPRINTING

By looking at the unique patterns of lines derived from the chemical basis of heredity, investigators can pin down the identity of a criminal. Since 1993, it has been possible to get usable DNA from even the most minute samples, even when they are no longer fresh.

But as impressive as DNA fingerprint technology is, forensic scientists need more. First, they need a computer database that contains genetic fingerprints of a large number of known subjects. Second, they need unequivocal DNA samples from the perpetrator. A useful comparison can be made only if one of the DNA samples can be definitely attributed to a given person.

The first success stories emerged from a database pilot program begun in 1990 that compared previously unconnected data from fourteen state and local laboratories that contained anonymous genetic fingerprints. In the United States, identical genetic fingerprints were found in many different databases. Finally, in October 1998, the FBI's National DNA Index System (NDIS) was established. Now, a DNA database infrastructure is available at the local, state, and national levels. DNA databases can link together a series of crimes over time that occur in different locations, meaning that criminals can no longer simply travel to another state to avoid discovery. It can take time to identify DNA and complete a database search, but once this is done, a criminal can be charged with all the misdeeds he or she committed, not just the ones where he or she was caught.

outrage, they made up an incredible lie: They told the media that the perpetrator always hid behind the victim. Only once, during the most recent rape, had he imprudently allowed himself to be seen by the victim, so only one Identikit picture existed, from the latest crime. Only now did they realize that they were dealing with a serial rapist, they claimed. They failed to notice that Paul Bernardo had crossed the well-guarded U.S.–Canada border regularly in his white Capri sedan and that they had received a number of reports of physical attacks and sexual molestations of which he had been accused. His file, containing all that information, remained well hidden in a bottom drawer.

When the first Identikit of the rapist was published, former Price Waterhouse colleagues recognized him immediately, but none of them got in touch with the police. Only one bank teller did what should have happened a long time before. He told the Scarborough police that his client, Paul Bernardo, resident at 21 Sir Raymond Drive, born August 27, 1964, was the man they were looking for.

But this statement got lost, too, and soon all hell broke loose.

Acting a Part

Paul Bernardo had graduated from weekend son to permanent guest at the residence of his future in-laws. The impression he left was that of a lovable, boyish, happy addition to the family. He became close friends with Karla's younger sister Tammy Lyn. Once in a while he went on long walks with her.

"If you really love me," Paul told Karla one day, "let me have some fun with your sister." Although (or maybe because) Karla knew about some of Paul's rapes, she did not like the idea that he now meant to accost her sister. She became jealous, in part because Tammy had always been the darling of the whole family. That is why she felt Paul should not get too close to Tammy. The older sister wanted to be, and to remain, number one.

Karla's self-confidence had declined since her wedding. She made up a list of resolutions that clearly showed how she felt about herself:

Show everybody that our relationship is perfect.
Always smile when Paul is around.
Be a perfect friend and a perfect lover to Paul.
Always remember: I am dumb.
Always remember: I am ugly.
Never forget that I am also fat.

To tie Paul more closely to her, she developed a plan that she thought was risky but still promising. She would support Paul in his pursuit of Tammy. Feeling like an ugly duckling—which she was by no means—she wanted both to help Paul and to put on the emotional brakes if he went too far.

One evening it developed further. Karla and Paul sneaked in front of Tammy's window and took a video of her while she undressed. In the days that followed, the two of them slipped into Tammy's bed when nobody was watching and Tammy was out for the evening. Karla then played the part of her younger sister for Paul.

Unfortunately, Karla's plans did not satisfy Paul. He wanted to have sex with the real Tammy, and he told Karla just that. To this end Karla put a strong sedative in the spaghetti she served her sister for dinner. The medication was for animals, and she had bought it so that her cat, Shadow, who had a bladder infection, wouldn't have to suffer so much. After Tammy had gone to sleep, Paul sneaked close to her bed and masturbated next to her on the pillow. Then he tried to rape her. But Tammy appeared to feel his touch, despite her drowsiness, and she moved. Karla and Paul then decided to leave well enough alone and went back to the living room.

Biological Traces

September 25, 1990, was a lucky day for Detective Irwin: The criminal biologist of the lab to which he had sent the traces of a rape scene from Scarborough found a tiny trace of sperm. The preliminary result was produced using blood group tests, which narrowed down the sample of possible perpetrators to about 13 percent of all males. Because there was also information on his face and age (about 30 years old) and because all the crimes had been committed in or near Scarborough, this was quite a step forward. Now, all men in that group could be asked for a blood sample for comparison. Had the police added the clues of the white Capri sedan and the name Paul Bernardo, which had been mentioned several times and whose home address and date of birth were known, the number of suspects would dwindle to one. But this information was still hidden in the police files, and because of the lack of computer database networking it was not easily available.

Still, the search for evidence with which to narrow down the list of suspects had begun. Detective Irwin went through all the paperwork at his disposal. He finally hit on the statement of the bank employee who had recognized Paul Bernardo from the Identikit. In addition, further clues in Bernardo's direction came from a woman named Tina Smirnis. She was the sister of his friends

Steve, Van, and Alex Smirnis. Unfortunately, in the intervening period the Smirnis family had moved away, and there had been almost no contact with Paul anymore.

Detective Irwin asked Tina to come to the police station. She came in the company of her brother Alex. It turned out that he had asked his sister to make the contact but that he actually wanted to say something. He had brought some photographs of Paul Bernardo. Alex said it was particularly suspicious that Paul suddenly wanted to move to St. Catharines. Why did he feel the need to leave Scarborough?

Alex Smirnis also supplied details supporting his suspicions. During a shared excursion, Paul once had coaxed a girl to come to his room. He got her drunk and then raped her. Also, Smirnis added, Paul always kept a knife in his car. There was no doubt in his mind that he must be the Scarborough rapist.

Although the police had no idea whether Alex Smirnis could be trusted, what he said rang a bell. Despite the similarity of his looks to the Identikit, Paul still did not show up as the number-one suspect. But when the police revisited the mountain of files on the rape cases, a particular piece of evidence showed up after having been lost in the shuffle for a long time. In the file on the Mary Both case, they found Officer McNiff's report, which had been filed in the wrong place. In it he had reported on Bernardo's cruelties against his girlfriend Jennifer.

After 2 months, an investigative team from the police department went to see the Bernardos. They found only Paul's parents but left their cards with the request that Paul come and see them. Paul called back very soon and said he would be happy to answer questions. He then happily told the investigators about his new love, Karla, and talked about what an odd coincidence it was that he was so similar to the police sketch. Rape did not interest him, he said; he always had enough girlfriends. The day the jogger was murdered, he was in Florida.

Paul Bernardo clearly knew what he was doing and saying. Being in charge was his favorite game. The investigators found him much more pleasant, more polite, and more intelligent than Alex Smirnis, who had brought Paul to their attention. The police officers were just a few years older than Paul, and he related well to them. They let him go after he had left a blood sample for further investigation. This blood sample was not lost but was sent to the crime lab as comparison material of a possible suspect. There, it was also supposed to be compared with the sperm sample that had been found on a rape victim. But a great deal of time elapsed before the comparisons were finally made.

Bernardo had barely left the police station when he lost his composure. He hastened back to Karla in St. Catharines. There he entered the house through the back basement window so that her parents would not see him. He then told Karla about the interview at the police station. Because she knew nothing about the last rape case, she tried to calm him down, but to no avail. The simple fact that connections were being made between the latest crime and the much earlier slaying of the jogging woman put the fear of God into him. Karla was confused. She would have no trouble giving Paul an alibi anytime. After all, on the evening before the last rape, he had been at her birthday party.

There was time for a little detective work. Paul and Karla went to the library and looked at the papers of the past few years. They jotted down the dates of all rapes by the Scarborough rapist on a writing pad, which also contained their marriage registry list. They added the time, place, and descriptions of all perpetrators. In doing so, they noticed that the police were completely in the dark and had no idea that Paul was a serious suspect. All clues that pointed in his direction, with the exception of the Identikit, appeared to have vanished.

Karla Performs an Experiment

On November 20, 1990, Karla tried to put together a new sleeping pill potion for her sister. She wanted one that did not have a bitter taste, as most drugs do. It also would act as an anesthetic so the person would feel nothing at all. Finally, she found something in an old issue of a yearly index of drugs, which she had taken from her veterinary office. There she read about a sedative–hypnotic drug called triazolam (Halcion); it had no side effects, and it was easy to get, especially because in her job as a veterinarian's assistant she was in charge of the daily procurement of medicine from the local pharmacy.

To be even more certain that her sister would be unconscious, she meant to add halothane. This anesthetic was routinely used in her veterinary office, and it was even easier to procure than the sleeping pills. On the negative side, halothane, unlike Halcion, could lead to fatal anesthetic accidents if taken in wrong dosage.

Be that as it may, Karla stole two bottles of halothane from her office and, to be on the safe side, said that the halothane mix apparatus wasn't working and that it used too much anesthetic gas. That would explain why such a large amount of the drug disappeared.

On Sunday, December 23, Karla and Paul planned a major "anesthetic day" for her sister. Unfortunately for them, Tammy made plans with a girlfriend and meant to stay overnight at her place. But again, fate appeared to play into the hands of Karla and Paul. In the early evening there was a severe storm, and

Tammy decided not to go out. Karla and Paul, on the other hand, went on their last Christmas buying spree. During this outing, they stopped their car and pulled out the Halcion sleeping pills that Karla had brought and ground them into powder. At about 7 P.M., they came home with armloads of gifts. All was ready for Christmas.

Paul pulled out his video camera and took movies of the Christmas tree, of Mother Homolka as she cooked dinner, and of Father Homolka, who was watching television wearing nothing but a pair of trousers. Then Paul prepared cocktails, very special cocktails for some of the party guests. Soon enough, Tammy was so inebriated that she asked Paul why he was holding two cameras. Not long after that, she staggered into her room, not to be seen for a while.

Karla got upset. Ever since the Homolka sisters were small children, there had been a picture of the two of them in front of the Christmas tree. "This year, it appears, that is impossible," Karla said in a fury. Paul's overly potent cocktails were to blame. To this day, we don't know whether this was bitter cynicism or pure denial. After all, Karla and Paul had mixed a dozen ground sleeping pills into Tammy's cocktail.

After the family Christmas celebration, when everybody except Karla and Paul had gone to bed on the upper floor, Tammy came staggering down the stairs. She sat on the couch and went to sleep immediately.

Paul started the camera and pointed it at Tammy. Karla pulled out the halothane and poured it over a piece of cloth, which she then held under Tammy's nose. In this fashion the amount of halothane used is very hard to control. But Tammy remained sleeping while Paul began to rape her in front of the running camera. "Hurry up," Karla whispered. "Just imagine if somebody comes down the stairs." She also asked Paul to use a condom because Tammy did not use contraceptives; having Tammy impregnated by Paul was the last thing she wanted. It would have turned her plans topsy-turvy. After all, maybe Paul would want to marry the mother of his child.

"Shut up," Paul answered in front of the video camera. "Just pay attention so that she remains quiet." The images on the video got more and more wobbly while Paul said, "Oh, Tammy, you're the best orgasm in the world by far." He then ordered Karla to rape her sister with her fingers. She obeyed, complaining bitterly because her sister had was having her period. All this time, she held the cloth with the halothane on Tammy's face.

After continued abuse, Tammy started vomiting. Karla and Paul got scared. They were worried not about Tammy's safety but about their own. Tammy had inhaled her own vomit and could suffocate. If somebody was awakened by all the noise and came into the room, that person would see the video camera

pointed toward a naked, half-dead Tammy in front of two power-hungry perpetrators who wouldn't know how to explain what was going on. So Karla and
Paul pulled the teenager, who was now having great difficulty breathing, into
her room, dressed her, and then called 911.

The medical emergency team arrived together with the police. They suspected from the start that it was a drug overdose. But Karla and Paul told them
truthfully that neither Tammy nor they had taken any cocaine or crack. The
police officer was baffled by something else. On Tammy's face, there was a
large flaming-red spot.

At 1 A.M., when December 24, Christmas Eve, had just begun, Tammy was
declared dead at the hospital. When the investigative officer came back to give
the Homolka family the sad news, Karla had disappeared. She had gone to the
laundry room, where she had already put all the blankets onto which Tammy
had vomited into the washing machine.

Although the police officer had been on the job for only 7 weeks, he was
present-minded enough to stop the machine. Still, it was too late; the wash
cycle had started, and the blankets were soaking wet.

The situation went from bad to worse. Karla put her arm around her other
sister, Lori, and cried. Paul screamed aimlessly, banged his head against the
wall, and ran around the house. This was probably the only sign of his oncom-
ing realization of what troubles he had started. Or was it only self-pity and fear
of the consequences?

A short time later, a senior detective entered the Homolka home. Karla and
Paul told him that Tammy had been sitting on the couch, completely drunk,
and finally, while watching television, simply stopped breathing. When the two
of them, who had nodded off a bit, noticed how poorly Tammy was doing, they
tried mouth-to-mouth resuscitation (which was true) and then carried her to
her room. The red spot must have happened while they carried her to her room,
when her head was dragging on the carpet. Even at the funeral, the flaming
red spot was still very visible. Later on, Karla told a neighbor that the discoloration was caused by acne. Nobody would surmise that, in reality, the spot was a
symptom of the anesthetics.

But this time, Paul and Karla did not get away quite as easily as before.
The coroner reported on that same night that the discoloration on Tammy's
face could not possibly be caused by scratches from being dragged through the
house. The police officer agreed that something wasn't quite right. The well-
rehearsed report of the young pair and the immediate use of the washing machine made them suspicious. On the other hand, this was the early morning of
Christmas Eve, and they all had better things to do on their holiday than this.

Halothane Destroyed the Dream

The anesthetic halothane played a different part in the case of serial killer Jürgen Bartsch. In fact, halothane put an end to his killing.

For forensic scientists, the Bartsch affair is not all that exciting. When he was arrested, the 19-year-old, through his confession, ushered in the end of the stuffy 1950s and 1960s for the German public. Like many normal boys, he came home punctually every day for dinner and joined his parents in their bed watching television. However, it turns out that before and after this daily routine, he was scouting for boys he could prey on.

Between 1962 and 1964, he coaxed four such victims into an old tunnel that had served as an air raid shelter. There he beat them up and killed them. After they were dead, he cut up the corpses, which aroused him sexually. He said later that he felt like an alien on Earth and a criminal superstar.

In private, most people in Germany agreed that he deserved the death penalty ("Put him against the wall," people would say to each other, even if not in public).

The old question of whether a person who is calculating and effective, and clearly not crazy, is fully responsible for what he or she has done arose clearly in the Jürgen Bartsch case. He must have approached hundreds of children, and he had let them run away if they offered the slightest resistance. He carried a briefcase for, he said, transporting diamonds for an insurance company. In addition, he had hidden a change of clothes in the vicinity of the air raid tunnel. He had stolen money from his parents' shop in order to finance his taxi rides and to pay for apple juice in bars, where he entertained his victims.

For a while, Bartsch actually walked around with a big suitcase of a size that permitted him to hide an "appropriate" boy. He preferred likable boys, with smooth skin, not too old or too strong. After someone in the street asked him what he was planning to do with this "children's coffin," Bartsch quickly disposed of the conspicuous item. Altogether, he did not appear clinically insane at all, and customers of his parents' shop called him friendly and alert.

On the other hand, most of his thoughts were directed toward finding more victims, which, of course, argues against his sanity. In a trial that ended in April 1971, Bartsch therefore was not given a life sentence, as he was in 1967, but rather 10 years in juvenile jail with subsequent internment in a psychiatric ward. This second sentence caused a great public outrage because it broke with the traditions of German psychiatry to date. Experts on sexuality and psychoanalysis were brought into the case, which would have been unthinkable in Germany in the 1950s.

Although Bartsch had frequently stressed that he would kill more victims if given the chance, he felt depressed in the psychiatric ward. He craved freedom, despite his sick instincts. One of the principal problems for him was that, in his confinement, this intelligent young man had no one to talk to. The wardens told him quite clearly that no professional was available for therapy. The other inmates were delighted at the magic tricks his mother brought him. All his fellow inmates liked him and chose him as their spokesperson. But this was not a life that could satisfy the now 29-year-old man.

The only two people with whom he maintained contact on a regular basis, in addition to his parents, were American journalist Paul Moor and chief investigator Armin Mätzler. Many letters and postcards written by Bartsch witness his attempts to regain his liberty. He even went so far as to marry Gisela, a partially paralyzed young woman with whom he had exchanged letters. Despite his ignorance of how to kiss and his continuing urge to prey on young boys, he thought this was a way to get out of the psychiatric ward.

In the 1970s, it was possible to apply for voluntary castration, but several physicians and fellow patients tried to dissuade Bartsch. First, they said, its effects were not entirely predicable, and sometimes it was ineffective. Second, it was a dangerous operation. Third, it might lead to unwanted physical changes. As a result, Bartsch wrote letters stating that he was opposed to voluntary castration.

In the fall of 1975, he made a full reversal and started arguing in favor of his castration. He wrote, "My fantasies have ceased; they do not carry any violence anymore. My perverted interest in sex has waned and is now at a normal level." He also argued that therapy and treatments with a drug that represses the male sexual hormone were unsuccessful. He continued, "For a sex offender who wants to become a *normal* human being, this operation means a *healing*. Since the body does not change, it leaves the possibility for normal sexuality but removes abnormal *urges*. The patient now is *100 percent in control. That means he will no longer be a sex offender*. I was wrongly accused of trying to maintain my sexual lust for an evil purpose. Those who say so are trying use the lowest form of argument to keep me in custody. But the *only* thing I want is to lead a normal life with my wife and to be able to satisfy her sexually. Otherwise she will give up on me, and I do not want to become a physical wreck. *That is all I want!* But the two medical experts are getting it all wrong. The only thing I am talking about is, please let two human beings be happy together, forever. To let *this* happen is human."

Bartsch's application, which was followed by several additional letters, was finally approved by the Medical Board of the Westphalia–Lippe district in 1976, despite the fact that it had been denied before. Even Bartsch's few friends thought he was dreaming if he thought this operation might lead to a happier life. Still, he thought that voluntary castration was the only way in which he might move closer to the normal life of his dreams.

And so the operation was performed some 6 weeks later, on April 28, in the regional hospital where he had been living since late 1972. At 10:30 A.M., he was declared dead due to cardiac arrest. This cause of death sounded odd because, ultimately, everybody dies of cardiac arrest. Could there have been an improper application of anesthetics?

Medical investigator Stichnoth and anesthetics expert Stoffregen did not find "improper details concerning the anesthetics used, nor concerning the operatic procedure." But then it turned out that a young nurse had administered the anesthetic because "the regional hospital did not have an anesthesiologist on its staff."

On May 6, the German weekly *Stern* published the true findings: Bartsch's heart had stopped because an overdose of anesthetic had stopped it. Just 6 days before the operation, a female patient had died in the same operating room. In both cases, somebody had filled the wrong evaporator for the anesthetic application with halothane.

The young nurse who had made this mistake could hardly be charged with any offense other than a lack of training. Rather, Josef Hollenbeck, the chief surgeon, was responsible for Bartsch's death. It turns out that there were seven different cases in which Hollenbeck had been charged with reckless endangerment or killing, but he had not been sentenced because of the statute of limitations. But he had lost several lawsuits in cases in which patients had suffered skin damage due to burning or cotton patches had been left behind when wounds were stitched up.

Bartsch's castration was a minor procedure and took only 8 minutes. At 8:30 A.M., it was finished, and it appeared successful. While wheeling the patient out of the operating room, nurse Stefan Gartner noticed that he could not feel Bartsch's pulse. That is when the final fight for the young murderer's life began. The 60-year-old surgeon opened Bartsch's chest to apply electrical impulses directly to his heart, to no avail. Bartsch had died of an overdose of halothane.

Later it turned out that Dr. Hollenbeck had a pretty odd notion of how to apply anesthetics. Journalist Paul Moor recalls, "The anesthetic applicator in the operating room of that hospital had two evaporators for two different anesthetics, and although there were highly visible large, yellow warning signs written in three languages on every evaporator, Dr. Hollenbeck had told the nurse who assisted him that it made no difference which medication goes in which evaporator. Hollenbeck was tried for medical malpractice, and was sentenced to nine months probation."

On May 4, Jürgen Bartsch was buried close to the psychiatric clinic where he had spent years of his life. Only seven people were given access to the ceremony, but 150 curious onlookers tried to get a glimpse of the scene. There was a police squad to keep them out and to restore order. It had turned out that in the few days before the burial, there had been threats not only against Bartsch (or rather his corpse) but also against the medical team that was responsible for his death.

At 6 A.M., everybody was at their wits' end. The investigation came to a halt over Christmas. When the police had left, Paul and Karla noticed, to their dismay, that somebody had removed the video camera.

But fate was still on their side. They found the camera in Karla's room. Somebody had put it there so it would not be in the way during the police investigation. One of the two videocassettes was lying on the floor next to the camera; the other one, which contained the recording of Tammy's rape and death, was still in the camera.

Movie Directors

These Christmas events did not discourage the murderous young pair; on the contrary, they became more unscrupulous. Karla went to get more sleeping pills the day after Tammy's funeral.

On January 12, her parents wanted to drown their despair by going on a trip to Toronto, where there was a large fireworks display. Karla's other sister was going to spend the night at her grandparents'; this opened the door for new misdeeds. Paul drove around in his car until he managed to pick up a girl, whom he raped and then sent on her way. Later, neither Paul nor Karla was able to say anything about that young woman, whom they simply dubbed "January Girl."

Still, Paul was not happy: Karla had killed his favorite toy, her sister Tammy. He reproached her repeatedly, fully aware that Karla actually had been very fond of her sister and that what happened at Christmas had been an accident.

To console themselves, the young pair decided to make a porno film in which Karla played the part of her dead sister. In the resulting video, the two principal actors appear in front of the camera, where they have a conversation that sounds confused but actually makes sense.

PAUL: Do you believe in family love?
KARLA: Well, I thought it was fun.
PAUL: And what did we learn from all of this?
KARLA: That we enjoy very young women.

After that, the pair discusses what they will do with girls they plan to entrap next. Finally, while the video is still running, Karla takes out Tammy's underwear and rubs it around Paul's penis.

Paul and Karla Plan Their Future

In the months that followed, Karla told people in the veterinarian's office that she was broke. Her colleagues took up a collection for her, and she accepted the money gratefully. She took every opportunity to bring more sleeping pills home.

In the same period, Paul smuggled more and more cigarettes across the border, making about $15,000 a month. One of his best clients was one of the Smirnis brothers.

Seventeen of his border crossings were registered in a computer. Customs agents do that routinely so that personal data and licenses are available when there is a need to search for criminals. After the truth surfaced, these data were used to reconstruct some of Paul's trips. Had the authorities compared their databases, Paul would have been caught much earlier, during one of his border crossings. But the customs computer data were never compared with the larger police database. As a result, the serial rapist happily commuted back and forth and was registered every time without consequences.

Paul became a regular at a tanning studio, bought a gold-colored Nissan, and thought about how to get into rap music. He considered himself a good rapper, and his idol was Vanilla Ice. Until the time of his arrest, he composed a good deal. On one of his horrific videos, one can hear Vanilla Ice playing in the background.

Now that money had become plentiful for them, they moved to a picturesque little village called Port Dalhousie (figure 16), a typical North American suburb with streets lined with white wooden houses. Their minds seemed to become more feverish: Karla thought that her new house was inhabited by ghosts, and Paul couldn't stand the stench in the rooms. Eventually, Paul closed the drainage holes. The odd smell became less obtrusive, and the "ghosts" appeared less often.

But their desire to make more videos did not diminish. On April 6, 1991, Karla was frightened when Paul raped a young woman at 5:30 A.M. on his way to the rowing club. When he arrived home shortly thereafter, in good spirits, Karla became very jealous. The wedding would be soon, so she made up her mind to prepare a gift for Paul that would tie him to her forever.

This gift was Jane. Three years earlier, when Jane was 12 years old, Karla had found her wide-eyed, standing in front of the vet's office. Karla permitted her to help a little, and they became close friends.

Jane was 15 years old when Karla implemented her plans. She invited the girl to come for a visit. Jane was beside herself with happiness. Karla engaged her in silly conversation and mixed cocktails. Those wonderful cocktails are the last thing Jane remembered the day after. As she woke up the next morning, she felt so sick that her parents put her to bed for the next 3 days, believing that their daughter had caught the flu.

But this was far from the truth, as the video of the night before shows. There, we see Jane in clothing that belonged to Karla's dead sister, Tammy. As Paul and Karla take turns raping her, she is fast asleep.

Still, Jane was lucky because the next victims of the power-hungry pair did not survive their tortures. Paul and Karla wanted to play their games with people who were awake, not with bodies in a trance. Looking at videos of the months that followed, it is clear that a few of the victims believed they had a chance of survival. One girl asked whether she could take a look at their dog on the way out. "We'll see about that," she was told. The girls were even allowed to ask for meals, which Paul quickly got from the nearby deli. The captives watched videos and listened to music. One of the girls was so exhausted that she fell asleep next to Paul on his bed.

All the victims were well aware that their lives were in danger and that their "hosts" could not just let them go. Still, they attempted to cooperate in the vain hope of survival. There were periods of perfectly normal behavior in between a sequence of rapes, masquerades, and beatings, so the girls held on to a little spark of hope. By 1993, at least three girls had died in the house of the recently married couple. Karla and Paul had passed every conceivable limit. But their ruthlessness appeared to pull them through.

The End Is Near—Or Not

When it became known what close escapes Paul Bernardo had repeatedly had, Canadians shook their heads. For instance, in July 1991 an attentive driver almost got him into custody. The young woman thought it strange that a gold-colored Nissan was constantly following her. She made a note of the license plate number and remained alert.

When, a short time later, she chased somebody out of the bushes in front of her parents' house, she got very frightened. That person must be the Nissan driver! She asked a friend to drive around the neighboring houses and look for that easily recognizable car. And sure enough, there it was, in front of a bar. The license plate number was the same one she had written down before. She reported this to the police, who politely took note.

A few days later, on July 22, the police appeared at the Bernardos' door, not because of the report of the suspicious gold-colored Nissan but because the Bernardos had reported a theft. After the wedding, while on their honeymoon, they told the police that gifts valued at a total of 30,000 Canadian dollars had been stolen from their house. Watches, cameras, a computer, jewelry, cash, and Paul's electronic musical instruments were reported stolen.

The police investigators smelled a rat immediately and suspected insurance fraud. In particular, they found it strange that the young pair had already prepared a neat list of all stolen items. The police officer didn't believe that this complaint was worth following up on. There were worse problems to attend to, such as the serial rapist in the neighboring town and the dead bodies of children that had recently been found. Let the insurance company take a close look at this possible fraud attempt. The gold-colored car of the man who had followed a young woman for several days was parked in front of the door. But the police officer did not notice because nobody at the station had passed on the report on the very recent incident.

The Gold-Colored Car

By 1992, the series of murders and rapes still had not been cleared up. Another young woman came forward with an interesting observation. On May 30, late at night, she was lounging around with a friend in a doughnut place close to Port Dalhousie. When she looked over the vacant parking lot outside, she saw a gold-colored sports car drive around slowly. The woman had the feeling that its driver was staring at them.

Next time the two of them looked out, the car was gone. Instead, they looked into the lens of a video camera pointed at them from the lower corner of the window. But it vanished as soon as they noticed it. That is all they could see because it was quite dark outside. At a quarter to three, as they left the place, they again noticed the gold-colored car parked close by.

The older one drove the younger friend home. As the younger one got out of the car, the gold-colored car slowly drove by. Now, she really got upset. Unfortunately, she did not make a note of the license plate, but she was determined to do something the next time; she would take care of that crackpot. When she got home, her anger turned into fear. The suspicious car was parked just a few blocks away from her parents' house. She called the police to report her observations.

Unfortunately, she still had not memorized the license plate numbers and letters properly. She said, "It is 660 NFM or 660 MFN," but the actual number of Paul Bernardo's car was 660 HFH. She was also wrong about the make of the car, which she reported to be a two-door Mazda, probably the model RX7.

Just by chance, however, she saw the car again the next day. She called the police station and gave them the correct license plate and the correct model:

a gold-colored Nissan 240 sx. But still, Bernardo's contract with his guardian angel was not yet up. The call to the police station was written down by a friendly young secretary, only to vanish immediately among the usual paper mess of the station.

Biological Traces and an Impossible Car Search

Slowly, Paul's incredible streak of luck was running out. In April 1992, more than a year after Paul had given a pointless deposition to a friendly police officer in Scarborough, Detective Irwin was ferreting around the lab reports of the samples that had been taken in this case. Among the blood tests of 230 men, Paul Bernardo's sample was the one that resembled the characteristics of the sperm that had been found in the underwear of one of the victims of the Scarborough rapist. With this match, the police had narrowed the field down to four men besides Paul, whose DNA traces were compatible. His DNA profile matched that of five men in total. DNA technology was not so advanced then; today it would have all ended here because the sample would have matched only Paul's.

Something should have happened now: a visit to Paul Bernardo, a search of his house, further depositions. The suspect did not live in Scarborough anymore, but it would have been easy to get to him through his parents. There was a good description of the suspect, so that Bernardo, one of the five suspects, should have had no chance to get away. But the system simply did not react. Once again, incredibly, no one followed up.

At this time, a new witness showed up and said that she noticed a struggle while driving by: One person had pulled another one into a parked car. At first she thought the people were playing a game. But when she heard of a search for a missing girl who had vanished at that exact location, she went to the police.

The officers asked about the car. The witness said she hadn't the foggiest notion of automobiles and could say only that the car had a light-colored exterior. But the police did not give up; they now felt they were finally on the right track. They showed her many books and publications with pictures of automobiles. They took her to car dealers, but to no avail. She finally said it might have been a Camaro, and in so doing she started one of the most abstruse wrong investigations in history.

The police first checked the local databank. They asked the Department of Motor Vehicles (DMV) for all car owners who had registered a Camaro before 1992. At the same time, a street search was started for all cream- or ivory-colored cars of this model—all, of course, to no avail. After all, the car into which the Bernardos had pulled that unfortunate girl was a gold-colored Nissan, but during her casual drive-by the witness had not noticed this.

When the requested list of cars arrived from the DMV, the investigators couldn't believe their bad luck. There were 125,000 Camaros registered in the province of Ontario. Some 5,000 of them belonged to people residing in the area where the crimes had been committed. But the police felt they were up to the challenge; with a little work, they could make it. And they would ask for help from the public.

A City Turns Paranoid

From then on, every Camaro owner was wise to leave his or her car in the garage. After the missing person reports were released, young girls were no longer allowed to go out by themselves. The hunt was on; huge posters, brightly illuminated, were shown along the streets, with images of the car type and a request to call the police.

The young woman who had reported Paul Bernardo's car to the police twice saw his golden Nissan again at just that time, on April 18. She realized that everybody in town was looking for a cream-colored Camaro, but this was not her case. Because the police had not reacted to her concerns, she followed this suspicious car from a distance.

The last thing she saw was the gold-colored car turning into Bayview Drive in Port Dalhousie and then vanishing from her view. The amateur detective came to the right conclusion: The driver must have put the car into a garage, and he must live on Bayview Drive.

The witness called the police a third time. She reported her most recent observation and explicitly mentioned its connection with her two previous reports. The woman on the phone promised her she would write it down to this effect—and so she did. But like its predecessors, this note landed in a dead file. No wonder, because the investigators had more urgent business. Everybody was looking for a Camaro. An ever-increasing number of people called, having seen a light-colored Camaro somewhere near the place where the girls had vanished. In fact, several mothers reported their sons driving such a Camaro.

With firm resolve, the police followed all clues. The new report about a gold-colored Nissan that belonged to a possible suspect simply had to wait.

An Old Friend

Suddenly, an odd clue in file number 241 gave the police a strong push in the right direction. A man who wanted to be anonymous (it was one of the Smirnis brothers) had talked to a police officer on May 1 to tell him that his old friend Paul Bernardo had been questioned as a possible candidate for the infamous Scarborough rapist. He said that Paul was extremely violent against women. What is more, Paul had raped a woman in Smirnis's presence. In addition, he said that Bernardo was a weakling who preferred young, weak women—certainly 15-year-olds. A further point: When rapes were reported to have occurred in Scarborough, Paul was out of town. Lastly, he added, he had no facial hair. (This last hint was confusing, but, looking back, it is important. Although Smirnis meant to suggest that Paul was a weakling, not manly enough to grow a beard, it appears to explain the fact that all witnesses described the Scarborough rapist as clean shaven.)

The police now pulled the file on Bernardo's criminal record. It showed that he had no prior convictions. Maybe he was the disgusting person Smirnis had described, but so far it had not been a matter for the courts. Still, to be on the safe side, two police officers drove to Bayview Drive.

Bernardo asked his visitors to join him in the living room. There, they saw a large wedding picture of Paul and Karla and a newly framed certificate from the Freemasons, which Paul had recently joined. Paul told the investigators that on the day when the most recent kidnapping of a young woman had occurred, he was at home writing words for some of his own compositions. This was something he did often, and he said he was well on his way to becoming a famous rapper. What car were they talking about? A Camaro? The only car he and his wife owned was the gold-colored Nissan parked in front of the house.

When the police officer left after just a quarter of an hour, Paul was relieved. He was quite certain that the police had not the foggiest notion of what he had been up to. They had been sitting in the very room where the crimes were committed. But Karla was afraid. What would they do if the police came back with a search warrant? They certainly must not get hold of the videotapes stored in the house. Paul agreed. As luck would have it, the insulation of the garage roof offered a fine place to hide the tapes. That was the end of that worry.

Paul Bernardo was removed from the list of possible suspects. Had the local police had any notion of the incriminating DNA evidence that was available in Scarborough, this would not have happened. The police departments of the neighboring towns did not share information, nor did they get together to consult. And why should they? In Scarborough there had been rape cases, but in the place where the pair now lived, girls had vanished. Why should there be a connection?

Bad Luck and the Consequences

As winter approached, and while investigators were still looking for a cream-colored Camaro, Karla and Paul acquired a new playmate: 17-year-old Norma. She had been a friend of Tammy. The pair invited her to dinner, took her along on outings, and bought her new clothes. Paul took videos of her turning cartwheels and other deceptively innocent actions. But Norma did not like to be touched. When Paul did not respect that wish, she left the house and did not come back.

Paul was furious. He told Karla that Norma's departure was her fault, and he beat her up. This was not unusual, but this time the beating was so severe that Karla was left with two black eyes.

A few days later an anonymous caller told Karla's parents to take a closer look at their daughter's face. Mrs. Homolka had no idea what this meant, but she drove to the vet's office. After some hesitation, Karla promised to leave Paul. That, of course, she did not do. Rather, she got another heavy beating by her husband. When her parents accompanied Karla to a doctor's office, the physician gave her sleeping pills and then sent the police to Paul. That did it. This time, Paul Bernardo—wife beater, professional smuggler, third-rate wannabe rapper, Scarborough rapist, girl killer, and unstable felon—was arrested.

A few hours later, he was back home, dissolved in self-pity. He sat down at his multitrack recording machine and recorded a sad love song for his lost love—for Karla. He wailed with such intensity that Karla's dog joined in the howling. The tape with the atrocious duet later was added to the evidence.

An Unexpected Telephone Call

Karla moved in with her uncle and aunt and spent her days writing down how awfully Paul had always treated her. She described even more past tortures, hoping that this might help her to extricate herself from her appalling involvement with the lethal rapes of young girls. She almost succeeded in this attempt. She wrote to more than ten of her women friends, "I was always frightened when Paul was around. In November, he stabbed me; in December, he strangled me; and he beat me up every day."

And at that time, after 5 years' delay, the phone rang in Detective Irwin's office in Scarborough. The forensic biologist who was on the line excused herself for being late in analyzing the DNA samples from the five suspects. One of her colleagues was taking a professional advancement course, another was on maternity leave, and she had been working hard on a number of murders; only now could she devote herself to the older rape cases from Scarborough. But finally she had analyzed the five DNA samples.

And the result, the biologist told the detective, was that it was Paul Bernardo who left biological traces in all three Scarborough rape cases. In other words, Paul Bernardo was the Scarborough rapist beyond any doubt.

To gather further evidence, police placed Bernardo under surveillance and tapped his phone line. The investigators in charge of the case also located in the police computer the report that Paul had recently beaten his wife.

At the same time, Karla was carefully interrogated in her aunt's apartment. The police were not yet aware that Karla might have known about the rapes Paul committed, and her black and blue marks seemed to make that unlikely. So they assured her parents that Karla had nothing to fear from the authorities; she was not suspected of having any involvement in the very serious crimes that they were investigating.

Karla knew that she had to extricate her neck from the noose as quickly as possible. With this in mind, she did all she could to play the part of the battered and oppressed wife. She poured out letters and phone calls with descriptions of the cruelties she had suffered to her acquaintances and, of course, to the police.

When the detectives returned to her house a few weeks after the first conversations, Karla's lack of experience in interrogations tripped her up. The police officer told her for the first time what they were investigating: Her husband, they said, was suspected of having raped several young women. Karla was clearly relieved because there was no mention of murder. It looked to her as though Paul had been identified as the Scarborough rapist. She then volunteered that she would not be shocked, hardly even surprised; in fact, she had been expecting the police to show up again soon.

The police were surprised by her attitude. Why, they thought, should the investigators come back so soon to the abused wife? Why wasn't the poor woman shocked at being told that her husband was a serial rapist?

They also were surprised to see Karla become upset when they asked questions that concerned not only the rapes in Scarborough but also the Port Dalhousie killings. When she asked how long convicted sexual predators might be put away, their patience came to an end; they took Karla's fingerprints.

That really inspired Karla. She now told them that she had never been able to stand Paul. She had not wanted to marry him; she did so because she considered it her duty. She had regained her composure only after moving away from their home, where her life had been nothing but torture. These tales may have seemed childish and simple-minded as they meandered between excuses and accusations. Still, they were duly written down. Karla did get some mileage out of the severe mistreatment she had recently endured. The police did not believe every word she said, but they thought it was very unlikely that, as a victim herself, she had been an accomplice in Paul's crimes.

The squad car had just left its parking place in front of her house when Karla called a defense attorney and made an appointment with him. Soon thereafter, she called the police station and made a point of asking simple-mindedly whether they would be kind enough to give her a ride to that attorney's office on February 13, 1993. The police didn't fall for her innocent-sounding request for taxi service, but they thought that they could coax a few remarks from their passenger that might be useful for their investigation.

But it did not work the way they had hoped. When the police dropped Karla off at her home later on, they had not learned anything new. The worst mistake Karla made during her blabbering was noticed only later on, when the "deal with the devil" had already been initiated. While riding with them, Karla told them how beautiful and romantic her wedding had been. Of course, this contradicted her earlier statement about having married Paul, who beat her up repeatedly, only because she felt she had an obligation to do so. But as skeptical as they were, the police did not catch on. They were still clinging to their notion of an evil culprit and his helpless victim.

Things went quite differently with Karla's lawyer, George Walker. He was deadly pale when he left his office after his first meeting with her. In fact, he was speechless. For a few minutes, he was incapable of uttering a word. Karla Homolka had told him, unexpectedly and matter-of-factly, that she was a partner not only in Tammy's death but also in the murder of two of the three teenagers whose largely decomposed bodies were found later. She also told him about videocassettes that recorded the sexual exploits at the expense of young women who had later been murdered. She did not know where to find these cassettes. She said she tried to take them from their hiding place in the garage when she left Paul, but they were gone.

Suddenly, Things Moved Too Fast

Karla dug herself deeper and deeper into the role of the abused woman. She read books on domestic violence and asked the police to tell her what sicknesses occur when women spend years as victims of an abusive man.

She was lucky. After her conversation with George Walker, he was visited by investigators from a different department. They told the lawyer that the authorities were ready to make a deal with Karla. If she told them all about

Paul and made a full confession of her own behavior, her sentence would be lenient. (In Canada, police investigators can exert considerable influence on the punishment imposed by the court.)

So, here it was, the deal with the devil. Her lawyer knew only too well that this was the best he could do for her. Karla was present during the murders and had helped to dispose of the corpses, and there was little that even a wily lawyer could do. There were videotapes that would help the prosecutor prove her involvement. Walker agreed under the condition that Karla would not be charged with involvement in the murders. Nobody can say how this deal sat with the lawyer's conscience. Maybe Walker was convinced that Karla had just stood at Paul's side when he committed his sadistic sexual acts. That same night, the police also told Walker that Paul was their principal suspect in the Scarborough rapes. The lawyer just shrugged his shoulders. Karla had not talked about that, and the sperm traces could not have come from her, so this was none of Walker's business. The police decided to take Bernardo into custody as soon as the deal with Karla was signed.

On February 17, everything appeared to be ready. George Walker had told Karla that she would be sentenced to jail—but for how long was still open. Karla agreed to the deal, but before she had signed anything, the local media discovered the story. There must have been a leak somewhere, so Bernardo had to be taken into custody before the evening news. The investigators had not completed their preparatory work, but the police had to act before the press showed up at his place.

At 4 P.M., two police officers rang Paul's doorbell, handcuffed him, and took him with them. He was wearing a black T-shirt and kept his cool, as usual. There was no proof that Bernardo had killed anyone, despite what Karla might say, but the police told him before driving off with him that he was going to be charged with multiple rapes in Scarborough and with multiple murders. Still, the only physical evidence they would be able to produce was the genetic evidence from the rapes.

When they got to the police station, there was a surprise for Bernardo. To shake his composure, the investigators had put up a screen illustrating family trees of the Homolka and Bernardo families next to the map of Scarborough. Then, there were big boxes with inscriptions in large letters saying "forensic objects," followed by a long list with the names of his victims and the genetic fingerprints. They had added a number of photographs of Paul's car, labeled "Bernardo's car: 1989 Nissan 660 HFH" in large letters.

"Remember me, Paul?" Detective Irwin, the first one who had paid a visit to Bernardo before, opened up the interrogation.

"No," Paul answered.

"He wipes a speck of dust off his trousers," Irwin's partner added to the transcript.

From this point on, Paul's only answer was "no comment."

Paul Bernardo and Karla Homolka had caused an entire town, and later an entire region of Canada, to become fearful and paranoid. In so doing, they had also taken away many people's trust in the efficacy of the police force. They confounded endless investigative attempts, and they inspired the creation of a Web site where people could bet on how long Karla Homolka would survive.

To this day, people in this region are still upset. Why? Karla's deal with the devil earned her only a 12-year jail sentence without parole, instead of a life sentence starting in July 1993.

The worst interference with the legal process was committed by Bernardo's lawyer, Ken Murray. The government tried to prosecute him in April 2000 after finding out that he knew all the time where the "lost" six videotapes could be found—the tapes that showed the rapes of the murdered girls (including 14-year-old Leslie Mahaffy and 15-year-old Kristen French). Had Murray given these tapes to the prosecution instead of holding on to them to protect his client, the deal with Karla would have collapsed. After all, the videos show that Karla had been an active and willing partner in all these misdeeds, not the brutally beaten victim who stood cowering to one side.

Following Paul Bernardo's suggestion, the lawyer had taken the videocassettes from their new hiding place in May 1993. Murray, who was accustomed to hot evidence items as a defense lawyer, declared later on that he would have stopped defending Bernardo if he had known of the evidence on those tapes, but Bernardo maintained that he did not even touch two of the girls seen on the video. Still, what the lawyer neglected to do was bad enough. He knew Paul would maintain his innocence as long as the tapes were inaccessible. To protect his client, he did not pass them on to his successor, defense lawyer John Rosen; he kept the tapes for an additional 16 months and remained silent about them. (Murray was acquitted because prosecutors could not prove that he had willfully obstructed justice.)

When the police submitted evidence of the genetic fingerprints, secured from the house in July 1994, it became more difficult for Bernardo to claim innocence. On the nightstand they found DNA samples from Kristin French and Leslie Mahaffy. They came from the stomachs of the two girls, who vomited when Paul orally raped them. Murray told Bernardo that there was now proof that he had mistreated the girls, even in the absence of the videotapes.

Bernardo didn't see it this way. He answered that there might well be samples of his sperm all over the house, given the sexual activities between Karla and him. He did not want to admit that this did not explain how the two girls, whom he said he had never touched, had vomited his sperm next to his bed. Murray decided he'd had enough, and he told his successor, John Rosen, about the videos.

On August 8, 1994, the court subpoenaed the videocassettes, and in September John Rosen handed them over. But it was too late: The deal with the devil was irrevocable because Karla had already been sentenced. The Canadian legal authorities either couldn't or wouldn't start new legal proceedings; they felt embarrassed and could not afford a new trial. The public was furious.

The videotapes were shown to the jury in 1995, when the court had to decide on Paul Bernardo's sentence. He was found guilty of murdering Mahaffy and French. Whereas he had been accused of forty-three sexual assaults when the proceedings began, he was now sentenced for life in prison for the double murders.

To this day, Paul Bernardo sits in a tiny, windowless cell with a bed, a table, and a television set, while his ex-wife (they were divorced in the meantime) sits in a more attractive cell and is permitted an occasional day's release. Having spent one-third of her sentence in this fashion, she will be able to petition for early release. As mentioned earlier, she was about to hand in such a petition when a media uproar ruined her chances of any such clemency. Karla Homolka's release is scheduled for July 5, 2005, "the day her second victim, Leslie Mahaffy, would have turned 29," reports *The London Free Press*.

Parents Last

The families of the murdered children had to deal with much more mundane problems. The Mahaffy and French families filed civil suits, and as of 1998, the unpaid invoices from their lawyers totaled more than $400,000. Even worse, their knowledge of the videos exerted enormous psychological strain. The videos were still among the court evidence, and there was a danger that they might be made available to the media at some point. To Leslie's mother, they were "poisonous garbage." Mrs. French felt that the mere existence of these tapes was like a continued assault on the girls.

In the fall of 2000, the court finalized the sentence against Bernardo that would keep him in jail for life; his ex-wife also would have to spend the full 12 years of her sentence in prison. Then, for the first and only time in the criminal proceedings of the Bernardo and Homolka case, something happened that felt liberating, reasonable, even good. On December 20, 2001, the originals and all copies of the tapes were burnt at an undisclosed location, by order of prosecutor general David Young in Niagara. He declared, "The families of the murdered children have suffered long enough. I feel honored that it is in my power to order the annihilation of these tapes." The authorities have kept nothing but a written description of the scenes shown on the tapes.

Leslie's mother had one closing comment when she said softly, "Quite a day."

Postscript: Dark Times

This sad case speaks for itself. This section began with the question of who, if anybody, deserves the death penalty, and with this question, the story ends. There is no answer to it.

Today, everybody knows that a bad start in life can lead a person to crime. Quite often, the most violent criminals start their lives far off the normal track. Take Jeffrey Dahmer: He was an introverted person before his crimes. His father, a soft-spoken, rather introverted chemist, believes to this day that Jeffrey was nothing but an awful likeness of his own inner self, somebody who would love to order the world his way, just as he, his father, orders the world of his flasks and test tubes.

Karl Denke, discussed in chapter 5, also turned away from a normal world. When he was a child, he was considered simple-minded, and so he turned more and more into a social recluse. How much of that was due to the world around him, how much to his genetic makeup, we will never know. Was he such an odd person to start with that other people were unable to connect with him, or did he find so little resonance with people around him that he became a recluse? Or was he simply mentally ill?

One thing is certain: There are plenty of "odd" people, ones who are most comfortable when they are out of contact with normal life. But they do not turn to crime. Does that mean that the line between good and evil is so narrow that we cannot see it?

Is there really a clearly defined separation between a telecommunication expert and an Internet pirate? What defines the difference between a scientific researcher who shuts himself away in his lab and a do-it-yourself bomber working in his basement? Are there clearly defined boundaries between the aggressive, cursing athlete and the abusive husband who turns into a murderer impelled by jealousy? Think of some quiet introvert: How many people has he or she killed in thought, how many haystacks has he or she mentally set on fire? Why do so many people crave crime novels or crime shows on television?

We will never know. But the next time we run into a criminal weirdo, he had better fear for his life. Our tendency to want to sentence him to death makes no sense. Even for severely mentally ill criminals, locking them away can prevent them from harming others.

One of these criminals was Rudolf Höss, commander of the Auschwitz Concentration Camp from 1940 to 1943. He was what we call today a screwed-up, unfeeling oddball, but nobody recognized this at the time. His dream job was to be a simple farmer. And that's what he dedicated his life to before he worked in Hitler's SS and what he returned to after the war, before he was unmasked.

Höss did not even speak to his wife about his desire to be a farmer. But he was upset about the lack of hygiene in his death camp and about the wardens' maltreatment of the inmates. He tried several times to obtain better-trained personnel but did not succeed.

He got just as upset when detainees escaped and he could not secure enough materials to build new fences around the camp, or when he felt that the people handling the dogs were lazy. On the other hand, he cultivated a childish friendship with the Gypsy detainees in his camp because they had such an uninhibited, playful demeanor. Still, when orders came to gas them to death, he did not mind being present to make sure all went according to the master plan given to him from above.

None of this makes sense, and we cannot categorize it.

Before Höss was hanged in 1947, he made a number of statements that show us how odd, how blurred our perception of the world becomes when we direct our eyes and our ears toward the abyss. His words will tell us that putting murderers such as Höss to death is no more than a helpless attempt to shut off the background noises of our own existence—or at least to turn down the volume.

In his memoirs, Höss wrote,

When I was a child, I had no playmates. So, the forest that began close to our house with its tall black fir trees had a great attraction for me, and even more so the big reservoir that held the water for the city. I spent hours listening to mysterious rumbling sounds behind its thick walls— and no matter what explanation the adults around me would have, I couldn't see any connection. . . .

And then, horses! I could not get enough interaction with them—stroking them, talking to them, offering them things they loved to nibble on. . . .

I already was, and developed more and more into, a lone wolf. I played by myself, I liked being alone and unobserved. I could not stand being watched. I had this craving for water, I kept washing up and taking baths. . . .

When I was seven, we moved close to the city of Mannheim, but we lived well outside its perimeter. I was unhappy to find out there were no farm animals, no stables. When I turned seven, I was given a pitch-black pony with sparkling eyes and a long black mane, whom I called Hans. He loved my companionship and followed me like a dog whenever possible. When my parents were not around, I went so far as to take him up to my room. Since I was on good terms with the domestic staff, they let me be and did not tell my parents.

And on it goes as the future head of a concentration camp talks about his earlier life. From the beginning, Höss was a faithful servant of his organization. He did not question the terrible system before the end of the war, and he did not make any decisions that were not in accordance with directions handed down to him. He integrated himself into the system that handed down orders. Seen from above, he was a good, orderly functionary who did as he was told, sometimes even more. Later on, after the war, when Höss was asked whether he could not simply have killed SS leader Heinrich Himmler so that the whole network of concentration camps would end, he said that such a thought never would have occurred to a member of the SS.

He went so far as to agree wholeheartedly with the motto "Work makes us free," which was painted on the entrance to Auschwitz. When he was himself imprisoned by the Weimar Republic before he joined the SS, he had concluded that prisoners needed some regular work activity to stay in shape, mentally and physically. Just sitting around and doing nothing would make them go to pieces. So he ordered the cynical motto to be painted on the entrance gate of the camp he commanded.

"In the concentration camp, I discussed this point with many detainees," he wrote in 1947; "all of them were convinced that life behind bars or behind wire fences was insufferable if there was no work—that, in fact, it would be the very worst punishment."

FIGURE 1 Author Mark Benecke on the grounds of the Forensic Anthropological Research Facility (Body Farm), University of Tennessee. (Photo: Mark Benecke)

FIGURE 2 The skull of a corpse in advanced decay on the Forensic Anthropological Research Facility (Body Farm), University of Tennessee. (Photo: Mark Benecke)

FIGURE 3 The Mannheim cornfield, showing the path where the corpse of an unknown man was found. The dark spot above the arrow shows the combustion area. (Photo: Walter Neusch)

FIGURE 4 Facial thickness. People of different ethnicities have different skin thicknesses within well-established ranges. These data are used for modeling flesh onto the skull.

FIGURE 5 Mikhail M. Gerassimov was the first "face finder." He developed facial reconstruction and applied it to very old skeletons but also used his knowledge for criminal cases. (From the cover of the English edition of Gerassimov's book)

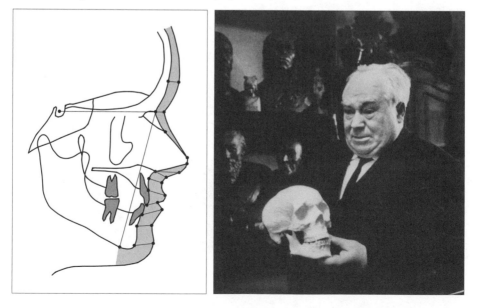

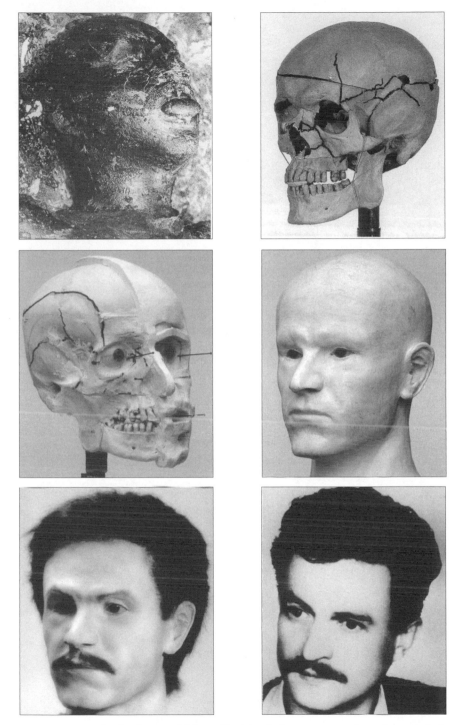

FIGURE 6 Murder in the cornfield outside Mannheim: reconstruction of the victim's appearance by Richard Helmer. F (*bottom row, right*) is a photo of the victim in life. (Photos by permission of Richard Helmer and Dieter Leopold)

FIGURE 7 Lenin's corpse (*foreground*) was preserved using an old recipe, although the winter frost was also helpful in the early stages of preservation. Behind the corpse can be seen (*left to right*) Professor Vladimir Vorobjov, head of embalming; Belinski, head of the Lenin Guard Unit; and Benjamin Gerson, Felix Dzerzhinsky's secretary. (Photo: Ilya Zbarski, Moscow/St. Petersburg)

FIGURE 8 Politicians and scientists responsible for embalming Lenin's corpse. Had they not succeeded in preserving the body after it had started to decompose, they certainly would have faced death. From left to right: (*foreground*) A. Schuravlev, B. Guerson, B. Zbarski, A. Schabadasch, A. Beliki; (*seated in 2nd row*) B. Weissbrod, W. Rozanov, K. Jatzuta, W. Tonkov, N. Melnikov-Raswedenkov, W. Worobjov, F. Dzerzhinsky, R. Peterson, A. Jenukidse, K. Voroschilov; (*back row*) unidentified. (Photo: Ilya Zbarski, Moscow/St. Petersburg)

FIGURE 9 Lindbergh's estate in Hopewell, from which little Charles was abducted. The boy's room was on the second floor (*arrow*). (Photo: UPI/Bilderberg)

FIGURE 10 George Parker and his little brother selling small replicas of the ladder from the Lindbergh case during the trial. (Photo: Corbis)

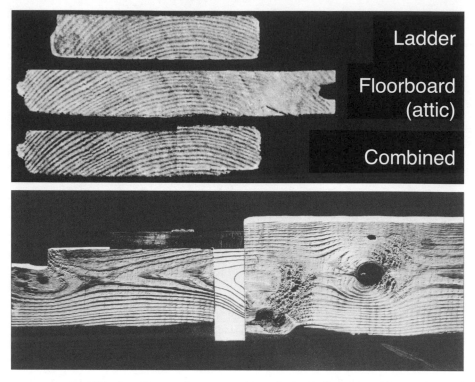

FIGURE 11 (*top*) Wood profiles were important evidence in the Lindbergh case. The tree rings and the grain of the wood of the ladder exactly match those of the floorboards found in Bruno Hauptmann's attic. (Photos from U.S. Forest Products Laboratory, Madison, WI; composite by Mark Benecke)

FIGURE 12 (*middle*) The wood grain from the ladder corresponds to pieces from the floor. In the middle, a missing piece (drawn by hand) connects the two ends. (Photo: U.S. Forest Products Laboratory, Madison, WI)

FIGURE 13 A gold certificate like that from the Lindbergh ransom. These certificates look very like today's dollar bills and could, in theory, be exchanged for gold from the U.S. Treasury. During the Depression, however, they were collected by the Treasury and not recirculated because they could no longer be exchanged for gold. (Photo: Federal Reserve Bank of San Francisco)

FIGURE 14 The parents of Jeffrey Dahmer (his father, Lionel, and his stepmother, Shari) during the sentencing of their son. They both showed incredulity and perplexity during the trial. Lionel Dahmer wrote a fine book describing his confusion but admitting that Jeffrey shared some of his characteristics in a more extreme form. (Photo: AP/Rick Wood/Pool)

FIGURE 15 Paul Bernardo and Karla Homolka seemed like a nice and intelligent couple. That allowed them to make friends with their juvenile victims before abusing them. Karla's mother considered Paul Bernardo to be the dream son-in-law. (Photo: *The Toronto Sun*)

FIGURE 16 Paul and Karla's house in a quiet neighborhood. For years, luck and mishandled evidence permitted them to kill three girls. These crimes robbed many Canadians of their trust in the police force. (Photo: Alan Wallace, © Mark Benecke)

FIGURE 17 This bench reportedly was a favorite place of Kristin French, a victim of Bernardo and Homolka. The city put up a memorial stone. (Photo: Alan Wallace, © Mark Benecke)

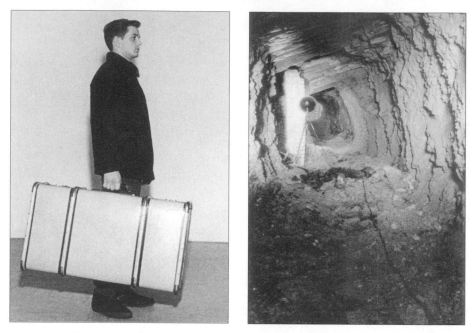

FIGURE 18 Jürgen Bartsch with his suitcase, dubbed a "children's coffin" by people who saw him carrying it around. He was dressed like this when he walked around carrying the suitcase, engaging boys in conversation and luring them to an old mine shaft. (Photo: Staats-Archiv NRW, Original case files; reproduction, Mark Benecke)

FIGURES 19 & 20 Pictures from the Bartsch case. When it became known that the corpses of three boys had been found in this mine shaft, the public came to see the site of the murders. These pictures (*top right and below*) show the shaft with its entrance at the time of the investigation. (Photos: Staats-Archiv NRW,Original case files; reproduction, Mark Benecke)

FIGURES 21 & 22 Today, the entrance to the shaft has been walled up and blocked by a huge steel barrier, ostensibly to prevent cars from hitting the hill. (Photos: Mark Benecke)

FIGURE 23 On June 11, 1964, Walter Seifert stood outside this classroom of the school in Volkhoven, a part of Cologne. The black spots on the wall opposite the window show that the flames reached all the way across the room (*arrow*). (Photo: Case files/Mark Benecke)

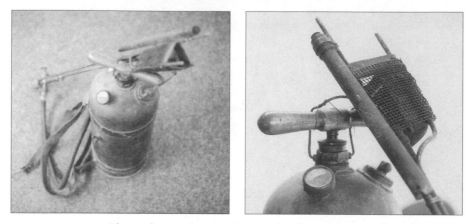

FIGURES 24 & 25 The garden sprayer reconfigured as a flame-thrower. Seifert built all the flame-thrower parts himself. (Courtesy of Cologne Police HQ; Photos: Mark Benecke)

FIGURE 26 The tip of the spear Seifert fashioned skillfully from a triangular scraper. (Courtesy of Cologne Police HQ; Photo: Mark Benecke)

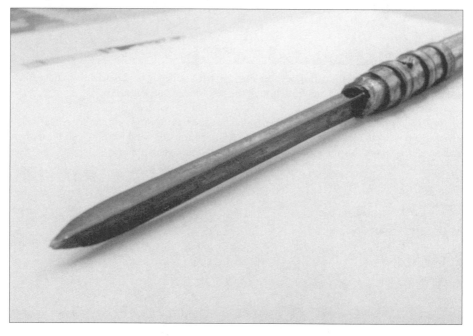

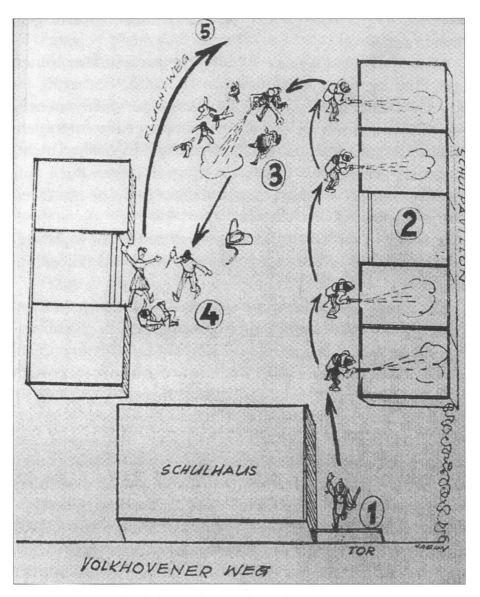

FIGURE 27 Diagram of Seifert's route: (1) From the gate (*Tor*) next to the stone school building (*Schulhaus*), he ran to the wooden annex (*Schulpavillon*, 2), shooting the flame-thrower through the windows into the classrooms. In front of the annex, he stabbed a teacher, Frau Bollenrat. Then he ran toward Frau Langohr's physical education class (3) and used the flame-thrower against them. From there, he ran to the other pavilion (4), where he killed teacher Frau Kuhr. His escape route (*Fluchtweg*, 5) led through an open field toward a railroad embankment. (Drawing by Haehn)

FIGURE 28 Karl Denke's rented apartment was inside this house. (Reproduction of an old photo by Mark Benecke)

FIGURE 29 Inside Denke's apartment. (Reproduction of an old photo by Mark Benecke)

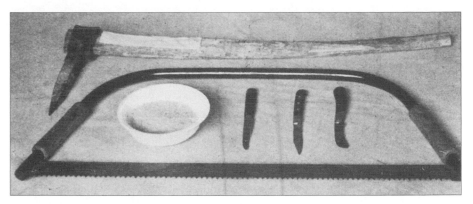

FIGURE 30 Karl Denke's murder tools. (Reproduction of an old photo by Mark Benecke)

FIGURES 31–33 Pieces of human flesh, human teeth, and suspenders and straps made out of human skin, as found in Denke's room. (Reproductions of old photos by Mark Benecke)

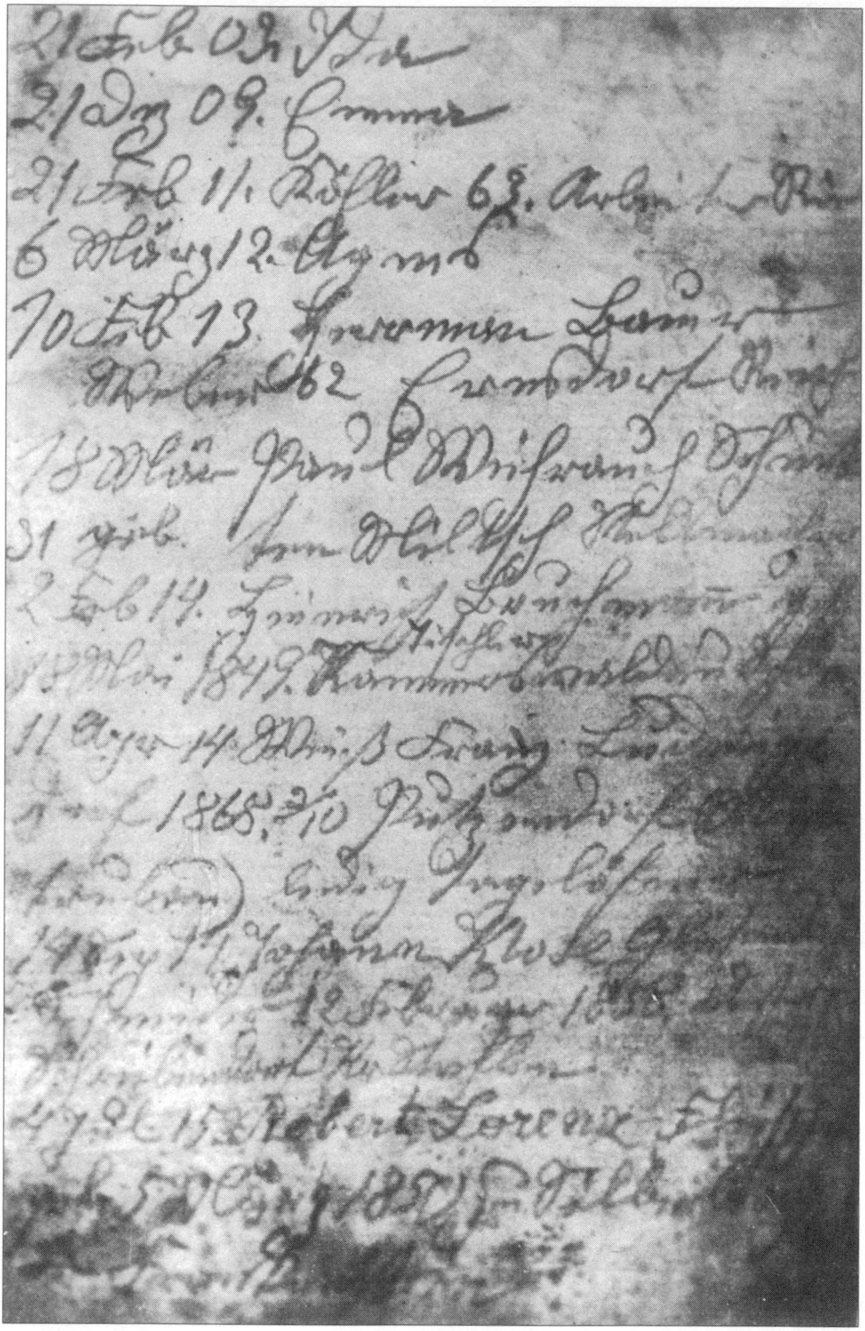

FIGURE 34 Denke's record of his victims, listing their names, ages, and weights.

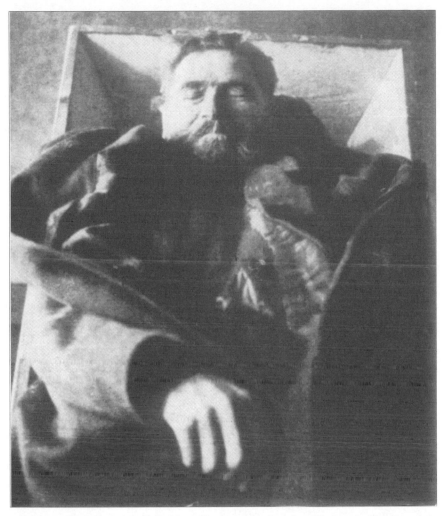

FIGURE 35 Karl Denke's body in his coffin. (Reproduction of an old photo by Mark Benecke)

FIGURE 36 This front page from the *Neues Münchener Tagblatt* (*Munich Daily News*) shows Kneissl as he appeared in court.

FIGURE 37 Robber Kneissl was erroneously fashioned into a Robin Hood–like hero, although he was in no way heroic. Later on, his story inspired novels. This one is called *Hiesel: A Thief but Still a Hero*. The young lady at his side is a more realistic figure. (Pamphlet from the collection of the library of the University Cologne; photo: Mark Benecke)

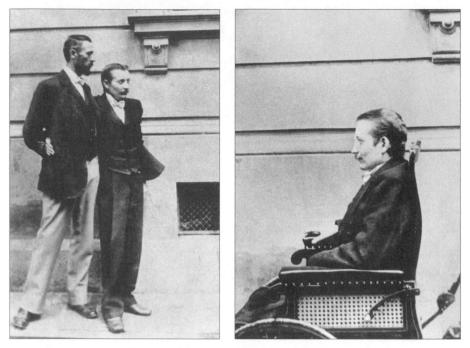

FIGURES 38 & 39 In reality Kneissl (*person on right and in wheelchair*) was much less dashing: A winter spent out in the woods and the wounds inflicted by the police when he was taken into custody clearly left their marks. (Reproduced from original photos by Michael Farin, Munich)

CHAPTER 5

WITNESSES, PUBLICITY,
AND DEAD SILENCE

It is surprising that so few crimes of the twentieth century are still vivid in the public's memory. In Germany, the most prominent are the murders committed by Fritz Haarmann in Hannover. His conversations with a psychiatrist were made into a movie in 1995. During Germany's economically hard times in the 1920s, Haarmann lived with his homosexual partner in a minuscule apartment. Haarmann, who was seen as a weakling, picked up boys at the railroad station, lured them into his tiny flat, and killed them. He then sold their clothes to his neighbors. He would also sell their flesh as meat. To this day, people in Germany remember a song about "Haarmann's little axe," which he used for his killings. In Britain, everyone knows of Jack the Ripper's crimes, even if no one actually knows who he was. A veritable industry of films and books continue to analyze and hypothesize about these brutal murders. In the United States the murders by Charles Manson's "family" likewise continue to horrify new generations.

Today, other crimes that created a great deal of excitement at the time, like Haarmann's, have been forgotten. Among these are the astonishing crimes of Peter Kürten, the Dusseldorf Vampire, which we looked at in chapter 4. Considering how extraordinary they were, you might imagine that his name would live on, but it seems not to. The same happened to the crimes of the robber Kneissl, who is remembered only in Bavaria.

From our vantage point, we can enumerate the elements of a criminal case that will make it remembered for generations: powerful emotions, mixed-up personal relationships, and, best of all, a good measure of sex, as we saw in the case of Pastor Geyer. If the case affronts common decency and morality, if it is sensational and somehow conflicts with the current culture, it will be remembered. Also necessary are legal proceedings that are picked up by the media and have nationwide impact. This is the only way in which the public at large can get a glimpse of written evidence. Take as a counterexample the case of Karl Denke, described later in this chapter: Certainly, it is one of the most terrible crimes in German history. But it has no element of sex, and there was no media coverage of the legal proceedings, which is probably why most people have never heard of this cannibalistic serial murderer.

In this chapter, I will juxtapose a few very well-known cases and a few that are less known or simply forgotten. You will probably agree that you don't really need a sexual slant to make a case interesting.

The O. J. Simpson Case

Arguably, the most famous murder story of the late twentieth century was the killing of Nicole Brown, the former wife of the football star O. J. Simpson, and her friend Ron Goldman. The public took a great deal of interest in this crime because it was the result of a simple human relationship turned upside down. A man of great physical strength, who was known to be extremely jealous and egotistical as well as violent, kills a person who was very close to him, together with her friend, in front of her house. In so doing, he leaves behind samples of his own blood and transports some of his victim's blood into his own bedroom. An open-and-shut case, you might think.

But this was by no means so. Take constant print and broadcast coverage, public expectations, lawyers' tricks, weaknesses of the prosecution, and advice from business-oriented counsel in the background, stir this concoction, and you wind up with the O. J. Simpson case—a modern parable.

First, there were the normal criminal proceedings, in which O. J. was acquitted, to the consternation of many of the people involved. Then there was the second trial, a civil suit, that had a very different result. Simpson was found liable to the tune of $33.5 million.

This entertaining story also shows the extent to which people can exercise poor judgment in legal proceedings if they are too certain of their arguments. In this case, the prosecution thought they had sufficient irrefutable evidence that a jury would not even consider an acquittal. But the men and women who had been chosen for the jury were more interested in prejudices than facts. Defense attorneys knew only too well how to play on human emotions in the criminal case.

The Facts

On June 12, 1994, O. J. Simpson's ex-wife, Nicole Brown, was brutally murdered, together with her friend Ron Goldman, between 10:10 P.M. and 10:30 P.M. Their bodies were found lying in a very large pool of blood close to the entrance of Nicole's house in Los Angeles. There were no surviving witnesses except the killer himself and a dog that had walked near the front yard, only to return to his master. O. J. refused to talk, and the dog couldn't.

However, the genetic fingerprints carried a lot of information: On Nicole Brown's lot, DNA samples were secured from seven different locations. Of particular importance were drops of O. J. Simpson's blood that were found on the path in front of the house. Only 1 in 170 million people would match the DNA configuration as it was found here. Simpson claimed that he had cut a finger on a piece of broken glass by the sink in a hotel. The resulting wound on his finger was still bleeding the day after, and that must be why it was found in the location where the bodies had been found.

A good deal of time was wasted on attempts to clear up this odd story— quite unnecessarily from a forensic point of view. It turns out that in and around O. J.'s home, in Brentwood, a different part of Los Angeles, blood samples were also found. Several traces indicated that O. J. was bleeding in his ex-wife's home and that he had transported her blood samples to his own home. That would not be explained by his bleeding finger. The most telling detail was three drops of blood that were found on O. J.'s socks, in his bedroom. With a probability close to certainty (1 in 21 billion), they were from his ex-wife. In other words, only one person on Earth could have left them: Nicole Brown.

Then there was a bloodstained right-hand leather glove that was found behind a brick wall of Simpson's house. The left-hand glove was found at the crime scene. One of the most talked-about photographs from the trial shows Simpson as he attempted to demonstrate that this glove could not possibly be his because it did not fit him. Because the defendant himself was to slip it over his hand, it was not hard for him to make it appear too narrow by stretching his thumb and his little finger apart as far as he could, as court reporter Jeff Toobin of *The New Yorker* magazine surmised. But even that was not really necessary. The leather had hardened from the moisture and had shrunk. Pictures of Simpson during this scene show a mixture of astonishment, smile, incipient hope, and embarrassment.

Eleven probes of the glove material put this matter in the proper context. The blood that was found on it belonged with a likelihood of 1 in 41 billion to Ron Goldman. Again, no other person on Earth would fit this DNA sample.

A bloody footprint completed the evidence on a macroscopic scale. Simpson owned a pair of very expensive Bruno Magli shoes; its impressions were identical with those found at the crime scene. Not only that, they were size 12, which is rare. The whole case was quite airtight: There was O. J.'s well-known jealousy; there was a long, aimless drive that could be seen as flight before the arrest; and there were several notifications to the police of his violent behavior toward his ex-wife. In the second trial, the civil suit, all this evidence was presented. Unfortunately, the criminal trial wound up as a kind of circus where the truth was never pulled from its many entanglements. These can be attributed not only to the lawyers but in equal measure to the police and the expert witnesses with their overly slow and overly fast conclusions.

The Experts

By the time of the Simpson trial, it was too late to register qualifying remarks against the reliability of DNA samples. This was a problem for the defense, given that the prosecution wanted to proceed as simply as possible. In this effort, they meant to rely mainly on genetic fingerprints and only a few other items of evidence.

Even Eric Lander from the Massachusetts Institute of Technology (MIT), who had testified in the late 1980s against a hasty use of blood samples for fixing probabilities by means of DNA analysis, was now of one mind with Bruce Budowle, the head of the FBI's DNA lab: "The battle over the validity of genetic fingerprints is a matter of the past."

Previous discussions about this matter had led to many improvements. Regular lab tests and computer-generated progress reports that document every step of an evaluation ensure that possible mistakes can be seen immediately.

It was unfortunate that, by sheer coincidence, the case of police chemist Fred Zain's fraudulent testimony in November 1993 became public knowledge. The lab tests from his blood sample equipment in West Virginia and Texas were freely invented. He had simply assumed that a suspect in a trial is the culprit. He also invented the expert opinions that, unsurprisingly, always wound up proving the guilt of the defendant.

Zain's colleagues had noted as early as 1985 that he seemed to read his results from an empty test plate. This primitive method of deceit couldn't last, given that every scientific finding must be replicated for verification. In 1987, when one lab test was challenged and had to be repeated, it became clear he was a fraud. All his expert testimony, given over a number of years, had to be rescinded.

This meant that U.S. courts had to revisit some 134 court cases in which Zain had acted as an expert witness. In one case, Zain's freely invented test results led to a sentence of 203 to 335 years in prison for a Huntington, West Virginia, man accused of armed robbery and sexual assault. After he had served 4 years in jail, Zain's test results were successfully refuted, and the sentence was annulled. Fortunately, the lying expert witness had not been involved in any death penalty cases. Fortunately, U.S. courts demand more conclusive evidence in such cases. Expertise on a blood sample or

A Bloody Shoeprint

In the O.J. Simpson case, a bloody trail of shoeprints led away from the corpses in the direction of the street. This track had its own exciting history.

On its left were a number of blood drops that matched O.J.'s genetic fingerprint. Because O.J.'s left hand had been cut, this was evidence that the shoeprints were his. If they were, it meant that he had walked through the dead people's blood on the ground. He strongly denied this.

The prosecution asked William Bodziak, an FBI expert on shoeprints, for help. He measured the bloody tracks and came up with eighteen different points of proof that the sole of the shoes—model Lorenzo, size 12—had been produced by Italian shoe designer Bruno Magli. To make sure there was no mistake, Bodziak flew to Italy in February 1995 to go to the designer and look for other shoe models in Bologna. This permitted him to confirm unequivocally that the tracks at the crime scene were made by soles produced by a company called Silga, of the type U-2887. And those were used for the Bruno Magli shoes, corresponding exactly to the tracks found at the crime scene in Los Angeles.

Lorenzo shoes were expensive, at about $200 a pair, but that presented no problem for Simpson. In the United States, there were only forty shops where this fancy Italian model was sold. In addition, it turned out that in the years 1991 to 1993 only 299 pairs of the Lorenzo model had been sold. O.J. denied ever having bought such ugly shoes, but a number of photographs were published that showed him wearing several different types of Bruno Magli shoes.

A shoeprint similar to those on the ground was also found on the back of Nicole Brown's dead body. That, said the prosecution, showed how the woman died. The murderer had put one of his feet on the victim's back, pulled her head up by her hair, and then used a knife to cut deeply into her neck. Even the scandal-mongering press put a black mark over the cut in its published illustration.

DNA structure is never accepted as the sole piece of evidence when a death sentence is possible,

The debacle of Dr. Zain's fraudulent testimony should have been sufficient to call into question the prosecutor's experts in the Simpson case. But early in the game it became clear that Simpson's defense was unable to exploit this connection. The blood samples had been tested by labs that had insisted on controlled and repeated tests of all their results. There was no way to exploit that angle in his defense.

Simpson's defense team used a different strategy to make the experts appear less convincing. They used plainly worded arguments and colorful illustrations to make their own findings understandable to the jury; then they used endless requests for further explanation of details that, in the end, none of the jurors was able to follow. After hours of further interrogation of the experts, the scientifically untrained jurors found themselves confused, and they stopped listening.*

In this way, the defense managed to push the scientifically definitive DNA evidence into the never-never land of the jurors' brains after they had tuned out.

Jury Versus Prosecutor

So who was on the jury in the O. J. Simpson case? And what connection is there to the outcome of the criminal proceedings? Let us look at the way in which a jury is selected.

In the O. J. Simpson case, which the defense had deemed hopeless, this game was played to the hilt. In the beginning, a fair number of people wanted to be part of such a prominent trial. Robert Shapiro, one of the most famous trial lawyers in the United States, asked Jo-Ellen Dimitrius, a well-known expert in jury selection, to help him find jurors who would be likely to follow his drumbeat.

Neither Shapiro nor Dimitrius trusted healthy human intellect in a jury pool, so they conducted a general survey of how people would be inclined to decide in a case such as O. J. Simpson's. They did not try to bias the survey. Initially, they did not ask why respondents felt as they did; they were interested only in the answers needed to reach the final goal of freeing O. J., not caring about the specific reasons.

---

* I have witnessed similar occurrences in the Manhattan Criminal Court. During a trial, I noticed that some members of the jury were fast asleep.

As it happens, prosecutor Marcia Clark dealt the defense team a very good card. Before jury selection she declared that she would not ask for the death penalty. As a result, the defense could immediately rule out all prospective jurors who, after having been provisionally selected, mentioned that they would vote for the death penalty if needed. It is well known that such people are more likely to vote in favor of a guilty verdict even in cases of severe doubt. Such people make up a dream jury for the prosecution. In this early selection step, which eliminated the hardliners, the prosecution lost its best allies.

In addition, the first survey showed that jurors of color would be likely to vote to acquit O. J., a black man. Prosecutor Marcia Clark didn't see matters this way. In fact, she insisted that black women in the jury would stand by her, given that black women often are beaten up by their husbands. That, she thought, would keep them from being lenient in a case against a man who was known for his violence against women.

Notwithstanding her prejudices, prosecutor Clark asked for the help of a consulting firm called Decision-Quest in jury selection. Five men and five women, six of them white and four black, were read parts of what was to be expected in the court presentation. She was amazed to find that the women's vote differed from what she had assumed: All black women voted against a guilty verdict for O. J., and all white women were in favor. Furthermore, neither side could be moved from its initial reaction, which appeared to be related to their skin color. The hypothesis that black women would make up a dream jury for the prosecution was disproved.

But Clark wasn't ready to concede. She told this test group to assume that blood found close to the dead bodies probably was O. J.'s and that one of his gloves was found at the crime scene. Again, all jurors of color were unimpressed. Three of the four black candidates voted not guilty in favor of O. J. The prosecutor started to pull her hair.

But things got worse as the Decision-Quest team continued its experiments. "You can't assume a man is a murderer just because he beats up his wife once in a while" was the opinion of the black jurors. "Every relationship has low points, and that means there will be some beating. That's life!" When the consulting firm made things even more specific and asked for number grades for O. J. and Nicole Brown, O. J. was given an average of 9.5 out of a possible 10 points of sympathy. His ex-wife got about 5. The fake jury considered defense lawyer Robert Shapiro "smart," "ready to pounce at the right moment," and "witty". Prosecutor Clark rated far worse. She was called "shifty," "strident," "deceitful," "unpleasant," and "a bitch."

Marcia Clark couldn't believe what she saw. She kept the faith in the good judgment of a real jury in the actual trial. That was one of the biggest mistakes she made in her career. But she didn't come to pay for her regrets. Right after the trial, she quit her job and made several million dollars from publishing a book about the O. J. Simpson case.

Be that as it may, the official jury selection started on September 26, 1994. Judge Lance Ito had asked for a jury pool of 900 people for the first round. When he declared that the members of the jury would receive no more than $6 per day and that they would have to live away from home for the duration of the trial, most candidates decided not to be available. After all, few employers in the United States compensate absent employees for jury duty.

Worse, Judge Ito frightened the jury pool: "I have never seen a case as unusual as this one," he said. "This is perhaps the most important decision you will make in your own personal life." This was nonsense, but it was good enough to frighten off those who had some doubts or those who were simply timid.

The judge dismissed everybody who had had enough after his initial talk. All they had to do to go free was to enter on the questionnaire that their employer would not pay them or that they had "private reasons" not to participate. Four days later the pool of possible jurors was down to 304, from which 12 jurors and 12 alternates had to be chosen.

This opened the door to questioning by the defense and the prosecution. They had assembled a total of 294 questions to ask the pool. For example, they asked, "Have you ever slept with a person of different skin color?" "Have you ever tried to get an autograph from a 'star'?" And then there were brief essay questions: "Where do you see the origin of using physical force in the family?" "Why is participation in sports activities good for the human character?" This resulted in a sea of ink and paper, and the O. J. trial sucked up time and public attention.

The defense did well during jury selection. White, educated men in the jury pool resented all the questioning by the prosecution. They left voluntarily, so that as early as October 12 the pool consisted of fully one-half black jurors, three-quarters of whom were women. Given the fact that the black population of the United States was only 11 percent and that black women constituted the least promising jury candidates, Marcia Clark didn't realize what was coming her way.

All the while, defense attorney Johnnie Cochran, who together with Robert Shapiro made up a black and white team, became quite proficient at handling the media. "We have the impression that the prosecution is trying to eliminate jurors of color—and their reason is simply that these people are black and that they like black heroes and one of these heroes is O. J. Simpson." This endless circular reasoning paid off for the defense. "The prosecution is taking aim at black jurors," read the title page of the *Los Angeles Times* the next morning. This trial was not just a matter of proof or denial but also of the skin color of the accused. Time and time again, the defense team was able to impute racial bias to the Los Angeles Police Department (LAPD). They suggested that the police probably had thrown Simpson's glove over the garden wall in order to plant evidence against him (which was not true). No matter how senseless this was, given all the evidence against O. J., the jurors were shaken in their perceptions and reverted to their preconceived notion: O. J. was a good man, incapable of killing anybody.

By the last week of the trial, the strain on the jury's forbearance was such that ten jurors had opted out, to be replaced by alternates. In the end, twelve people voted on O. J. Simpson's culpability. In his book *The Ruin of His Life*, Jeffrey Toobin, journalist and staff writer for *The New Yorker*, sums up some features that characterize them:

> None of them read a newspaper regularly.
> Just two of them had finished college.
> Not one of them had been to graduate school.
> All of them, with no exception, voted for the Democratic party.
> Five of them had—either themselves, or through members of their families—had bad experiences with the police.
> Five were of the opinion that it was perfectly okay to use force here and there in the family.
> Nine of them were convinced O. J. could not possibly kill his wife, given that he had been a top-notch football player.

The Police

The police unintentionally helped the defense to make racism—in itself irrelevant in this case—an object of the proceedings. The LAPD was well known for handling blacks insensitively, even more so when they were poor. Cochran and Shapiro had their work cut out for them; after all, O. J., was an exception to the rule. Although he pretended differently later on, Simpson had never shown any interest in black people's problems, and he had always been treated well by the police. He had invited some LAPD members to parties at his house, and his invitations had always been accepted gladly.

Still, their search for instances of racial prejudice proved successful. One of the local police investigators turned out to be a fitting sacrificial lamb:

the pompous Mark Fuhrman, who was called to the witness stand on March 9, 1995.

Nobody, not even Cochran and Shapiro, could have foreseen that Fuhrman would wind up being the trump card for the defense. He was living proof that the LAPD happily practiced redneck racism and was even self-congratulatory about it. The defense didn't care that Fuhrman had played only a small part in the early investigations of the O. J. Simpson case. The surprise element that was played up later left no room to the prosecution or the judge to explain to the jury that the affair involving Fuhrman was nothing but a big and unexpected distraction.

In the beginning, all went well. As he testified, Fuhrman appeared to be a run-of-the-mill police officer who was interested in clearing up the facts of the case, not adding to the circus atmosphere of the trial. He did know that a real estate agent had shown up to talk to the defense team about the Officer Fuhrman she remembered. Several times in 1985 and 1986 he visited friends of his not far from her office. On one of these occasions he told her that he always made a point of stopping a "nigger" if he saw him sitting next to a white woman. In boasting about it, he was clearly admitting that he was prejudiced. He then told the agent that it would be wonderful if all "niggers" were rounded up and killed, maybe by a bomb exploding in their midst.

This story had been reported in the newspapers long before. That gave an appearance of careful strategy on the part of the defense team, which otherwise played up every hint of racism before the jury. When one of O. J.'s lawyers asked Fuhrman whether he might have smeared some of the victim's blood on O. J.'s glove only to throw it behind the house, everybody present thought this was nothing but a bad joke. For one thing, Fuhrman didn't know whether O. J. was in the country when the murders occurred. Second, he would have been concerned about the possibility of contracting HIV from blood samples of unknown origin. Finally, there were other investigators close by who certainly would not have permitted such evidence tampering. Then, when Fuhrman was asked whether in the last 10 years he had used the word *nigger* when describing people, he denied it vehemently and swore to the fact. Fuhrman clearly was taking a risk, but at worst it was his word against that of a real estate agent.

Fuhrman Loses

Four months after Fuhrman's first appearance in court, an anonymous phone call was placed to Johnnie Cochran's office. A writer named Laura Hart McKinny had conducted an interview with Fuhrman in 1985, trying to learn more about investigative work in general. She then wrote an article about how hard things were for newly hired women in the LAPD. In the interview Fuhrman told her immediately that police work was no job for a woman. The two of them met several times for similar conversations.

On April 2, 1985, McKinny recorded conversations with Fuhrman. She promised him $10,000 for any insider information he might pass on, and she was particularly interested in his misogynous tirades. She transcribed all the tapes of her 12-hour conversations and sent copies to Fuhrman. She also asked women on the police force about their experiences in the LAPD. That was turned into a television script, which was ultimately not selected for broadcast.

On July 28, 1995, O. J.'s lawyers got hold of these tapes. They couldn't have dreamed up anything better. Fuhrman was swearing and frequently using the word *nigger.* The lawyers couldn't publish the text because the tapes were not admitted as evidence in the trial. So a writer named Larry Schiller, a man who didn't mind dirty work as long as it might help O. J., took care of this angle.

Schiller had written a book called *I Want to Tell You* for O. J. In this book, published in 1995, Simpson tells his fans from jail what a wonderful family man he was and how he could never kill another human being. It is notable that this book does not address the question of what O. J. did at the time of the murders. Rather, this absurd literary and pictorial concoction includes many letters he received in jail and many photographs of his family.

To counter the allegations that O. J. beat up his wife repeatedly, Schiller (ghost-writing for Simpson) quotes a letter he received in jail from someone called J. Miller: "Mr. Simpson, one thing I wanted to say, everyone is focusing on the alleged abuse you inflicted on your ex-wife. No one has mentioned the abused she inflicted on you. . . . I commend you for striking out at something else and not at her."

After this book appeared, author Schiller, now in possession of the Fuhrman tapes, had a new task. He fed to the media parts of the Fuhrman interviews. Leaking the information was illegal, but the defense saw this as an unimportant technicality compared with the many dirty tricks that were used on both sides. Because no one wanted the trial to fall apart over such technicalities, it was worth the risk of leaking information.

On August 14, the tapes were played for the judge. While Judge Ito listened, he heard that in his voluble talks Fuhrman had made offensive remarks about Mrs. Ito, who had been his superior in the LAPD 10 years earlier. Strictly speaking, Judge Ito should have recused himself. After all, there was a danger that he would not deal objectively with a witness who had offensive things to say about his wife. On the other hand, had Ito thrown the tapes out, he would have to suppress evidence already brought to the proceedings. That would have resulted in a mistrial, and the prosecution would have to start anew. Ito therefore decided that he need not recuse himself, despite the offensive remarks about his wife. But the tapes were not played publicly once the jury and the people directly involved had heard them.

That was not what the defense had in mind. They wanted to influence not just the jury but the public. If there was a broad recognition that Fuhrman was a bad cop, no juror would be able to vote against O. J. without having to suffer the consequences at home later on. In only 2 weeks Cochran and Shapiro, with help from the media, had pushed Judge Ito into a corner. He now permitted the publication of the tapes, and that meant that the trial was lost for the prosecution as the jury heard the following:

> Two of my buddies were shot and ambushed, policemen. Both alive, and I was the first unit on the scene. Four suspects ran into a second story in an apartment project—apartment. We kicked the door down. We grabbed a girl that lived there, one of their girlfriends. Grabbed her by the hair and stuck a gun to her head and used her as a barricade. . . .
>
> Anyway, we basically tortured them. There were four policemen, four guys. We broke 'em. Numerous bones in each one of them. Their faces were just mush. They had pictures on the walls, there was blood all the way to the ceiling with finger marks like they were trying to crawl out of the room. They showed us pictures of the room. It was unbelievable, there was blood everywhere. All the walls, all the furniture, all the floor. These guys, they had to shave so much hair off, one guy they shaved it all off. Like seventy stitches in his head. . . . We had 'em begging that they'd never be gang members again, begging us. So with sixty-six allegations, I had a demonstration in front of Hollenbeck station, chanting my name. . . . That's where the Internal Affairs investigation started. It lasted eighteen months. I was on a photo lineup. . . . I was picked out by twelve people. So I was pretty proud of that. . . . They didn't get any of our unit—thirty-eight guys—they didn't get one day [of docked pay]. I didn't get one day. . . . I mean, you don't shoot a policeman. That's all there is to it.

Unfortunately, this story was true. And that is why tape recordings of utterances of a racist, brutally macho police officer who perjured himself in court, who broke the law while on duty, who took hostages without any justification—all of which had nothing whatever to do with O. J. Simpson—decided this case. One-time football star, actor, and playboy O. J. Simpson was acquitted on October 3, 1995, at 10 A.M. Thus ended the trial of a suspect accused of murdering his ex-wife and her friend, who was only trying to return her sunglasses, which she had left in the restaurant where she dined with her parents and O. J.

When the jury left the courtroom, most were crying and hugging each other. Then there was just silence and rigidity, a result of the tremendous pressure they had been exposed to, all the while far from their families.

One of the female jurors broke the silence: "Let's make sure we protect ourselves." And that was the end of this particular show—at least for the time being. In December 2001, O. J., who had lost most of his friends in the meantime, was in the news again. After a 2-year investigation (dubbed Operation X by the FBI) he once again had to open the door to the police. He was accused of working with a smuggling ring importing Ecstasy from the Netherlands and trying to sell data that had been illegally downloaded from TV satellites.

Shortly before, on October 24, 2001, he had been found guilty in a minor proceeding in Miami. O. J. had pulled the sunglasses from the face of a driver who had not respected his right of way. In so doing he had scratched both the sunglasses and the man's face.

Witnesses

Most jurors and witnesses have a problem in common when in court: They have no experience evaluating dry scientific evidence. How would they? In most people's daily life, it is not facts that count but opinions, feelings, personal interests, and zest for life. In court proceedings, most people without a legal background show more interest in what they perceive as the character of the accused rather than the facts of a case. That is only natural.

Unfortunately, this opens the door to the practice of bringing into the court proceedings a confusing mixture of assumptions. We showed this in the Lindbergh case. Recall that examination of a piece of wood in a ladder showed clearly that Hauptmann was the culprit. Still, simply by omitting and twisting some of the evidence it was possible to create the impression that he was nothing but a small-time miscreant who had accidentally slid into the investigation.

In the same fashion, it would be difficult to appreciate the facts in the case of the killing of Pastor Geyer's wife if there weren't solid pieces of evidence. For instance, consider his girlfriend's assumption as told to the German magazine *Stern:* "If he did it, he pushed it out of his mind. He has always fled from reality in threatening situations, even if those were of his own making. I know that he had been contemplating her death before. When I heard about the crime, I thought, he finally got what he wanted." And the pastor maintained that he was innocent.

Many people would accept his girlfriend's remarks as incriminating. But why should we take the assumption of his lover more seriously than the pastor's declaration of innocence?

For someone who wants to keep a clear perspective, personal statements are nothing but a small part of the mosaic that makes up a complicated case. If there are scientifically clear pieces of evidence, it is better to forget all personal opinions. After all, their veracity often is very hard to prove.

By concentrating on factual proof, a jury usually can save itself sleepless nights. It is up to the judge to evaluate opinions and character quality when he or she decides on sentencing.

Let us not forget that it is not always possible to evaluate witnesses' opinions and observations. Recall the case of Manuela Schneider, in which children managed to confuse the investigators with their freely invented statements.

Similarly, the Geyer case contains an impressive scene of this kind. One witness stated that he saw the pastor in a location close to where his wife's body was found, at the critical time. Consider this report in the German paper *Berliner Zeitung:*

Geyer's defense attorney, Börner, said about the many witnesses who attested to having seen him either with or without his wife on the day in question, "None of them has consciously said a falsehood." But for identification purposes, they were shown only pictures of Reverend and Mrs. Geyer. This helped to make their recollection more and more precise the more they heard about the case.

The witness who attested to having seen the pastor at the critical location was considered the most reliable by the prosecution. He made a whole string of precise observations in just a couple of seconds. "That is more than an observational genius would be capable of," said the defense lawyer.

Maybe the defense was mistaken but the witness had been paying attention. Take these comments from a Frankfurt newspaper:

A fifty-six-year-old pharmacist said he observed Pastor Geyer on the day his wife disappeared close to the location where her body was found two days later. As he drove by, he noticed a red vw station wagon parked on a side path. He was a hunter looking for an acquaintance. But the only person he saw was "a man with a receding hairline who looked at me in a way that took me aback."

The witness continued that he had the impression that that person appeared to be highly agitated. Although he had no more than two seconds of observation through his car window, he saw the profile of the man standing behind his car.

When questioned by the police, that witness had originally stated he wasn't quite sure whether he could identify the man. However, when he saw him six weeks later during the initial proceedings, he was quite certain, and he picked Geyer from a line-up of seven people of similar appearance.

The question of whether witnesses or jurors are reliable has been much discussed by psychologists. Recent results from a study at Cornell University confirm that the most explicit exhortations don't necessarily make a jury open-minded and dispassionate. The Cornell psychologists showed that repeated instructions to look at nothing but the facts and weigh them against one another had little effect. As in the first O. J. Simpson case, the jurors had made up their minds before the proceedings started.

In our daily lives, it is usually accepted that we rely on what we have learned over years rather than weigh facts presented in a particular case and come to conclusions. Otherwise, we would not be able to make decisions quickly. But the rules of decision making are different in court proceedings than in shopping, chatting, or driving around, so most modern nations prefer to leave the necessary decisions to professional judges rather than laypeople.

Our perceptions are particularly sensitive when there is an appearance of supernatural influences. Time and again, young people with a sick craving for notoriety have managed to hoodwink many others. That can happen only if our fears—or hopes—of things from the "other side" are stimulated long enough to make the ordinary citizen forget about his or her healthy, normal perceptions.

Take lawyer Herbert Schaefer, who spent years in Germany fighting "otherworldly happenings" that were arranged by a 15-year-old boy. In the beginning, the boy just arranged rocks on top of a door in his grandmother's apartment. Whenever the door moved, the rocks fell down. Perhaps they were the actions of a poltergeist?

Then he threw rocks through the window from the outside at night, but he told everybody he was inside when it happened. In the basement of the shop where he worked, he destroyed large amounts of china simply by stacking it at skewed angles so that it appeared to fall down without reason. Sometimes, when no one was looking, he simply threw broken pieces of china onto the shelves. Even firefighters who came to check the building were convinced these were otherworldly happenings. Schaefer, who proudly called himself a ghost-buster, remarked, "Selective attention and unconscious fears, together, make people blind."

The famous stage magician Harry Houdini performed dangerous tricks and succeeded at times only by bribing key bystanders (such as police officers, who carefully chose the manacles they handed him). One of his best-known tricks was to step into a big tank, which was tightly locked with keys and filled with water right up to the brim. Minutes later, Houdini stepped out, beaming. Onlookers who believed in miracles were convinced that Houdini was a sorcerer. Even Houdini's friend Sir Arthur Conan Doyle was of that opinion. Houdini exposed people who, for profit, pretended to participate in transcendental séances, making himself many enemies. This behavior also broke up his friendship with Conan Doyle. From that point on, the "sorcerer" declared at the beginning of every show that the water torture trick had nothing to do with magic.

Only once did Houdini not manage to stay above the fray, and that was in Cologne in 1901. The economy was in shambles, and people were particularly sensitive when they thought they were being taken for a ride. When Houdini appeared in the Corty–Althoff Circus as the principal attraction, competitors in Circus Sidoli tried to ruin his reputation by seeing to it that the journal *Rheinische Zeitung* published this story, told by Cologne police officer Graf: "Houdini tried to bribe me with 20 reichsmarks into appearing with manacles that had been 'tested by the police.' In reality, the manacles were easy to open." In addition, the newspaper reported that Houdini was a fraud because his tricks were illusory.

Houdini successfully defended himself against the accusation of bribery. He was happy to no longer be seen as a sorcerer. The onlookers still were not convinced that the fake criminals on stage were opening their manacles on their own. But then they learned that you cannot always trust your eyes.

Our excursion into the world of witnesses, juries, and human perception ends with three cases that show basic differences from the O. J. Simpson case. These violent events occurred without any circus, without fanfare, and were quickly forgotten. The first two crimes in this category, those of Seifert and Denke, did not enter public discourse as the Simpson case did. This may have been because they were too awful to talk about, even just in water-cooler talk.

In addition, the perpetrators died soon afterward, so no urban legends or myths developed.

The third of these crimes, Kneissl's, was not quite so repugnant; that may be why, in southern Germany, it was still making the rounds as a folk tale in the late twentieth century, although it was based on crimes that occurred about 100 years earlier.

The Seifert Case

There are cases that can no longer be evaluated by criminalists, but their evidence is quite plain. With a little imagination, you can even discern the culprit's motives. Consider the Seifert case, which kept a good part of the city of Cologne in suspense for years. To this day, one should not mention June 11, 1964, to older residents of the Volkhoven suburb of Cologne.

Karl Kiehne, who was at that time the head of the Cologne Criminal Investigations Unit, reports, "It all happened at a Catholic elementary school in one of our suburbs. The school is protected from the street by a 5-foot-high solid wall, and has a double iron gate that leads to the entrance door. In the courtyard, on the left-hand side, there is a massive old school building. On the opposite side, there is long wooden single-floor building with four classrooms."

Such lightweight buildings generally were called "barracks," and you can still see them today. In the 1960s and 1970s, they permitted easy expansion of old schools, and sometimes they were the only buildings available.

This elementary school encompassed grades one through eight. There were seven barracks around a courtyard: four stood in a straight line on one side of the courtyard, two were connected by a little pavilion on the other side, and one stood by itself on the third side.

Investigator Kiehne continues the story:

> The four-room part of the school had black stains inside and outside; they must have been made by the heat. In the hallway, there was a puddle of blood about 2 feet across, and several bloodstains were on the floor in front of the entrance door. Facing this building across the yard was a smaller building with only two classrooms. In front of it, there are some patches of garden separated by a paved walkway that leads to the school-yard. About two yards from the entrance stairways of this pavilion, there was another puddle of blood on the ground.

While I was trying to grasp the extent of what had happened here, two 13-year-old pupils walked up to me and gave me a wooden peg that they had found by the iron entrance gate to the schoolyard. They told me what they had seen.

One of the boys had served as a school crossing guard, whose job was to see to it that the younger children could safely cross the street on their way into the schoolyard. After that, he usually went home because his own lessons were scheduled for the afternoon.

But on this day, the diligent boy came back at 9 A.M. to help dispense chocolate drinks to the students. At 9:25 A.M. he was seen, with only two helpers, in the courtyard. At the other end of this area, there was a gym class. Just as the three youngsters started to carry bottles full of the chocolate drink into the classrooms, a stranger appeared.

"At 9:30 A.M., a man came to the door of the schoolyard," a young witness told one of the investigators. "I did not know the man. He was wearing blue denims. He was carrying an insect spray canister on his back. I know this kind of thing from our own garden. The man entered through the small door, which could not be locked because the lock was broken. He had a big wooden peg that he pushed below that door after closing it. It had nails on its bottom. I asked him, 'What are you doing there?' But he did not answer. I thought he might be there to fix the lock. That's why I told him, 'It's about time you fixed that lock.' Again he did not answer; he just shook his head."

At that point, the man (whose name was Walter Seifert and who was within in a week of his forty-third birthday) walked up to the gym instructor, Mrs. Langohr. As he got close, he opened the valve of the insect spray gun he was carrying. The small flame that normally would burn under a protective net at the end of the sprayer now turned into a 3-foot-long flame. The teacher, already engulfed by the flames, screamed, "Fire!" She fell back into some bushes and collapsed there. The crossing guard said, "I thought that man was just pulling off a joke and that the fire was nothing but some gold spray."

But the fire was the real thing. The assailant sprayed a mixture of used motor oil and paint thinner from his pressure sprayer, which was ignited by the hot metal net, which held a functional torch. Seifert turned away from the dispersing, panicky gym class and walked back to the first barrack, the one closest to the entrance gate.

He then used a homemade iron device that was held by a chain like a sling, broke the windows of the barracks, and pointed the 18-foot flame into the full

classroom. The flame reached all the way to the opposite wall, as the scorched traces showed later.

One of the students, named Heribert, was agile enough to jump out the window, but he landed next to Seifert. When he fell to the ground after jumping, the attacker pointed the flame directly at him. The same happened to a number of children who came running out of the classroom with burning clothes, only to be sprayed again by the flame.

The boy who meant to dispense chocolate drinks later told the police, "When I saw all this, I knew that it was not some kind of joke. Together with two other boys, I pulled the wooden peg from under the little gate so it would open again. It wasn't easy to remove it. When I ran away from the school buildings, I remembered that my bicycle was still leaning against a tree in the schoolyard. So I ran back and saw the man standing by the first-grade classroom. He directed his fire spray gun into the class. So I took my bicycle and rushed to the police station as quickly as I could."

By that time, the fuel was used up, and Seifert threw the device and the empty canister on the ground (figures 24 and 25). It is probable that his short supply of the incendiary fluid saved the lives of many of the 380 children who were in the classrooms at the time.

Still, this was not the end of the horror. Seifert produced a homemade triple-edged spear (figure 26). A female teacher who ran up to Seifert was killed immediately as Seifert pushed the spear into her stomach.

Now, two additional classes that were being taught just behind the entrance of one of the pavilions were in danger. The two teachers tried to hold the door to their classroom closed, but to no avail. Seifert opened it with one strong push. One of the teachers fell down a couple of stairs into the schoolyard, where she received two stabs from the spear in her upper thigh and then a fatal stab in the back.

The murderous Seifert did not know that the peg had been removed from the courtyard entrance door; he thought he had locked himself in with this peg. So he ran to the opposite side of the schoolyard and climbed the fence, with his weapon, and fled in the direction of the railroad tracks, across a barren piece of land.

By this time, the fire brigade had arrived and began to extinguish the fire in the barracks. Meanwhile, many curious spectators had shown up; they told the police officers where Seifert had fled. The police ran after him, and he was caught immediately. Seifert resisted by turning around and trying to hit a police officer with the spear. They had to shoot him in the thigh to disable him.

The homicide squad arrived quickly, and detectives tried to get a statement from Seifert at the scene:

Q: Do you understand me? Can you speak?
A: Yes.
Q: What is your name?
A: Walter Seifert.
Q: When were you born?
A: June 19th, 1921, in Cologne.
Q: What is your occupation?
A: [unintelligible]
Q: Where do you live?
A: Volkhovener Weg [a street name, the number unintelligible, understood to be 54].
Q: Why did you do this?
A: They tried to kill me!
Q: Who?
A: The medical examiner . . . he was trying to kill me!
Q: Did you know one of the teachers?
A: No, none of them!
Q: Did you have any trouble with this school?
A: No!

Seifert's words were as confused as his thoughts. He was convinced that in 1961, doctors had caused the death of his wife, Ulla, and his newborn child. In reality, the child had been born prematurely. His wife had died soon after, at the hospital, of a venous occlusion. Since then, Seifert had carried fresh flowers to their grave regularly. "He must have loved his wife above all," a florist remarked to the police.

The emergency doctor who arrived in the meantime made sure that Seifert was taken to the hospital. His mental state went from bad to worse. Next to his incendiary equipment, a small bottle with pesticide, parathion, was found. Had Seifert taken any of it?

The police investigators did not let up. After medical treatment, they continued their questioning.

Q: Can you hear me?
A: Yes.
Q: Why did you do this?

A: [no response]

Q: Can you see me?

A: Yes.

Q: Why did you do this?

A: [no response]

Q: Did you know one of the teachers?

A: No.

Q: Did you know one of the children?

A: No.

Q: Did you know this school?

A: No.

Q: Can you tell me why you did this?

A: Yes, all of this is a bad thing.

Q: But why is it a bad thing?

A: Yes, it is a bad thing.

Q: So when did you plan this? When did you start thinking about it? For a long time, or just a short time?

A: For a long time.

Q: And why did you do it?

A: [no response]

Q: Why did you do it? Give me a reason.

A: Those damned doctors.

Q: Which doctors? Give me a name.

A: Dr. M.

Q: And?

A: Dr. C.

Q: Why, anything to do with the pension money?

A: Yes, that too, but that was not the main thing.

Q: What differences of opinion did you have?

A: [no response]

Q: Why did you go after the children?

A: Can't tell you now, it is too complicated.

Q: Will you tell me tomorrow?

A: Yes, tomorrow.

Q: Are you sorry? Are you ashamed?

A: I'll take a stand on this later. I have to take responsibility for all this.

Q: And why those children? Can't you stand children?

A: I sure can.

Q: But why then?

A: Maybe it was a depraved idea.

Q: And why those three teachers?

A: They ran toward me.

Q: You know what you did?

A: Yes, I know.

Q: So what is it that you did?

A: I built a flame-thrower.

Q: And what did you do with it?

A: I attacked people.

Q: But why? Did you attack them only with the flame-thrower, or did you have another weapon?

A: I had a spear.

Q: What did you do with the spear? Do you recall?

A: I used it to kill one of the teachers.

Q: How many people did you kill with it?

A: Three.

Q: Two or three?

A: Three [in reality it had been two].

Q: Why those people? Why those children? Why this school?

A: Pure coincidence.

Q: Are you sorry? What do you want me to tell your mother?

A: Just tell her the facts.

Q: And your brother? He has been with us.

A: Same thing.

Q: How long did you plan this action? Yesterday, the day before yesterday?

A: [Seifert shook his head]

Q: Did you attack a newspaper woman a year ago?

A: No.

Q: How long have you been planning this? For a day, for a week, for a month?

A: [no response]

Q: When did you build the spear?

A: Some eight weeks ago.

Q: And when did you built the flame-thrower?

A: Just before that.

That was all Seifert told them. At 8:30 P.M., he died of the poison he had swallowed.

For days the police didn't know what to make of this. As often happens after particularly gruesome and unpredictable murders, the neighbors remembered Seifert as inconspicuous, as somebody who would always help others and who loved children.

Such neighborly opinions often are quite superficial. Compare them with what Seifert's brother, 6 years his junior and working as a telephone operator, had to say about him: "Before his wedding in 1955, I had a falling-out with him. He had a plan that I thought was totally idiotic."

Not just idiotic, it turns out; it was the precursor of what led to the killing of ten students and two teachers. His older brother had planned to stash girls away in his basement, to help himself to their "services" whenever he felt like it. He meant to catch them by lying in wait on a country path. He would then knock them unconscious and put them on his motorcycle.

"I certainly thought my brother was serious about this," said the younger brother. "You could see it in his face." Twice he had managed to talk Walter out of such abduction plans.

Motive and Method

The younger brother added, "Until yesterday, the only trouble I knew my brother had was some dispute with sewage workers. We also talked a bit about TV programs, but there was no indication that he was planning some violent deed."

Clearly, this was a rosy description of Walter Seifert's mental state of mind. For years his mind was tangled up in a mental maze of bizarre logic. His mind always started from the "fact" that two doctors were responsible for his wife's and newborn infant's death. He wrote a document some 100 pages long to the authorities, to medical people, and to pharmaceutical companies.

"Physicians are the worst mass-murderers in human history. . . . What can we do about that? Should we appeal to their conscience? That is totally useless. People who act like that don't have a conscience. Should I take the facts I have accumulated to court? No, the medical clique will create terror—they feel that in our pluralistic system they can judge themselves. But terror can be gotten rid of only by counter-terror from the other side. The system that denies me protection by law forces me to take up arms."

The man who had come to this conclusion felt it was up to him to fight the system. He chose the same methods that had been adopted by the "enemy of society," the medical profession: Terrorize weak people. The tools for his vindictive actions he built from the materials that he found in the shop where he had learned to use the drill and the lathe.

It was easy to believe that he chose his actions at random, as he indicated during the interrogation. The elementary school he attacked was close to his apartment, so there was no need for psychoanalysis to figure out why it became the target of his action: It was next door. Seifert probably had nothing against those children. They became his victims because of his crazed need for vengeance.

This was not the first time Walter Seifert took on the system. As a 20-year-old mechanic, he had been called to serve in the Army during World War II. After only a year he was sent home because he had tuberculosis. This illness was not cured but did not get worse either. Still, Seifert was unable to do any physical work and remained unemployed.

Seifert was resentful, certain that his illness was a consequence of his military service. He had been infected by other soldiers. Since 1955 he had been in medical care for his lung disease. In 1960, he was declared an invalid: no longer employable, but with a right to state support. He fought for a higher pension, which was denied. He kept sending a barrage of new applications to the head of the Public Health Authority and protest letters to Max Adenauer, the senior city manager of Cologne.

A medical expert told the public health officer that Seifert's illness predated the war. That rankled him not only because it meant his illness was unrelated to his military service but most of all because it had been disclosed from his public health files without his permission. When he heard about this report a few days before his rampage, he told his parents-in-law that there was no justice in the world. The old couple was particularly dismayed that Seifert again started to talk about his long-deceased wife. "Wouldn't it be lovely if Ulla were still with us?" That was just 2 days before his attack on the school. "After he lost his wife and child, I had the impression Walter was going mad," his father-in-law remembered.

Bewilderment and Denial Remained

The media reacted with great excitement, horror, and compassion. A Cologne newspaper commented on page one, "The parents and everybody else who is worried about the injured children are horrified by this unbelievable act. . . . We can only tremble at this display of what one man is capable of doing and to what extent we are helpless when faced with criminals like that." The attack was also reported in many other European newspapers, often on the front page.

Still, his mother-in-law couldn't believe it: "I cannot grasp this, this is impossible," she told a journalist who informed her of the crime. "Our Walter, that reasonable person, is supposed to have done this? He wouldn't hurt a fly. Had you told me that the skies had fallen down on Volkhoven, I would have less trouble believing you. Walter—such a good boy."

When Seifert died the evening after the attack, the postwar German public, who were still rebuilding their economy, felt that his crimes were too horrible to even think about. For years, they simply shut them out of their minds. The whole matter was incomprehensible. There was only one explanation that was repeated here and there: One of the teachers resembled Seifert's dead wife. Had he even tried to describe the true reasons for what he did, maybe people could have come up with some understanding, some acceptance. As it was, any mention of Seifert's crime was greeted with silence in Volkhoven for almost 40 years. Nobody wanted to think about it. Today, Seifert may have been diagnosed as a paranoid schizophrenic, but of course no one had the opportunity to make such a diagnosis at the time.

THE FORGOTTEN CANNIBAL: KARL DENKE

People such as Walter Seifert, who cannot explain their motives for what they do, can spread anxiety and terror through their actions alone. However, they don't give the media anything exciting to report. This is well illustrated by the case of Karl Denke. His name and his horrific deeds, as incomprehensible as they were, are pretty much forgotten, whereas more talkative murderers such as Jeffrey Dahmer, Ed Gein, and Charles Manson have gained cult status: Their images can be found on cups, T-shirts, and Web sites.

We have to live with the notion that there are deeds for which we cannot understand the motives, just as we accept modern quantum physics although we may not know how to reconcile its theoretical principles with what we see. One basic question has not been answered to date: What turns one person into a criminal and another person with a similar background into a nurse, police officer, carpenter, or district attorney? As long as we cannot answer such questions, there will be criminals whose motives challenge our understanding. This can be illustrated by the case of Karl Denke.

Serial Murder

The movie industry and the psychiatric and forensic communities have paid little attention to the case of Karl Denke, so I shall state the facts just as they were understood at the time. Although Denke committed his crimes well before the serial misdeeds of Ed Gein (who was taken into custody in 1957 and whose exploits inspired such movies as *Psycho* and *The Silence of the Lambs*), Denke might have had a more convincing claim for inspiring the psychological horror movie wave that followed. But Denke remained silent, so he did not inspire indignation over his lack of emotion or remorse.

His case was presented to the Congress on Forensic Medicine in Bonn in 1925 by Dr. Pietrusky from Breslau, and it was published the next year in the *German Journal of Forensic Medicine* (*Deutsche Zeitschrift für die Gesamte Gerichtliche Medizin*).

Before the serial killer Haarmann was punished for his crimes, there appeared reports of a series of crimes in Münsterberg that, if anything, were even more hair-raising than his. Over a period of 21 years, Karl Denke had murdered more than thirty-one people. Their flesh had served him as meat, which he also offered to others as part of meals. Not only that, he used parts of the corpses and made tools out of them. This case shows us that things we would consider impossible do occur.

The facts as I present them here rest on the investigation of the entire case file, which was sent to the Forensic Institute in Münsterberg. These files were generously put at my disposal by the chief prosecutor of the case, the mayor of Münsterberg, and the local chief of police.

Münsterberg, close to the city of Breslau,* is a small country town of some 9,000 residents. On its periphery it looks more like a village with small houses, surrounded by gardens, spaced every 20 to 50 yards along the streets. There were farmhouses on both sides of Karl Denke's house. Next to his house but further back from the street was Denke's woodshed. Further from the house, about 80 yards, there was a 10-foot-deep small pond, which he had installed 3 years before. In the back, there trickled a brook called the Ohle.

The house was shared by three families. The front part served as living quarters for a teacher and his family who had been expelled from Upper Silesia by the Polish authorities at the end of the war. Karl Denke lived on the ground floor of the back part of the house and shared the corridor and the entrance to his apartment with a working couple who lived on

---

* Now the city of Wrocław in Poland. In Denke's time, this was a German city. Münsterberg is now known as Ziębice in today's Poland

the upper floor in an apartment. The man was hard of hearing and appeared limited in intelligence. His wife seemed quite intelligent.

Denke's apartment on the ground level consisted of just one room, measuring less than 60 square feet. This was where he slept, ate, and worked and also where he committed murder and sliced up the corpses. The filth in his room was beyond imagining. I shall describe the other objects connected with the murders in more detail later, but there was a great deal of salt and piles of clothing he had taken from his victims.

The municipality issued the search warrant for his apartment for the following reasons. In December 1924 a young journeyman named Vincenz Olivier came to Denke begging for money; Denke in turn asked him to write a letter because, he said, he was so short-sighted that he had trouble writing. He would pay him 20 pfennigs for the service. This man, to whom I later talked in his jail cell, reports that Denke's dictation began with the words "You fat paunch." He considered these words rather strange and turned around just in time to avoid a pickaxe that was directed at his head—but not fast enough to avoid a wound on his right temple. In frustration, Denke threw himself onto the journeyman. The latter, although strong, had a very hard time defending himself. Asked later about the reason for the fight, Denke did not give an explanation. He just sat there red-eyed, with a vacant stare and distorted features, his teeth gnashing, his whole body twitching. Denke had a good reputation in town, but when the journeyman insisted, Denke finally was arrested.

Many people in town thought it inexplicable that the police would take a quiet member of their town into custody as a result of what some vagrant told them. In his jail cell, Denke committed suicide by hanging himself in a horizontal position, just a couple of feet above ground, after fashioning an open sling from his handkerchief and attaching it to rings that were meant to tie up suspects. His relatives refused to pay for the funeral. In order to take stock of what he left behind, his apartment was searched 2 days later, and that is when parts of human bodies were found.

Many events became public knowledge only later on but should have contributed to an earlier discovery of Karl Denke's activities. Some 2 years before, another journeyman was seen coming from Denke's apartment covered with blood and running away without stopping. A little later, a vagrant complained to people living across the street that Denke asked him to write a letter and that, when he sat down to do so, Denke suddenly put a chain around his neck, trying to strangle him. A strong man, he managed to get away. Also, a year and a half earlier, the other people living in the house had noticed a particularly disagreeable stench percolating out of Denke's apartment. The women living above him complained to their fellow occupants. They approached Denke about it, and that was the end of the stench. Also, it was later reported that even at the time of the worst inflation in Germany, Denke was always very well provisioned with meat. He carried it in open containers from the stables, across the courtyard, and into his room. His other house occupants did not give it too much thought, assuming that it was dog meat. They remembered having found a dog pelt in front of the apartment. It was illegal to slaughter dogs, but they couldn't have cared less. They did not ask themselves how Denke might have access to that many dogs, either. In addition, nobody paid any attention to his carrying full buckets of bloody water or blood into the courtyard. Nor did they pay attention to the hammering and sawing noises coming from his flat throughout the night. They just assumed he was working on the keys that he manufactured and sold.

In retrospect, it was considered a bit strange that he left the house at night carrying a parcel and that he would come back quite late without it. Sometimes that happened several times in the same night. It was reported that he offered used clothes and shoes for sale and that he burnt some of them in his garden. Bones that were found once in a while were assumed to be animal bones.

The first things that were found during the apartment search were bones and various pieces of meat. The latter were preserved in a salt solution in wooden containers. There were fifteen pieces of it, complete with skin. Two of them must have come from a hairy chest. They had been cut horizontally in the center about 2 inches above the navel. Their lateral extent went as far as the forearm. Then there was a piece of the stomach area with the navel in the center. The remaining pieces came from the sides and back. The largest of these pieces measured some 16 by 12 inches. It was noticed that the anal opening had been cleaned carefully and was well prepared on both sides.

The meat was reddish-brown and did not look as though the body had lost a great deal of blood before it was cut to pieces. On the other hand, parts of the back showed bluish discolorations, which experts call death spots. They suggest that the body was cut up several hours after the victim's death.

There is no indication from the cut-up parts of any vital reaction, that is, an indication that some of the cutting was done while the victims were still alive. There were no skin or muscle parts of the neck among the meat segments, nor were there extremities, heads, or genitals. From these pieces there was no way to determine how death had been induced or what butchering tools might have been used.

There were three medium-sized pots filled with some kind of sauce. It looked like cream sauce with boiled meat that was still covered with skin and human hair. The center of this meat was light pink. Those pieces appeared to have been cut from the posterior region. One pot was only half filled; Denke must have consumed the other half before his arrest.

There was no indication that he had ever sold any of his victims' flesh. (It was assumed that Fritz Haarmann did just that, but there was no proof because the meat Haarmann sold was consumed.) It seems certain that Denke offered this meat to the vagrants he picked up. There was a third pot containing many segments of human skin and parts of human aortas.

A bowl was found on his table containing amber-colored fat, looking very much like human fat. Biological lab tests indicated that it contained human protein.

In the shed where the pieces of meat were found, there was a barrel containing large amounts of bones that had been neatly cleaned of tendons, muscles, and other tissues. They must have been boiled before being stored. An investigation of the first shipment of bones from the shed revealed that these were six upper parts of the ulna that had belonged to three different people. In addition, there were large numbers of carpal and tarsal bones. A look behind the shed revealed more bones. In the pond Denke had dug behind the shed, the investigators found a piece of a human lower leg.

Further away, in the city forest, there were many more skeletal remains. Here is what was sent to the lab: sixteen lower parts of the femur, a few of which looked astonishingly strong, two pieces delicate; six pairs of femurs and two additional left femurs; fifteen middle section long bones; four pairs of upper ulna bones; seven radius heads; nine lower parts of the radius; eight lower parts of the ulna; one pair of upper tibia ends; and one pair of lower radius ends and lower ulna ends that had not been separated yet and were quite moldy. Then there were two lower parts of upper arms, one pair of upper arm heads and a pair of collarbones, two shoulder blades, eight heel and ankle bones, 120 sections of toes and fingers, sixty-five metatarsals and metacarpals, five first ribs, and 150 parts of ribs. With very few exceptions, the bones were lightweight, porous, and devoid of fat.

In addition, vertebrae were found in the city forest, as well as four sections of a carefully prepared male pelvis that showed clear indications of having been sawed off. Only one piece of skull was found, a part of the left side that looked broken, was unevenly severed in front, and appears to have been cut off by a sharp saw on top. A cross was drawn on this piece in ink.

Judging from the size of these bones, we can conclude that one of the people to whom they belonged was particularly strongly built, two of them were frail, and another had had misshapen hips (the medical term is *coxa vara*). Because most of the bones in the shed had been boiled, information is available only for the bones deposited in the city forest. Taking the temperature and the weather conditions of the recent past into account, we concluded that only 1 or 2 months had passed since their death. That would correspond to the age of the pieces of meat found in the house, although we cannot be certain about the age of the meat because nobody has forensic experience in determining the age of salted human flesh.

The areas where flesh had been separated from the bones showed signs of brute force, maybe created by the back end of an axe or hammer. Also, there were areas where a saw had been used. In some places, a sharp instrument, probably the sharp end of an axe, had been applied. There are also knife marks at the joints.

Judging from these findings, we were able to state that the bones must have belonged to at least ten different people.

Denke's collection of teeth provided a lot more information. We were sent a total of 351 teeth. They were found inside a money pouch, two metal boxes on which the words *salt* and *pepper* had been written, and three paper bags that had originally held pepper. They were sorted in part by size. Molars were in the money pouch, whereas the others, separated into good and bad teeth, were found in the two boxes and one of the paper bags. In another paper bag, there were teeth that must have all belonged to the same person. Finally, there were three lower front teeth that were badly atrophied and probably belonged to an old person. All but six of the teeth were well preserved.

Dr. Euler, director of the local dental institute, was kind enough to write a report on what we found and also provided pictures. From the teeth, we hoped to determine how many victims there were; of what age, sex, and probable occupation they were; how the teeth were extracted; and how much time had elapsed since they were killed.

These investigations gave us useful results. Whereas the bone evidence established that there were at least eight victims, other circumstances indicated that it must have been a much larger number. We learned from the teeth that there must have been at least twenty different people because twenty left lower canine teeth were found.

The fact that most of the victims had a gum disease called periodontitis and that the canine teeth are particularly susceptible to this illness again argues in favor of a much larger number of victims. Given that there was no sign of dental care and that there were indications of advanced age, Dr. Euler set a lower limit of twenty-five people.

The teeth had been removed in different ways: Some of them had been loosened by age or illness; with others, force had been used. Many of them still had parts of the tooth socket sticking to them. There were a few characteristic fractures in the molars and premolars that could not have existed while the victims were alive. Then there were indications of the use of pliers with sharp edges. Some of the roots indicated that the jawbones had first been boiled. A few teeth—broken during extraction—had been glued together by Denke.

Then we hoped to determine the age of the victims. In a list [figure 34] Denke recorded the names, ages, and weights of his victims. There were no children among them. However, when we studied four of the wisdom teeth, certain features emerged that are characteristic of 15-year-olds. Evidence from the other teeth suggests that at least 80 percent of the victims must have been a lot older. Dr. Euler finally concluded that there was one person who was no more than 16 years old, most were much older than 40, two were between 20 and 30 years old, and one was between 30 and 40 years old.

Additional attempts to determine the sex of these victims gave no useful information, just as useless as the attempts to find out what their occupations might have been. Also, there was no information about how long ago they had died, although it could be seen that a few of the teeth had been extracted years before. The tooth extraction from the young person must have happened several weeks before.

Altogether, the evidence from the tooth collection provided a great deal more information about the number and the age of the victims than could have been obtained from the bones alone. There weren't that many bones, and they were all broken. Still, Dr. Euler could not have been produced his results without his expert knowledge of the appropriate scientific methods.

Three pairs of suspenders were found, made of human skin. They were about 2 1/2 inches wide and 2 1/2 feet long. The skin was not smooth; it was broken in several places. That tells us it was not tanned but simply separated from the lower tissue and subsequently dried. In one place, there was clear evidence that the skin was cut so both nipples can still be seen. Then there are four places where the skin was sewn together, and it was taken from the victim's pubic region, as can be seen from the hair. Microscopic studies showed that some of the hair had nits and pubic lice. It was clear that Denke had worn all the suspenders; in fact, he was wearing a pair when he died.

In addition to the suspenders, Denke also produced straps from human skin, which he used to tie his shoes and to bundle laundry. Many of these straps also show human hair, but we cannot tell from which body parts they originated.

All over Denke's apartment there were old clothes; in his bed alone there were forty-one bundles of rags of various sizes, held together with straps. One of them held pieces of an old, worn rug, another held scraps of window curtains. Many of the pieces of cloth couldn't be identified as coming from a particular item from their shapes. Mostly, they consisted of remainders of linen, wool, and cotton. It is interesting that small rags of just a few inches in size had been carefully preserved and bundled together. Most of them showed signs of having been divided and washed. Many also had been neatly folded and ironed. In a larger bundle there were small pieces of the same cloth stacked together, folded at the edges. It is not likely that they were used to patch other pieces of clothing. Rather, the evidence suggests that their collection and the manner in which they were bundled had been nothing but a game.

Another odd feature was Denke's "coin collection." It consisted of flat, round pieces of terra cotta of sizes between those of pennies and quarters. He had scratched the denominations onto one side.

There were many personal identification papers and private notes from several people in Denke's room and lists of income from his garden products, hours that he had worked, and similar items, all marked down fairly orderly. More notably, there were thirty names of men and women, with a date in front of each name. Those dates must refer to the dates they died. For the last one—number 31—there is no further entry. All of this information was arranged chronologically. The numbering began with the eleventh name. For women, there was only the first name; men apparently deserved more detailed annotations, including the date and place, their social status, and their profession. It makes sense to assume this was the list of his victims, particularly because the personal ID cards of several of these people were found in his room. Their whereabouts had been unknown, and some of their clothes were identified by family members who said that the owners had disappeared. Judging from the appearance of these papers, the list had not been put together in one day.

On one page, the first letters of their names were written, with a number afterward; these numbers probably are the living weights of these people. On another paper the names were followed by notations such as "dead, 122; naked, 107; slaughtered, 83." The last numbers were next to the last person's name in the last table.

Then a set of numbers arranged in three columns of ten rows was added. The first column lists the weights of the last ten people. The middle column lists the weights of the group next to the last, and the last column lists the weights of the first ten. In each of these columns the individual weights were listed in ascending order. The number 31 carries neither a name nor any other descriptive detail in the table, except one number that must be the weight of that person.

Only the second name on the list, that of a woman named Emma, is not followed by a weight indication. It turns out that a man called T. was sentenced to 12 years in prison for having killed a woman with that first name whose body had been hacked to pieces before it was found in Münsterberg in 1909. He completed his sentence, but a retrial of the case exonerated the man who had spent all this time in prison.

To hack his victims to pieces, Denke used three axes, a large wood saw, a pruning saw, a pickaxe, and three knives. The police took them to look for human blood. This investigation was successful; it also proved that for the easy sawing jobs at the pelvis and at the head, Denke used a more precise tool: a pruning saw. More human blood was found on the pickaxe Denke used in his last murder attempt. The instrument is 18 inches long and tapers off at the head. The knives had no special features.

Talking to relatives and acquaintances of Denke and digging through a lot of documents, I have come up with the following personal information. Karl Denke was the third son of a small-time farmer, born in Oberkünzendorf in Silesia in 1860. In neither his paternal nor maternal family history is there any mention of insanity, alcoholism, or suicidal tendencies. His father was reported to be quite pedantic. His brothers and sisters became small-time farmers and married in the same social circles. They are now advanced in age and in good health.

No details about his birth are known. As an infant, he developed very slowly, had trouble learning, and started talking so late that his parents assumed he might remain mute. Only at the age of 6 years did he manage to speak a few words.

At the end of his sixth year, he started school, where it took weeks for him to utter even the vaguest sounds. His teacher reported that he was afraid Karl Denke was an idiot. He moved his body as slowly as his mouth. He rarely answered questions. When somebody put out a hand to greet Denke, he might lift his right hand just an inch so that the other person had to lower the hand to grasp his. He was a very poor student in his early years and was often punished. Later on, his grades improved to "satisfactory" and "good." Still, his report cards speak of a lack of attention and of being obdurate, and there is no praise. A year later, there is a note that "things have improved." He rarely interacted with his fellow students, and he had no friends.

As a boy, Denke was moody and sullen. He didn't want to go to school, and often his brother or his fellow students had to carry him to school. He never lost his slow speech. He retained into his later life a tendency to wet his bed.

During his time in school, he was close to his older brother. But when he left school, they parted company. Even when asked, he would not join his brother in any activity.

After graduating from school, Karl Denke worked in his father's pub. But his tendency to stay by himself became stronger. He was uncommunicative and would not interact with people his age, or anybody else, for that matter. He never went out for amusement. When he was 22 years old, he sneaked away from his parents' house. For 9 months he disappeared, and his family did not receive a single sign of him. Finally they found out that for months he had worked as a handyman, cutting cobblestones for a construction company. When he finally returned home, he didn't talk about his reasons for his going away, nor did he describe what had happened to him. He was closed-mouthed and indifferent, as usual.

After his parents' death, which did not appear to touch him at all, his siblings tried to keep him with them. They considered him unable to fend for himself. He busied himself a bit in the pub, but not much. He returned home more and more sporadically. It turned out that he wandered about the forest, staying there as late as midnight. Finally, he didn't return home anymore. A while later he appeared at the family house with a horse and buggy. Without saying a word, he loaded up his personal belongings and took them to Münsterberg, where he had rented an apartment. Soon after, he bought a piece of land there. The seller took advantage of his lack of business acumen, causing his brothers and sisters concern about his modest inheritance. They thought he was dangerously limited in what he could understand in such transactions, and they filed for a petition of incapacitation. In the written filing they demonstrated that he had paid three times the normal price for a lot he had acquired. They also mentioned that they thought him to be of very limited mental capacity.

In the ensuing paperwork, there are written opinions of other townspeople who had known Karl Denke for a long time. They all agreed that he would not be able to take care of his inheritance. But the petition was withdrawn when medical advice cautioned that such circumstances might send people like Denke into a "fit of rage so that other people in the streets would have to fear for their lives." For many years, the magistrate kept asking about Denke's behavior.

After the petition for legal incapacitation was withdrawn, Denke became more and more suspicious of his family. Still, most of the time he was easy to get along with. He got a bit upset when he felt somebody was looking him over. There was a rumor that he was "neither man nor woman." Certainly his feelings were different from those of normal people. For instance, he felt no fear or disgust. His family thought him devoid of all feelings. Other people who met him considered him tight-lipped. They never mentioned that they considered him sick, and they insisted that they had never seen any sign of brutality or a violent temper.

It was hard to make him say anything, but once in a while he would answer if he felt he was being teased. A butcher who occasionally worked for one of his cousins said that Karl Denke was particularly curious when he cut up the slaughtered animals. A former tenant in the same house as Denke said that she had always been a bit "scared of that shy person," and she never dared to enter his apartment. She gave no reason, just that "he seemed eerie."

He had almost no contact with his brothers and sisters. Of many invitations, he accepted only one. On that occasion, he devoured about 2 pounds of meat; he was generally considered a glutton.

His neighbors considered him a well-meaning oddball whose income came from what his garden grew and what the bread dishes would fetch when he sold them. Vagrants and traveling workers considered him a minor benefactor; rarely did one of them leave his place without a gift from him. He was often called "Father Denke" (without religious connotation).

During the period of inflation in Germany in the early 1920s, he sold everything he owned and lived in a small room of the house he had previously owned. Every necessary household task he did himself, with the exception of his laundry.

About his sexual life little is known. He never had relations with women; he was considered a misogynist. There was no indication of homosexual tendencies. Also, he was not known to have a drinking habit.

I took careful note of his autopsy and will report a few relevant details here. He measured 5 feet 4 inches; he was muscular with a solid bone structure and perhaps overweight. The hair on his head and in his beard was gray. His body was quite hairy. He had both testicles in his scrotum. On his neck, just under his thyroid cartilage, he had an old rope mark running horizontally, up to the ear on the right side and 1 inch beyond the ear on the left side.

The cranial dura mater was of normal thickness, smooth and shiny, and separate from its surroundings. The vessels of the other membranes were filled with blood to their very ends, and were smooth and tender as well as shiny. There was no indication of brain damage.

The sutura sagittalis (the suture uniting the two parietal bones of the skull) sharply deviates to the right; the sutura lambdoidea (on the back of the skull) is more strongly curved on the right side than on the left. There it is quite flat.

The inner organs of his chest and stomach did not show any abnormalities or signs of illness. The inner walls of the arteries were smooth. The stomach contained some 5 cubic inches of partly digested food, where I recognized pieces of meat. His testicles, the size of a walnut, showed no indications of illness. The same goes for the epididymis and the adrenal glands. The seminal vesicles were filled with a slimy substance containing a few spermatozoa. None of the inner organs showed any abnormalities or outgrowths. His tongue was grayish-white, without scars. Near the tip there was a bluish-red discoloration of the muscles close to the surface, forming a bruise the size of a pea.

Obviously, there was much interest in Denke's mental state. But knowing the media, it may be just as well that Karl Denke's suicide freed him from any assessment of his mental state.

Furnishing an expert opinion simply on the basis of the data often is a thankless job. A person's deeds alone say little or nothing. It makes no sense to consider them as the effects of a sick brain when we don't understand the person's motives. There must be knowledge of a complete personality, but in this case we have only the observations of people who had only superficial contact with Denke, given his odd habits.

At first glance Karl Denke seems to be a highly psychopathic person whose motivations must be seen in terms of some sexual perversion, but his early development and life speak against this assumption. His habits of cutting out and preparing the anal area, severing the skin across the breast nipples in order to turn them into clothing items, and making suspenders with human skin from the pubic area, when seen together, do indicate some sexual perversion. Still, the assumption does not explain all of his actions. It is easier to assume Karl Denke to have been a schizophrenic.

There is no information that hints at a hereditary influence on his development, except perhaps his father's meticulous and controlling behavior. His prepuberty development certainly was abnormal. He started speaking quite late, and there are reports of mental debility; his teacher considered him an idiot. His sullen, stubborn, and solitary behavior in boyhood was so strong that it indicates that he had already started to suffer from a mental disturbance. His state worsened in puberty. As mentioned earlier, his brother told us that their friendly relations stopped when he refused to take part in any activities with him.

His tendency to avoid others went from bad to worse. He never went to bars or pubs and did not participate in dances; instead he roamed through the forest by himself throughout the night. Not that he was interested in nature—he was totally uninterested. He ran away from home without uttering a word. When he returned, almost a year later, he didn't consider it necessary to tell anybody what had happened in the meantime. He did not care that his family had been worried. He stood by his parents' gravesite showing no indication of sadness or any other feeling. Not that he was unpleasant—he never went into a rage. He did jobs assigned to him without interest, but he did them. He was kind to animals.

`Below the surface, however, clearly his emotions and thoughts were out of control. He killed dozens of people, and he butchered them like animals. He weighed their bodies, cut them to pieces, and used them for his own meals. He made suspenders and other straps from their skin. He kept meticulous statistics of their weight, totaling the resulting numbers, categorizing hundreds of their teeth, and keeping them like poker chips. For reasons of his own, he washed rags made from their clothes and wrapped with human skin using a system that he invented for this purpose. He even made money from them.

On one side, he was a kind, well-meaning old loner; on the other, he was a murderous beast who killed his guests, helping himself to their flesh as meat and to their skin for straps and suspenders. And both of these sides made up one person: Karl Denke.

Should we diagnose that as schizophrenia? I'm not sure. We have to accept both sides of his nature. In the end, our memories of Karl Denke will consist not only of a despicable monster but also of an unhappy man who lived on the periphery of normal social behavior.

The Denke case is a low point in our observation of human error: a dark object, inscrutable and sad. The last photograph taken of him shows this serial murderer, his beard well-combed, clad in a thick coat, in a simple casket (figure 35). It is known that the dead tend to have peaceful facial expressions, but in this case the onlooker does not know whether the face shows stress or maybe even peaceful bliss.

In the summer of 2003, I found more information on the Denke case. In the attic of an abandoned monastery in the town of Herbrechtingen, I gave a lecture about confusing criminal cases from the past century. When a group of listeners did not want to let me go after 3 hours, I started to mention the Denke case, with which I meant to close my presentation, but with no luck. One woman got up and told us that her mother had sung the following street ballad, written 80 years ago. I had never heard it before. So this woman started to sing the *Song of Denke:*

> Münsterberg, my fair village,
> Münsterberg, my lovely town.
> That's the home of "Father Denke,"
> who cut up so many guests:
> Good-looking, young vagrant workers,
> he invited to his house.
> He cut them up and put them
> neatly into vessels.
> Recently, there came a handyman,
> asking for a slice of bread.
> Denke asked him in for writing,
> but he meant to kill him dead.
> The poor devil foresaw the danger,

of this murderous design.
And with bleeding, wounded head,
he attacked his host—that beast.
But tough luck, policemen enter,
not believing what he said,
but instead they only offered,
this poor sinner a bed in jail.
Had not Denke hanged himself,
butchering would still go on.
But this opened up the record
and the veil was off and gone.

How and why the mother of this woman knew these verses and why she sang them to her daughter, I did not find out. We are told that this text originally was sung to the accompaniment of a barrel organ, and images were displayed at the same time.

A similar poem is recited to this day in Germany about homosexual serial killer Fritz Haarmann. But we must not forget that the Haarmann case was known all over Germany, whereas Denke's murders have been almost completely forgotten since World War II. Here is the Haarmann song:

Wait, just wait a little while,
Haarmann will soon come and see you.
He'll bring his little pick-axe and a smile,
and from the living he will free you.

Whoever finds this to be too scary answers,

Haarmann, you just wait a while,
and expect we'll come and see you,
we will bring a bigger pick-axe
and from your living days we'll free you.

THE ROBBER KNEISSL

Crimes do not always spread terror—certainly not when the miscreant is a country boy, son of a miller, who made trouble only for those in higher places. The case of the Robber Kneissl is notable in this context. He never considered himself a Robin Hood, as many of his compatriots did. He was right about that; he was indeed no Robin Hood, just a man who went astray with no way of getting back.

His ill-tempered parents were of unknown origins. In 1886, they stopped running their little inn and bought a mill in the desolate Bavarian hinterland, somewhere between Augsburg, Munich, and Freising. It was called the Schacher Mill, and it was hard to reach, deep in the woods, shrouded by the thick moss.

At that time, millers had a bad reputation. Formerly, they were considered, together with shepherds, to be dishonorable because in times of war they had to stay home to maintain the food supply. But people who did not join the armed forces to defend their country in battle were seen as unpatriotic. When Kneissl, who was later called the Robber Kneissl, was born on August 4, 1875, the bad reputation of millers and shepherds had been almost forgotten—but not quite.

Small-time criminals often were guests at the Schacher Mill, a strategically remote location. When Kneissl's father was involved in plundering the pilgrimage church of Herrgottsruh, he was taken into custody in the town of Dachau, and he died soon after, for reasons unknown. His mother was already in police detention. Those were tough times for the boys, Alois and Mathias, who were left to their own devices. They had never been good students. Twelve-year-old Mathias found this on his report card: "He is not totally devoid of gifts, but he is lazy beyond imagination. He never pays attention, and his output doesn't exist. It is useless to scold him or punish him. He has no love of school whatsoever."

His 10-year-old brother, Alois, didn't fare much better: "He is an idiot student, living up to no expectation whatsoever, but he does have some musical talent. Whatever his education has been at home, he does not show it in school. Attendance inadequate."

When their mother, who liked shooting bucks or wild boars for food, was jailed, her sons failed to go to school and went poaching instead. This did not endear them to the local police—not that the people in this rural community minded, because the green-uniformed country constables were regarded as representatives of the bourgeoisie and the military. In contrast to the work of the honest farmers and common folk, their job was talking, not working. And they had a reputation for taking advantage of the common folk. Whoever wasn't on good terms with them was treated like a vagrant. Even worse from their perspective, these gendarmes came from Franconia, a northern region of Bavaria. Franconians were considered more like their Protestant cousins in the north, particularly with their admiration for law and order. The true Bavarians considered themselves quite the opposite.

"As my bad luck would have it," Mathias Kneissl told a court 12 years later, "I had to go to the same school right up to my seventeenth year, just because Pastor Endl could not stand me and kept harassing me. Many of my friends left school long before I learned as much as the others. For the final exam, I was the only one told to do a calculation on the blackboard. I didn't want to do it. I don't accept unfairness. I will not bow even if it kills me."

Kneissl's final days at school were an indication of what would happen to him later on, and he must have known it. On February 21, 1902, he was be-headed in Augsburg.

Kneissl Turns to Robbery

Kneissl's criminal history began when, on November 2, 1892, police officers Gösswein and Förtsch visited the Schacher Mill to stop the two boys from poaching once and for all. Unfortunately, they had not considered the boys' determination to resist. The boys took their firearms and locked themselves in the attic. After the first shot had targeted Förtsch, Gösswein climbed the stairs slowly while talking to Mathias—the quieter of the two brothers—only to become the target of Alois's two shots. He never recovered from the wounds he sustained. After escaping from the mill, the brothers were caught a few days later. They were arrested for receiving stolen goods and for robbery, attempted murder, poaching, and resisting arrest. Alois was sentenced to 15 years in jail, and Mathias was sentenced to 6 years.

After Mathias was released in 1899, he took to living in the woods near his home. He was well liked by the farmers because he provided them with veni-son. He dreamed of emigrating to America. But to do so, he needed money, which he tried to steal whenever the occasion presented itself. But he never had enough.

It was the early evening of November 30, 1900, that turned Mathias Kneissl into Robber Kneissl, who later became the hero of poems and adventure sto-ries in the region. He knocked on the door of the Fleckl family farmhouse in Irchenbrunn, meaning to ask for overnight hospitality because it was raining and he was hungry.

The farmer's wife didn't want to open the door, but she sent him to see her husband, who was at the local inn. However, Kneissl didn't want to be seen by the other guests, who might recognize him as a habitual thief. Farmer Fleckl came outside with two beer steins and various sausages. He took Kneissl back to his living room, where the two of them talked until 11 P.M. The dog started barking, there was a knock on the door, and voices outside said, "Open up, Farmer Fleckl! Police here!"

Farmer Fleckl acted the part of the outraged citizen and didn't permit Commissioner Brandmeier and Constable Scheidler to enter. However, Kneissl became suspicious. He guessed that when the farmer got the beer and sausages, he must have told the others at the inn where to find Kneissl. The motivation was clear. Although Fleckl himself lived on the border between legality and illegality, he did not want to forfeit the reward of 400 marks.

Kneissl grabbed his rifle and retreated to the back of the farmhouse. The police officers came in, followed by some neighbors who were trying to help. Kneissl held his breath as Brandmeier walked past him. Kneissl then pulled the trigger. The six neighbors who accompanied the commissioner and the constable took off as quickly as they could. It turned out that Kneissl's bullet hit the commissioner in the upper leg, but the shot had damaged his artery, and he bled to death. Only after the constable returned fire did Kneissl aim at him. Still, Constable Scheidler was hit only in his right foot, but 3 weeks later he died of an infection of his wound.

And Thus Began a Legend

If we believe what the Kneissl legends say, we are ready to call him a hero, an innocent lamb. It was reported that Mathias really wanted to run away when he saw the police officers with their injuries. And sure enough, he did run. Too bad that a wanted poster was pinned to the wall in every railroad station and printed in every newspaper: "Twenty-five years old, medium height [Kneissl measured 5'5"], blond, blue-eyed, speaking with a strong Bavarian accent. Old bullet scar on the upper thigh . . . black hat, dark suit . . . striped blue shirt with stiff collar, black socks and yellow shoes."

Now it was serious. Local police officers began interrogating people who had had Kneissl as a guest. In one instance, sixteen officers went to the Popfinger farm; the owner was known to have been acquainted with Kneissl's father. But Popfinger said he had never run across the son. Five police officers turned everything upside down in the house, while the others watched from the outside, with no result. After the police left, Farmer Popfinger just shrugged his shoulders, harnessed two horses, and made them pull his liquid manure cart toward his fields. That is when Kneissl jumped out, smelly but still free.

His adventures continued. Soon, a postcard that poked fun at the authorities made the rounds. Stories galore—many of them freely invented—were told in the living rooms of the farmers in winter. Without even trying, Kneissl had become the darling of the farmers. On local stages, there was always someone impersonating Kneissl, in his local dialect, ridiculing the "fat authorities" who couldn't even speak the local dialect.

Unfortunately, reality was not quite that amusing. Kneissl had to stage one escape after the other but was lucky enough to wind up in accommodating female arms in between. People who hosted him were not being generous; they made him pay dearly for the courtesy of letting him sleep on a straw sack and under a blanket. "When I gave them a 10-mark coin, they would just give me a meager meal and a stein of beer," Kneissl said in court later on. "And nobody gave me any change. I had to accept that; otherwise, they might have told on me."

Kneissl could count on help from his family. His sister gave him a warm coat when he needed it in February. She met him for this purpose in a place they chose carefully: the Rosenau Inn. This was a tourist destination, and nobody would have suspected that Kneissl would go there for fear of being recognized. But nobody noticed the new folk hero.

Reward

Kneissl could not hide out forever, but it wasn't his imprudence that finally turned Kneissl in; it was investigative work.

Things started to go downhill when Kneissl's 20-year-old cousin, Voest, was apprehended in Munich. He could get a stiff penalty because he had been forbidden to enter the city after previous run-ins with the law. One of the officers who took him in, Commissioner Joseph Bössert, noted that he was related to Kneissl. This made him grill the poor fellow as best he could. He offered him the reward of 1,000 marks if he was able to tell him where to find Kneissl.

Such an offer would get him out of poverty—hardly an offer he could refuse. As a result, a police squad entered the Aumacher Farm of Mr. and Mrs. Merkl. This couple admitted to the police that Kneissl was somewhere in the house. When called, he did not show himself; instead, he barricaded himself somewhere in the house.

On March 4, 150 police officers showed up. Still, nobody volunteered to force the robber out of his hiding place. It took another day before forty-three officers fired shots in the direction where Kneissl was hiding out. Then they pulled the heavily wounded robber from his hole, hitting and kicking him on the way. It took the Munich police to protect Kneissl from further physical abuse by the local police, who felt that he had made a fool of them for years.

Kneissl's Last Days

Kneissl had become a folk hero, a position he certainly had never intended to occupy. But he was badly wounded, and the parish priest administered the last rites to him to be on the safe side. A horse-and-buggy team took him to the railroad station, from which he was to be taken to jail. But the train could not stop at the Munich station because of the enormous crowd waiting there. The train had to back up all the way to the station at Bayerstrasse so that Kneissl could be taken off the train.

He then told the police chief, in his best Bavarian dialect, "Look here, there were several occasions when I could easily have shot you dead, but I didn't want to." The chief, in the same vein and dialect, answered, "When I saw you in your hiding place up there, I could also have killed you." Kneissl retorted, "You would have missed me; my rifle is better than yours."

There were two pieces of evidence that Kneissl did not immediately start shooting when cornered. First, he said in court, quite convincingly, that he would have given up long before, when he was caught at the Fleckl Farm, had he known at that time that he would be running away forever. At the time he did not aim at a person when he pulled the trigger of his gun. He just pointed his gun downward in order to chase the police away. The police also found a rifle and a handgun in the attic where Kneissl had been hiding. Both of them were loaded, and neither had been discharged.

Altogether, Kneissl kept his head and maintained a clear appreciation of what was going on. During the trial in November 1901, he remarked quite correctly—while his hands and feet were tied up—that the whole thing looked like a staged event, like a play. The pimps and the prostitutes made up the audience, and the prosecution and the defense were the actors. He himself appeared in court quite well dressed. His mother had bought him a dark suit and a light blue tie, a breast pocket handkerchief, and carefully polished shoes.

But then Kneissl became ill. He made friends with the nurses, who saved his life with their good care—for the guillotine.

The robber was certainly no innocent lamb, and the prosecutor said bluntly, "Kneissl needs to be expunged from human society. To put him into jail for 15 years would not do. He has been charged with murder, and the proceedings have shown that the charge was justified. I would consider it a bad mistake if somebody like him were set free after 15 years. We cannot assume that he would then join a normal profession. Rather, Kneissl would return to his larcenous lifestyle. Ladies and gentlemen of the jury, please do your duty and see to it that this murderer is put out of operation forever."

The defense had no trump card, and it took only an hour and a half before a verdict was handed to the judge. The judge handed down the sentence: 15 years in prison for willfully injuring Scheidler (who subsequently died of his wounds) and the death penalty for killing Brandmeier. Kneissl turned white, and his mother shouted from the audience, "Murderous justice!" And when, on February 21, 1902, he was executed in Augsburg, his mother spent 60 marks in gold to obtain his body.

Before his execution, Kneissl drank six glasses of beer. To the last minute he insisted, "I die in the knowledge that I did not mean to kill those two policemen." Was he kidding himself? There is no way to know.

Positive Consequences

The story of Robber Kneissl spread as far as the Rhineland. The papers there published stories about his arrest within a day. The first version in the papers reported that he was taken in while drinking heavily with two women, having been turned in by a prostitute. It took only 2 days in Cologne—where people loved to celebrate and tended to loathe the authorities, as the Bavarians did—to find the correct version:

> We see that the frequent assertion that it is country folk who are most supportive of authority is incorrect.... The authorities should ask themselves how the people can be encouraged to improve their social behavior. Maybe that could best be accomplished by improved economic conditions and educational institutions with sincere teachers who teach students how to think freely. Let us recall that Kneissl, who had been penalized for poaching, had no trouble finding employment as a craftsman and that his bosses were pleased with the work he did. They let him go only because the police so closely scrutinized his actions.

As mentioned repeatedly in court proceedings, the reintegration of ex-convicts into the job market is difficult, even if employers mean well. These days, ex-convicts are pushed out of their jobs by clients of their employers, not by the police.

Kneissl's skull was on exhibit at Munich University until 1944, when U.S. bombardment destroyed the anatomical collection. The Kneissl song survived.

As recently as 1966, plates were manufactured with inscriptions and illustrations of the story of that popular but reluctant folk hero.

This spark of recognition posthumously benefited a taxi driver a few years later. When the man died, his obituary mentioned that during his career he had provided transportation not only to novelist Ludwig Thoma but also to the folk hero Kneissl.

EPILOGUE

There will always be new, unexpected criminal activities. Each crime puts demands on society. When airplanes crashed into the World Trade Center on September 11, 2001, forensic scientists had to acknowledge their most recent error. With the beginning of the new millennium, a belief had arisen that the last problems of forensic investigation had been solved: The discovery of genetic fingerprinting, the development of DNA technology, and the resulting computer databases moved us as far in this direction as we had ever dreamed. But only a fraction of the victims of the World Trade Center's collapse could be identified by this new technology. Most bodies had been destroyed and had become part of the debris and ashes of those buildings. Few biological traces survived.

And so we find ourselves in a position not unlike that which existed when forensic science first blossomed at the end of the nineteenth century. Today, there are new demands and new technical challenges with uncertain outcomes. Only one thing is certain: Reality will always remain more exciting than any fiction we can imagine.

REFERENCES AND FURTHER READING

Ahlgren, G., S. Monier. 1993. *Crime of the Century: The Lindbergh Kidnapping Hoax.* Boston: Branden Books.

Anonymous. 1984. "Auffallend vorsichtig. Kriminalistische Bilanz der Heineken-Entführung." *Kriminalistik* 38:53. [Heineken case]

Anonymous. 2000. *See* www.geocities.com/byebyekarla/ [Web site predicting the death of Karla Homolka; offline since November 2004]

AP (Associated Press). 2001. "Police: FBI, DEA Serve Warrant at Home of Former Football Great O. J. Simpson." AP, 12/4/2001.

Baden, M. M. 1983. "The Lindbergh Kidnapping Revisited." *Journal of Forensic Sciences* 8:1035–1037.

Bassenge, F. 1937. *Ehre und Beleidigung.* Berlin: Duncker & Humblot. [Dueling]

Bayerisches Oberlandesgericht. 2000. "Beschluss vom 23.02.2000 zu Aktenzeichen 5 St RR30/00. Zit." *Deutsches Auto-Recht* (DAR) 2000:277. [Insult caught on hidden camera]

Benecke, M. 1996. "Die DNA-Beweise im Fall Simpson." *Kriminalistik* 50:481ff. [Simpson case]

Benecke, M. 2004. "Forensic Entomology: Arthropods and Corpses." In: M. Tsokos (ed.), *Forensic Pathology Reviews*, vol. 2. Totowa, NJ: Humana Press, pp. 207–240.

Benecke, M. 2006. *Kriminalbiologie: Genetische Fingerabdrücke und Insekten auf Leichen*, 3rd ed. Bergisch Gladbach: Bastei Lübbe Taschenbuch. [Forensic biology]

Bene[c]ke, M., M. Rodriguez. 2002. "Luis Alfredo Garavito Cubillos. Kriminalistische und juristische Aspekte einer Totungsserie mit über 200 Opfern." *Archiv für Kriminologie.* [Serial killer Luis Alfredo Garavito]

Benecke, M., M. Rodriguez, A. Zabeck, and A. Mätzler (in press). "Two Homosexual Pedophile Sadistic Serial Killers: Jürgen Bartsch (Germany, 1946–1976) and Luis Alfredo Garavito Cubillos (Columbia, 1957)." *Minerva Medicolegale.*

Benecke, O. 1889. *Von unehrlichen Leuten. Culturhistorische Studien und Geschichten aus vergangenen Tagen deutscher Gewerbe und Dienste*, 2nd ed. Berlin: Wilhelm Hertz/Bessersche Buchhandlung. [Criminal careers]

Brandon, R. 1993/2001. *The Life and Many Deaths of Harry Houdini.* London: Secker & Warburg/Pan Books.

Bruce, R. G., M. E. Dettmann. 1996. "Palynological Analyses of Australian Surface Soils and Their Potential Use in Forensic Science." *Forensic Science International* 81:77–94. [Pollen]

Burnside, S., A. Cairns. 1995. *Deadly Innocence. The True Story of Paul Bernardo, Karla Homolka, and the Schoolgirl Murders.* New York: Warner Books.

Cairns, A. 2000. "Karla: Prison Party Girl." *The Toronto Sun*, 9/2/2000.

Cairns, A. 2001. "Bernardo Allegedly Got Smut from Guard. Kingston Prison Suspends Staffer in Contraband Probe." *The Toronto Sun*, 5/24/2001:20.

Carlson, K. A., J. E. Russo. 2001. "Biased Interpretation of Evidence by Mock Jurors." *Journal of Experimental Psychology: Applied* 7:91–103.

Connors, E., T. Lundregan, N. Miller, T. McEwen. 1996. "Convicted by Juries, Exonerated by Science: Case Studies in the Use of DNA Evidence to Establish Innocence After Trial." Alexandria, VA: U.S. Department of Justice & National Institute of Justice/Institute for Law and Justice. [Zain case]

Court TV. 1996. Reporter's daily transcript. Superior Court of the State of California for the County of Los Angeles. *Sharon Rufo et aliis, plaintiffs, vs. Orenthal James Simpson et aliis, defendants*. Santa Monica, CA, 11/21/1996.

Dahmer, L. 1995. *A Father's Story*. New York: Avon Books.

Dalcke, A. 1913. *Strafrecht und Strafprozess. Eine Sammlung der wichtigsten, das Strafrecht und das Strafverfahren betreffenden Gesetze.* 13th ed. Berlin: H. W. Müller. [Slander]

Dietel, M., P. Krietsch. 1996. *Berliner Medizinhistorisches Museum an der Charité.* CD-ROM. Berlin: Blackwell. [Dueling]

Dietrich, S. 1998. "Hier ist ein Gesicht zerstort worden." *FAZ*, 4/17/1998, 89:II. [Geyer case]

dpa. 1976. "Jürgen Bartsch beigesetzt." *Rheinische Post*, 5/4/1976. [Bartsch case]

Dvorchak, R. J. and L. Holewa. 1992. *Wer ist Jeffrey Dahmer? Das schockierende Porträt des Milwaukee-Mörders.* Bergisch Gladbach: Bastei Lübbe Taschenbücher. [Dahmer case]

Eckermann, W. 2001. "Ein diffuser Auftragsmord. Oder: Der mysteriose Tod einer Ehefrau." *Kriminalistik* 55:264–270. [Nearly perfect murder]

Express Düsseldorf: (a) Schmährufe an Bartschs Sarg. Nur der Pfarrer predigte: "Herr, gib ihm Frieden, den ihm die Welt nicht geben konnte," 5/4/1976:3; (b) "Bartsch starb an Narkosemittel . . . , das behauptet Illustrierte," 5/6/1976. [Bartsch case]

Express Köln, 5/14–17/1997, 10/28/1997 [Rhafes case], 3/11/2001 [Geyer case].

Farin, M. 1999. *Polizeireport München 1799–1999.* München: Belleville. [Kneissl case].

Fisher, J. 1999. *The Ghosts of Hopewell: Setting the Record Straight in the Lindbergh Case.* Carbondale: Southern Illinois University Press.

Frankfurter Allgemeine Zeitung. 1998. "Pastor Geyer bezeichnet die Anschuldigungen als gemein." *FAZ*, 2/3/1998, 28:12. [Geyer case]

Frankfurter Allgemeine Zeitung. 1998. "Staatsanwalt fordert acht Jahre. Pastor des Totschlags angeklagt." (dpa-Meldung vom 3/24/1998). *FAZ*, 3/15/1998, 71:II. [Geyer case]

Friedrichsen, G.. 1998. "Wie Falschgeld herumlaufen." *Der Spiegel*, 2/9/2001, 7:70. [Geyer case]

Gerassimow, M. M. 1968. *Ich suchte Gesichter. Schädel erhalten ihr Antlitz zurück. Wissenschaft auf neuen Wegen.* Gütersloh: Bertelsmann. [Facial reconstruction]

Gera[s]simow, M. M. 1971. *The Face Finder*. Philadelphia, New York: Lippincott. [Facial reconstruction]

Gerlach. 1962. 30. StGB §§185, 179; Beleidigung durch unzüchtige Handlungen, OLG Stuttgart, Urt. v. 7.07.1961–2 Ss 213/61. *Neue Juristische Wochenschrift* 1962 (1/2):62ff. [Redbeard case]

Graham, S. A. 1997. "Anatomy of the Lindbergh Kidnapping." *Journal of Forensic Sciences* 42:368–377.

Gronau, H. 1933. *Der Hiesel. Ein Räuber und doch ein Volksheld.* Freya Heidenau, H. 43 (von 105). [Kneissl case]

Helmer, R. 1984. *Schädelidentifizierung durch elektronische Bildmischung.* Heidelberg: Kriminalistik Verlag. (Schriftenreihe Kriminalistik, Wissenschaft & Praxis, Bd. 16.) [Facial reconstruction]

Helmer, R. 1998. "Identifizierung unbekannter, unkenntlicher Leichen mittels bildtechnischer oder rekonstruktiver Verfahren." In: D. Leopold (Hrsg.), *Identifikation unbekannter Toter.* Lübeck: Schmidt-Römhild, S. 449–476. [Facial reconstruction]

Helmer, R., S. Röhricht, D. Petersen, and F. Moer. 1989. "Plastische Gesichtsrekonstruktion als Möglichkeit der Identifizierung unbekannter Schädel (II). Eine Überprüfung der Zuverlässigkeit der Rekonstruktionstechnik durch einen doppelten Blindversuch." *Archiv für Kriminologie* 184:142–160. [Facial reconstruction]

Henke, J. 1995. "Die Bedeutung der DNA-Analysen im Prozess gegen O. J. Simpson." *Der Amtsvormund,* Juli 1995:788–802. [Simpson case]

Hillman, H. 1992. "The Possible Pain Experienced During Execution by Different Methods." *Perception* 22:745–753. [Death penalty]

Hinder, L. 1997. "Zwischen Himmel und Hölle." *Stern* 12/4/1997, 50:200. [Geyer case]

Höss, R. 1947. *Meine Psyche. Leben, Werden und Erleben.* Hrsg. unter dem Titel *Kommandant in Auschwitz v. Martin Broszat (1963).* München: Deutscher Taschenbuch Verlag. [Death penalty]

Houdini, H. ca. 1920. *Miracle Mongers and Their Methods. A Complete Exposé* (reprinted 1993). New York: Prometheus Books. [Houdini and alleged supernatural powers]

Iscan, M. Y. and R. P. Helmer (Hrsg.). 1993. *Forensic Analysis of the Skull: Craniofacial Analysis, Reconstruction, and Identification.* New York: Wiley-Liss.

Juhnke, A. 1998. "Der Hinrichtungsjournalismus hat mich zerstört. In einem einstündigen Schlusswort bat Pastor Geyer vor Gericht um Freispruch." *Berliner Zeitung* 4/1/1998, 77:12. [Geyer case]

Juhnke, A. 1998. "Der 'Todes-Pastor' und die Schäfchen. Im Prozess gegen Klaus Geyer gibt es keine eindeutigen Beweise: Das Publikum ist voll auf seine Kosten gekommen." *Berliner Zeitung* 4/9/1998, 84:2. [Geyer case]

Kaya, H. 2001. "Die Bedeutung des Ehrbegriffs im türkischen Kulturkreis. Hintergrundinformationen bei Totungsdelikten und schweren Körperverletzungen." *Der Kriminalist* 10:411ff. [Honor and the Rhafes case]

Kennedy, L. 1996. *Crime of the Century: Who Kidnapped the Lindbergh Baby?* New York: Penguin Books.

Kern, E. 1912. *Die systematische Abgrenzung der Verbrechenselemente bei der Beleidigung.* Breslau: Schlettersche Buchhandlung/Franck & Weigert. [Dueling]

Kiehne, K. 1965. "Das Flammenwerferattentat von Köln-Volkhoven." *Archiv für Kriminologie* 136:61–75. [Seifert case]

Kimmel, A. 1966. "Eigenartige Zufälle bei der Aufklärung von Erpressungen." *Kriminalistik* 20:352f. [Blackmail cases]

Koehler, A. 1933. *Report of Examination of Ladder for the New Jersey State Police. Sum-*

L220

mary of Observations and Conclusions. West Trenton: New Jersey State Police Museum. [Lindbergh case]

Koehler, A. 1935. "Who Made That Ladder?" *Saturday Evening Post,* 4/20/1935. [Lindbergh case]

Koehler, A. 1937. "Technique Used in Tracing the Lindbergh Kidnapping Ladder." *Journal of Criminal Law and Criminology* 7:712–724. [Lindbergh case]

Kohut, A. 1888. *Das Buch berühmter Duelle.* Berlin: Alfred Fried. [Bismarck–Virchow duel]

Kölner Stadt-Anzeiger: Seifert case, 6/12/1964; Mohammed Rhafes case, 2/11/1998.

Kristl, W. L. (n.d.). *Kneißl. Bayerns Kriminalfall der Jahrhundertwende.* München: Pflaum. [Kneissl case]

Krönke, G. 2003 (August). "Der Amerikaner und die Hutmacherin. Von 1957 bis 1974 hatte der berühmte Flieger Charles Lindbergh eine zweite Familie in München." *Süddeutsche Zeitung* 176(2–3):3. [Lindbergh's second family in Germany]

Lenk, E. and K. Kaever (Hrsg.). 1997. *Peter Kürten, genannt Vampir von Düsseldorf* Frankfurt/Main: Eichborn. [Kürten case]

Linke, D. 2001. *Kunst und Gehirn. Die Eroberung des Unsichtbaren.* Reinbek b. Hamburg: Rowohlt. [Beheading and consciousness]

London Free Press. 2001. "'Evil' Bernardo Tapes Burned: The Families of His Teenage Victims Say They're Relieved." *London Free Press* (Canada), 12/22/2001:A1.

Maisel, J. 1976. "Gutachter genehmigte Eingriff. Im Herbst hat Jürgen Bartsch einen Antrag auf Kastration gestellt." *Rheinische Post,* 4/28/1976. [Bartsch case]

Manchester Union Leader. 1990. "Dear Abby." *Manchester Union Leader* (New Hampshire, USA), 12/23/1990. [Lindbergh landing]

Marks, M. 1995. "William M. Bass and the Development of Forensic Anthropology in Tennessee." *Journal of Forensic Sciences* 40:741–750.

Moor, P. 1978. "Ganz gewöhnliche Schlamperei. Juristisches Nachspiel zum Fall Bartsch. Die Kunstfehler des Dr. Hollenbeck." *Die Zeit,* 4/28/1978:12. [Bartsch case]

Murder in Mind. 1998. "Bruno Hauptmann." In *Murder in Mind,* vol. 37. London: Marshall Cavendish. [Lindbergh case]

Neue Ruhr Zeitung. 1976. "Bartsch war das zweite Todesopfer in Eickelborn." *NRZ,* 5/18/1976. [Bartsch case]

Nowak, R. 1994. "Forensic Science Goes to Court with O. J." *Science* 265:1352ff. [Simpson case]

Oppermann, K. 2000. "Personenerkennung: Daktyloskopie." In: R. Jäger (Hrsg.), *Kriminalistische Kompetenz,* Bd. I, Abschnitt KT 6. Lübeck: Schmidt-Romhild. [Fingerprinting]

Ottawa Sun. 1998. "Families Call for Help to Keep Tapes Secret." *Ottawa Sun,* 2/21/1998:6. [Bernardo and Homolka case]

Pennsylvania Gazette. 2000. Dr. William Bass III, "On This Farm, Corpses Are Cultivated." *Pennsylvania Gazette,* Alumni Profiles, University of Pennsylvania, August 2000. [Body Farm]

Peter, B. 2004. *Das Herz der Stadt stand still: Das Flammenwerfer-Attentat von Köln-Volkhoven.* Köln: Sh-Verlag. [Seifert case]

Pietrusky, F. 1926. "Über kriminelle Leichenzerstückelung. Der Fall Denke." *Deutsche Zeitschrift für die Gesamte Gerichtliche Medizin* 8:703–726. [Denke case]

Polidoro, M. 1998. "Houdini and Conan Doyle: The Story of a Strange Friendship." *Sceptical Inquirer* 22:40.

Pozsár, C. and M. Farin (Hrsg.). 1995. *Die Haarmann-Protokolle.* Reinbek b. Hamburg: Rowohlt. [Haarmann case]

Pringle, K. 2000. "Inside the Mind of Jeffrey Dahmer. FBI Files Detail Orgy of Sex, Murder and Cannibalism." In: APBNews.com, 8/10/2000. Internet: *See* www.apbonline.com/media/gfiles/dahmer/dahmer0814.html?s=pb_dahmer (accessed November 2001). [Dahmer case]

Quatrehomme, G., S. Cotin, G. Subsol, H. Delingette, Y. Garidel, G. Grévin, M. Fidrich, P. Bailet, and A. Ollier. 1997. "A Fully Three-Dimensional Method for Facial Reconstruction Based on Deformable Models." *Journal of Forensic Sciences* 42:649–652.

Reidl, M. 1971. *Der Räuber Kneißl. Vierundvierzig Holzschnitte über den bayerischen Kriminalfall um 1900 mit dem Text des Kneißl-Lieds und einer Chronik der wirklichen Ereignisse.* Ebenhausen: Langewiesche-Brand. [Kneissl case]

Rheinische Zeitung: (a) "Der Rauber Kneißl," "Die Gefangennahme des Raub-morders Kneißl," "Die Affäre Kneißl," "Die 'Affäre Kneißl,'" 3/6–22/1901 [Kneissl case]; "Houdini," 7/6/1901; "Der geheimnisvolle Koffer," 7/15/1901; "Houdini," 7/25/1901; "Zirkus-Anzeigen," 7/5/1902. [Houdini and Graf case]

Roberts, T. D. M. 1954. "Cortical Activity in Electrocuted Dogs." *The Veterinary Record* 66:561–567.

Rodriguez, W. C. and W. M. Bass. 1983. "Insect Activity and Its Relationship to Decay Rates of Human Cadavers in East Tennessee." *Journal of Forensic Sciences* 28:423–432. [Body Farm]

Rossa, K. 1966. *Todesstrafen. Ihre Wirklichkeit in drei Jahrtausenden.* Oldenburg: Stalling. [Chessman case, beheading, dueling]

Schäfer, H. 1994. *Poltergeister und Professoren: Über den Zustand der Parapsychologie.* Bremen: Fachschriften-Verlag Schafer. [Parapsychology]

Schmiedel, H. 1992. *Berüchtigte Duelle.* Leipzig: Koehler & Amelang. [Dueling]

Schmuck, M. O. 1976. "Die letzten Tage des Jürgen Bartsch." *Rheinische Post,* 5/5/1976. [Bartsch case]

Schneickert, H. 1940–1941. "Die Entführung des Linderberg-Kindes und der Mordprozess gegen Hauptmann." *Archiv für Kriminologie:* 107:125–138; 108:28–33, 90–97; 109:18–39, 87–97; 110:39–43. [Lindbergh case]

Schneidereit, P. 2004. "Six Months, 23 Days to Homolka's Release." *The Halifax Herald,* 12/14/2004.

Shapiro, E. D. and S. Reifler. 1996. "Forensic DNA Analysis and the United States Government." *Medicine, Science, and Law* 36:43–51. [Simpson case]

Smith, S. L. and P. H. Buschang. 2001. "Midsagittal Facial Tissue Thickness of Children and Adolescents from the Montreal Growth Study." *Journal of Forensic Sciences* 46:1294–1302.

Snyder-Sachs, J. 2001. *Corpse. Nature, Forensics, and the Struggle to Pinpoint Time of Death.* Cambridge, MA: Perseus Books. [Body Farm]

Steiner, O. and W. Gay. ca. 1956. *Der Fall Kürten. Sachdarstellung und Betrachtungen.* Hamburg: Kriminalistik. [Kürten case]

Stephan, C. N. and M. Henneberg. 2001. "Building Faces from Dry Skulls: Are They Recognized Above Chance Rates?" *Journal of Forensic Sciences* 46:432–440.

Steuerer, E. 1978. "Die Rekonstruktion von Entfuhrungswegen." *Kriminalistik* 32:396–400. [Manuela Schneider case]

Stoney, M. B. and T. D. Koelmeyer. 1999. "Facial Reconstruction: A Case Report and Review of Development of Techniques." *Medicine, Science, and the Law* 39:49–60.

Supreme Court of Appeals of West Virginia. 1993. Investigation of West Virginia Police Crime Laboratory, Serology Division; Post-Conviction Habeas Corpus. Ross A, Special Prosecuting Attorney vs. Castelle G, Chief Public Defender of Kanawha County; Justice Miller deliv. opinion of the court, filed November 10, 1993, Case 21973. [Fred Zain case]

Szibor, R., W. Pohle, U. Düring, and D. Krause. 2001. "Pollenanalyse als Hinweis auf die Jahreszeit des Todes." In: M. Oehmichen, G. Geserick (Hrsg.), *Osteologische Identifikation und Altersschätzung*. Lübeck: Schmidt-Römhild (*Research in Legal Medicine*, 26):41–53. [Pollen]

Szibor, R., C. Schubert, R. Schoning, D. Krause, and U. Wendt. 1998. "Pollen Analysis Reveals Murder Season." *Nature* 395:449f.

TAZ. 1998. "Wie viele Fragen verträgt eine Ehe?" *TAZ* 2/13/1998, 5457:7. [Geyer case]

Thies, H. 1998. "Ein Dorf verliert seinen Pastor. Beienrode nach dem Schuldspruch: Die Kirchengemeinde singt gegen ihre Trauer an." *Die Zeit* 4/23/1998, 18:20. [Geyer case]

Thies, H. 1998. "Ein Pastor außer sich. Hat Klaus Geyer seine Frau erschlagen? Seine Glaubwürdigkeit im Prozess schwindet." *Die Zeit* 2/2/1998, 9:62. [Geyer case]

Thies, H. 1998. "Pastor hinter Gittern. Der angesehene Gemeindepfarrer Klaus Geyer soll seine Frau erschlagen haben. Zuspruch von Reemtsma." *Die Zeit* 1/15/1998, 4:16. [Geyer case]

Toronto Sun. 2000. "'He Was Going to Lie': Murray Quit When Bernardo Told Him to Suppress Videos." *Toronto Sun,* 4/20/2000:4.

Tyrrell, A. J., M. P. Evinson, A. T. Chamberlain, and M. A. Green. 1997. "Forensic Three-Dimensional Facial Reconstruction: Historical Review and Contemporary Developments." *Journal of Forensic Sciences* 42:653–661.

Ubelacker, D. H. and D. R. Hunt. 1995. "The Influence of William M. Bass III on the Development of American Forensic Anthropology." *Journal of Forensic Sciences* 40:729–734. [Body Farm]

Wallace, A. 2000. Personal communication.

Wälter, H. and N. Westphal. 1995. "Entführung: Eine infame Spielart der Erpressung." *Kriminalistik* 49:629–636. [Manuela Schneider case]

Weir, B. S. 1995. "DNA Statistics in the Simpson Matter." *Nature Genetics* 11:365–368.

Winnipeg Sun. 2000. "Bernardo Ex-Lawyer Grilled About Tapes." *Winnipeg Sun* (Final Ed.), 4/26/2000:14. [Bernardo and Homolka case]

Wittig, H., W. Pohle, U. Düring, K. Jachau, M. Laufer, and D. Krause. 2001. "Analyse des Pilzsporen-Spektrums im Nasen-Rachen-Raum zur Eingrenzung von Sterbeort und -zeit." *Rechtsmedizin* 11:26ff. [Fungal spores]

Wolf, H. 1976. "Jürgen Bartsch: Nach grauenvollen Morden jetzt ein rätselhafter Tod." *Bild-Zeitung,* 5/4/1976. [Bartsch case]

Zarbock. 1995. "Das DNA-Verfahren im Strafprozess und in Vaterschaftsfeststellungen am Beispiel des Simpson-Prozesses in Los Angeles." *Der Amtsvormund,* Juli 1995:788–802. [Simpson case]

Zbarsky, I. and S. Hutchinson. 1998. *Lenin's Embalmers,* trans. Barbara Bray. London: Harvill Press.

INDEX